Fulfilling Your Divine Plan

Kim Michaels

The Avatar Revelations, vol 3

Fulfilling Your Divine Plan

Kim Michaels
More to Life

Fulfilling Your Divine Plan

Copyright © 2019 Kim Michaels. All rights reserved. No part of this book may be used, reproduced, translated, electronically stored or transmitted by any means except by written permission from the publisher. A reviewer may quote brief passages in a review.

MORE TO LIFE PUBLISHING
www.morepublish.com
For foreign and translation rights,
contact: info@ morepublish.com

ISBN: 978-87-93297-53-1

The information and insights in this book should not be considered as a form of therapy, advice, direction, diagnosis, and/or treatment of any kind. This information is not a substitute for medical, psychological, or other professional advice, counseling and care. All matters pertaining to your individual health should be supervised by a physician or appropriate health-care practitioner. No guarantee is made by the author or the publisher that the practices described in this book will yield successful results for anyone at any time. They are presented for informational purposes only, as the practice and proof rests with the individual.

Content

Introduction 7
1 | How you make your Divine plan 9
2 | Invoking a higher vision of my Divine plan 25
3 | Overcoming the fear of being wrong 37
4 | Invoking freedom from the fear of being wrong 53
5 | You are not on earth to solve problems 69
6 | Invoking freedom from solving problems 87
7 | Christhood and your Divine plan 103
8 | Invoking Christ discernment about my Divine plan 121
9 | The revolutionary aspect of your Divine plan 145
10 | Invoking the revolutionary aspect of my Divine plan 157
11 | Conscious versus unconscious choices 173
12 | Invoking awareness of my choices 187
13 | The reward for service is freedom 207
14 | Invoking the ability to admit being "wrong" 223
15 | The judgment of Christ and your Divine plan 239
16 | Invoking the vision of my personal Christhood 257
17 | The omega perspective on judgment 285
18 | Invoking peace with being here 301
19 | Withdrawing space from certain imbalanced conditions 321
20 | Invoking my buddhic potential 333

INTRODUCTION

This book is one of the workbooks building on the novel *My Lives with Lucifer, Satan, Hitler and Jesus*. The novel introduces the idea that many spiritual people have come to earth as volunteers or "avatars." We have then received deep spiritual traumas as a result of what we have experienced here. Many of us still carry these traumas with us, and it can explain why we sometimes can feel as if we are not making progress on the spiritual path or why there are certain issues we cannot overcome. How to overcome these traumas is explained (along with practical exercises) in the book *Healing Your Spiritual Traumas*.

This book contains further teachings on these concepts, but it also explains how to execute your Divine plan, a plan you made along with the ascended masters before coming into embodiment.

Please note that it is recommended that you read the novel and *Healing Your Spiritual Traumas* before using this book. The reason is that these books contain many important teachings that can help you make use of this book

This book contains a number of invocations that you are meant to give aloud. If you are not familiar with giving such invocations, you can find further teachings and instructions on the website *www.transcendencetoolbox.com*. You can also give the invocations along with a recording and you can purchase recordings of the invocations in this book on the website *www.morepublish.com*.

1 | HOW YOU MAKE YOUR DIVINE PLAN

I AM the Ascended Master Mother Mary, and it is my great joy to open this gathering for the purpose of teaching you about what we have called your Divine plan.

"What's in a name?" as the Bard said. Well, whenever we give a concept, we, of course, face the reality that we have to use words in order to communicate these ideas that are truly beyond words. We also face the reality, that not very many people think about, which is that words are interpreted differently by different people, depending on their background, their culture and their individual psychology.

When we give a name, such as a "Divine plan," well it cannot necessarily reach everybody because some people will have a prejudice against the idea. They will not be open to even hearing more about the concept because they have a reaction to the word "divine" or they have a reaction to the word "plan." It causes their minds to go into this state, that is so common on earth, where you reject without truly considering with an open mind and heart what is hiding behind the words, what is being said that is beyond the words.

Focus on one of the four lower bodies

I wish to give you a little bit of a view of how it is for us as ascended masters. Now, I want you to imagine that you, with your present level of consciousness, were transported to wherever you see us residing—whether it be in a higher energetic realm or however you can conceive of it. You are transported to the level where we reside and you are now with us, looking down at the earth. You see what you may never have considered, or at least what most people have never considered. You see how many different types and groups of people there are on the earth. You now see that which you cannot see with your physical sight but you can see this from our level: How all of these groups of people are in a certain state of consciousness. You see what you already know: Each person has an individual psychology, an individual state of consciousness made up by their four lower bodies. You see how people have a physical level of the mind, an emotional level of the mind, a mental level and an identity level.

Now, you see that each human being, of course, has what we have called the conscious mind. You see that each human being has the conscious mind focused in one of its four lower bodies. For some people it is the physical body they are mostly focused on. Other people pay more attention to their emotions and live their entire lives in their emotions. Others are focused on the mental realm and are always thinking and analyzing, and a few are more focused in their identity bodies or their identity minds.

You see that when we give a teaching, one of the goals of that teaching is to reach the person's conscious mind and cause the person to have a conscious insight, a conscious revelation, an "Aha experience," if you will. This causes them to shift their consciousness so that they see something they did not see before and they have a broader, more mature view of life or of their personal situation. Therefore, they can shift into doing things they could not do before: overcoming certain emotional patterns, overcoming certain mental patterns or even shifting their identity to a higher level.

In order to do this, we need to give a teaching that reaches people's conscious minds, we need to somehow, from our level, penetrate through to people's conscious minds. Now, you also see that in order for us to reach a specific person's conscious mind, the ideas and concepts we give have to pass through those of the four lower bodies that are above where a person's conscious mind is focused. If a person is focused in the emotional level, our ideas have to penetrate the identity and mental minds of that person before they can reach the conscious mind. It may even have to penetrate some aspect of the emotional mind.

Now, you see that each person has certain filters, certain barriers, certain beliefs, certain attitudes, certain emotions that might actually block the ideas we are releasing from reaching the person's conscious mind. Mind you, this is not simply a matter of the person hearing, finding or reading the ideas. It is entirely possible that a person can read a book that contains our ideas but as the person is reading the words, the higher levels of the mind of that person are blocking, are filtering out, the concepts from really reaching the person's conscious mind, connecting and having an impact. In other words, the person is reading the words but is not truly absorbing them, connecting to them, grasping them.

Limits to understanding

I am deliberately not saying "understanding" because it is not just a matter of understanding; it is a matter of truly connecting to the idea so that it shifts your consciousness. Too many people focus on *understanding* and that is because many of the people who have found the spiritual path are focused in the mental mind. They are focused on understanding an idea but there are many, many examples of people who have a great intellectual understanding of spiritual concepts but it does not shift their consciousness. That is because they have not truly connected, they have not actually had an intuitive experience of the idea. It is blocked by their mental mind's desire to understand the idea, to categorize and label it so that the mental mind can put it in a nice little file folder in the database where it feels like it has the idea under control.

My beloved, it is not a matter of having an idea under control because if your ego and your mental mind feels that it has a spiritual idea under control, how is that idea going to shift your consciousness? It will just be filed away as something you know and understand at an intellectual level and it does not shift your consciousness.

If you could see what I have now told you, you would see that there are many, many people on earth that are completely unreachable for the ideas we can bring forth from our level. You will also see that there are many, many people who are actually open to a spiritual teaching, who are maybe even open to an esoteric, metaphysical, New Age or even an ascended master teaching. They still have so many prejudices, filters, preconceived opinions and ideas they are not willing to question, that it is very difficult for us to come up with an idea, to formulate an idea in words, that can actually reach these people's conscious minds.

If you were to see this with your present level of consciousness, it is very likely that you would be so shocked that you would feel almost hopeless and discouraged because what could you actually say that can reach people? Some of you will even have the experience of knowing people that you have attempted to tell about what you believe. You also run into the limitations of the words so that whatever you say does not connect to the peoples' conscious minds, does not really shift them.

Why the masters are not discouraged

If you could see the situation that we face, you would, with your present level of consciousness, most likely feel discouraged. Now, I am, of course, not giving you this teaching in order to make you feel discouraged because we do not have your present level of consciousness, we have ascended. There are two aspects of this that I wish to bring to your attention.

The first one is that we have, of course, truly integrated and experienced the reality of free will and therefore, we have no desire to change other people against their free will. We have actually accepted, as we have even said in some of our latest books, that when you consider that the earth is an educational institution that is meant to give certain people the experiences they desire, then we have no frustration about working with earth.

Now, you may go back, if you are familiar with previous ascended master dispensations, and you may be able to actually find dictations where there, even in the wording or in the vibration of the wording, could be detected a certain sense of frustration or impatience on behalf of the ascended masters. You may even go back and find some of the early dictations given in this dispensation where you can find that sense. I wish to make you aware here that if you detect such a vibration in an ascended master dictation, then that frustration, that vibration, came from the three higher bodies of the messenger. There is no other explanation when you are talking about a sponsored messenger because we, of course, do not have any frustration. If we had any kind of frustration about working with earth, we would have long ago experienced what you on earth call "burn-out." I can assure you that this phenomenon does not exist in the ascended realm. An ascended master does not go down with stress, does not have a nervous breakdown.

We have ascended because we have overcome the desire to change people against their free will. It is true, of course, that there are many phenomena on earth that we would like to see changed because they obviously cause people to suffer. You should not reason based on that and say that we are impatient or frustrated because these conditions have not been changed. You realize that from our perspective, we do not have any kind of frustration. Therefore, we are, of course, not feeling discouraged. We are working with people and we are in acceptance of the fact that every human being has free will and therefore has the right to be in their present state of consciousness.

Not one absolute truth

We can say that your four lower bodies form what we have called a self, but we have said there are many different selves, there are many different internal spirits. There is the ego, there is the conscious mind. Let us just call it a personality, just too use a word that you are somewhat familiar with. The totality of your four lower bodies form this personality and inside of that personality is the Conscious You at a certain level of consciousness. It has a greater or smaller identification with the four lower bodies, the contents of the four lower bodies, the selves that are in those four lower bodies. We accept that this is how free will is outplaying itself. We accept that the earth is a low-consciousness, high-density planet. We fully accept that our role is to work with people at whatever level of consciousness they are at and seek to help them come up higher.

Based on this, the idea I want to convey to you is that it is not the goal of the ascended masters to bring forth one highest, absolute, universal truth and get all people on earth to accept that truth. It is not our goal to do this. I know this will contradict what some of you believe. I know this will contradict what many people who have studied previous ascended master dispensations believe. I am sure that some people will go out and find quotes from previous ascended master dictations and say this contradicts what Mother Mary is saying through Kim Michaels—and this is perfectly all right. The reality we are giving you, who are ready to step up to a higher level, is that we are not sitting up here with one, ready-made, predefined, universal, absolute truth that we are seeking to bring into the physical realm and get all people to accept. The reason for this is that we recognize from our level very clearly that it would be impossible to bring forth one teaching and get all people to accept it. There are simply too many different levels of consciousness between the lowest and the 144th level. There are too many different groups of people (from different backgrounds, different planets, whether they are from the earth, whether they are fallen beings, whether they have come from a myriad of different planets) that you cannot bring forth one teaching that all can accept.

This is partly due to the fact that they are from many different backgrounds and of many different levels of consciousness. It is also to a very great extent a product of the fact that the earth is a low-consciousness, high-density planet. Therefore, words, the words that is the primary means of communication on earth (which it would not be if the earth was of a lesser density) are so limited that it is impossible to express a truly universal, absolute, highest truth with the words that are available today.

Our role, our goal, is clear. We seek to work with any person or any group of people that are open to anything we can bring forth. In order to reach through all the barriers, all the filters, of a specific group of people, we have to look at what is their background, not only their culture and history on this planet but even their cosmic background. Where do they come from? What prejudices do they have in their minds? What ideas do they have in their minds that they are not willing to question?

The ideas people will not question

You recognize, my beloved, that almost all human beings have a certain aspect of their mind that is open to new ideas. There are some people who do not have this openness, they are not open to any new ideas but most people have a certain openness to new ideas. They also have a certain aspect of their minds where they believe here are their most cherished, most fundamental, most trust-worthy ideas that they are not willing or able (but it is really the same thing because if you are willing, you are always able), they are simply not willing to question.

We know that in some cases, we must work within very narrow boundaries because people will reject anything we give them if we question their pet ideas, their mental holy cows, so to speak, their taboos. There are many people, many groups of people, on earth where there is very little we can do for them. Still, we attempt to bring forth some idea, to inspire some person to write some book that can move them a little bit. Then, of course, you can go higher and higher and you find a range of people who are gradually more and more open, have fewer and fewer of these mental holy cows that are untouchable. We have more and more options for working with these people.

Based on this, you might look at yourselves and say: "Well, where are we at?" Well, if you are open to the teachings we are giving through this messenger, and if you have not been scared away by the book about *My Lives* [*My Lives with Lucifer, Satan, Hitler and Jesus*], then you are at a very high level of openness. This means that you are ready to actually step up to a higher experience of your own Divine plan. You may say: "Well, why haven't we given more teachings about the Divine plan earlier?" The reason for this is very simple. We have gradually given you a number of teachings and tools so that when we give you a teaching about what blocks your Divine plan, you have the teaching, you have the tools so that you can begin to work on this, as you see it individually.

First of all, the book about *My Lives* is a very important healing tool. I dare say that not even the messenger has with his outer mind grasped how many layers there are to this book. Of course, none of you need to grasp all of the layers, you just need to recognize that there are layers in this book. That means you can benefit from reading the book many times because it is a very important tool for shifting your consciousness.

Overcoming the linear mind

My beloved, one of the ways you need to shift your consciousness in order to come up to a higher grasp of your Divine plan is that you have to overcome this focus on the linear mind. As I said, many, many spiritual students have their conscious minds focused in the mental mind. You are trying to study and understand, you want to understand analytically. You often want to have a very linear time line, a linear grasp of concepts. This has not been wrong for you up until this point, but there does come a point on the spiritual path where you cannot go higher if you are focused on the linear mind, if your consciousness is, so to speak, attached to or trapped by the linear mind. Why is this, my beloved? Well, is it not obvious?

We have told you that the lowest aspect of your mind is the physical, the next is the emotional, the next is the mental and the highest is the identity mind. Well, I can assure you, my beloved, that your identity mind is not linear and analytical, it is the highest level of intuition you can reach while you are in embodiment. If you are going to shift your focus from the mental level to the identity level, you cannot do this through the linear, analytical mind. You cannot analyze your way into the identity mind. You can only do this by opening your intuitive faculties. It is not a matter of knowing, understanding and grasping. It is a matter of experiencing intuitively because what is in your identity mind is subtle. These are the teachings we have given you about the cosmic birth trauma, the primal self [See the book *Healing Your Spiritual Traumas*]. These things are subtle and they have facets, many facets.

Teachings for many different levels

Your primal self cannot be defined in a very simple, linear, analytical way. It is not a matter of creating a mental label and saying: "Ah, now I understand my primal self. This is what it is, and now I can let it die." Well, if you do this, it will still have hidden aspects that you have not even started to see because you can only see those in an intuitive way. How will you progress on the spiritual path beyond the mental level? Well, not through the analytical, intellectual, linear mind. Only by shifting into the spherical, intuitive mind that looks at the wholeness, looks at the bigger picture and is willing to grasp, to experience, the truth of what I have just told you, namely that we are not seeking to give forth one absolute, linear truth.

We are seeking to give forth many different concepts and ideas because what is our purpose for interacting with earth? It is not, *it is not*, my beloved, our purpose to bring forth an absolute truth. Our purpose is to raise people's consciousness, each person's state of consciousness, and this must be done individually. That is why we must look at certain groups of people and say: We can give a teaching for a certain range of consciousness and then we must be satisfied that it will reach a certain amount of people and then we give other teachings for other levels of consciousness.

No messenger is meant to reach all 144 levels of consciousness; it would simply be impossible. We give teachings for a certain level and I dare say, my beloved, that we have now given teachings through this messenger where you can start the Course on Self-Mastery, the Path to Self-Mastery, at the 48th level, and you can work your way up to the 96th level. Then, you have all of the teachings, Maitreya's book [*Master Keys to Spiritual*

Freedom], my books on the abundant life [*A Course in Abundance*], the *My Lives* book and the teachings on how to overcome your trauma, that can take you higher. I can assure you, my beloved, that the book on *My Lives* can be read by people from the 48th level all the way up to when they are almost ready to ascend and they will still be able to find something new in it, something that can shift their perspective.

It is a book given for a very broad range of consciousness and that is why there are certain things that are put into this book that are deliberately put in there as a provocation—because, what is the purpose? As I said, there comes a certain point where, in order to bring you further, we have to take you beyond the linear mind. The linear mind is the *linear* mind—it is like a computer. It will do what it always does: It will analyze, it will categorize, it will label.

The linear mind cannot see the linear mind

My beloved, we can say all of these things. You can think: "Yes, but I understand this intellectually about the linear mind." My beloved, the linear mind may be able to *understand* the linear mind but it will never be able to *see* the linear mind itself from the outside. The linear mind cannot step outside itself. Only the Conscious You can step outside of the linear mind, outside of its current identification. How can we help you switch out of the linear mind by giving you a teaching that conforms to the linear mind's way of thinking? It cannot be done, my beloved.

That is why certain Buddhist sects have the concept of the koan that is deliberately given to confuse the linear mind. What is the sound of one hand clapping? Well, this entire book [*My Lives*] is a koan. There are multiple koans in there that are meant to help people shift out of various levels of consciousness, not only the linear mind but also the emotional and even shift their identity. This is done by giving you an experience that is so surprising, so provocative, so non-linear, that people must either completely reject it, and thereby reject the book, or they must shift to a higher level of consciousness. There are very few people who can read this book and not be touched or provoked by it—very few people. Of course, there are some (most of them will be below the 48th level of consciousness, some can be a little bit higher) who can be very closed, very prejudiced. They can have certain ideas that they are absolutely not willing to question, and when they find that the book questions those ideas, they will reject it. Very few people can read it without having some reaction and this is a very, very important tool when you understand this correctly.

The wrong planet for comfortability

There are many of you who have been ascended master students for a long time, some of you for decades. You need to be aware that there can come a point where you know so many teachings, you have read so many teachings, that you almost become comfortable. You think that the ascended masters cannot surprise you anymore. There is an aspect of your mind that does not want us to surprise you because you have become comfortable at the level you are at.

Well, my beloved, I will tell you one thing. If you have a desire to be comfortable, you sure picked the wrong planet because this is not a planet on which to try to be comfortable. Throughout the ages, many, many people have tried to create certain physical, outer situations in which they felt secure or comfortable. It is understandable, but look at history. The wheels of history have ground them all into dust. All the mighty empires have been ground into dust. You cannot, on a planet like this, be truly comfortable.

The challenge I put before you here is this: Do you want to know your Divine plan or do you want to be comfortable? Because you cannot do both. Most of you already have some conscious awareness of your Divine plan. I understand that you do not see it in full detail, but we will explain later the reasons for this. You have some idea of your Divine plan. Most of you have been following your Divine plan to a large extent throughout your lives, even if you have not been consciously aware of this.

What I put before you is that you have reached a level now where there are certain aspects of your Divine plan you have not seen. Again, you have seen *some* aspects of your Divine plan, you have followed your Divine plan to a large extent, but there is something you have not yet seen. You need to ask yourself: "Am I willing to see what I haven't seen?" If you are, then you need to recognize that you need to give up your comfortability in order to see this. The reason you have not seen it is that you have adapted a certain outlook, a certain attitude, a certain understanding and you do not think you need to go beyond it. If you do not go beyond it, you cannot see the aspects of your Divine plan that are still hidden from you. This is the decision you need to make and *you* need to make it. Basically,

I am asking that as you to go to sleep tonight, you make a call to be taken to whatever ascended master retreat you would like to go to, whatever is closest to your heart. Then, I ask you to seriously ask to be shown, so that you can remember this tomorrow morning, what it is that you are too comfortable with that blocks your vision of your Divine plan. You will not get the maximum benefit from this teaching if you are still holding on to that comfortability. I am not saying that this is necessarily some big terrible thing you are doing. It could be a very subtle thing. You understand that most of you have reached a level of the spiritual path where there is not a risk that you will make a major mistake and start going downhill, fall into a lower state of consciousness or miss your ascension. You have reached a good level, you have made good progress but if you want to step up higher, you cannot allow yourself to be comfortable.

This can be a very subtle thing where you feel that you have a certain comfortability, certain things you do not need to change. Again, I respect your free will. I am simply saying that if you really want to know the hidden aspects of your Divine plan, you need to become aware that they are hidden, not because some dark force is obscuring them, not because we of the ascended masters are withholding them from you, but because there is some level of comfortability in your mind that is preventing you from seeing them. This is the determination you need to make at this first day of the conference so that you can be more open to what we will give you in the coming days.

How your Divine plan is made

Now, my beloved, I wish to also talk a little bit about how your Divine plan is made. In the book by Nada [*The Mystical Initiations of Peace*] she talks about the fact that your Divine plan is not made from the ascended state of consciousness even though, of course, you have ascended masters that are helping you. When you come into this lifetime, you have a high potential and a low potential. In other words, you have a potential that you could reach a certain level of consciousness—if you keep transcending yourself and really apply yourself. If you live a, so to speak, "normal life," you will reach a lower state of consciousness. Your Divine plan is made from the highest level of consciousness to which you have the potential to rise in this lifetime. In other words, when we meet with you and we make the Divine plan with you, you are not at the same level of consciousness with which you left your last embodiment or with which you come into this embodiment. You are at the highest level of consciousness you have the potential to reach. Therefore, you can see what you can see from that level of consciousness when you make your Divine plan. I can assure you that when you make your Divine plan, it is not made with the linear, analytical mind. We are not sitting there with the linear mind, analyzing every aspect of your past, your psychology or this and that. We are not like people on earth where you see business people or army leaders that are making a detailed plan and all of the things that have to fit into place for this plan to be executed. This is not how a Divine plan is made. It is not linear or analytical in that way.

This is another reason that in order to grasp these hidden aspects of your Divine plan, you have to overcome the linear mind. Many of you have become comfortable with the linear mind. You have even used the teachings of the ascended masters to create a linear view of the world where you feel you have figured out how the world works. You have an idea of past history and cosmic history and this and that, and you are comfortable with this. I am telling you that you need to step up higher in order to grasp the highest potential in your Divine plan. That is why you need to be willing to step beyond this. You need to recognize that the goal that both you and we have when we make your Divine plan is, of course, to have you reach the highest level of consciousness you have the potential to reach.

If this is your last lifetime on earth

A substantial portion of you have the potential for this to be your last embodiment so that you can ascend, either immediately after this embodiment or at least some time after, when you have resolved the last psychology and you are ready to ascend. This means that the question we ask ourselves when we are making your Divine plan is that we look at the lowest level of consciousness, the level of consciousness you attained at your last embodiment and with which you will come into this present embodiment. Then, we look at the highest potential and we say: "How can we shift your conscious mind from that lowest consciousness to the highest? What are the prejudices, the filters and the holy cows in your four lower bodies that you need to challenge and see beyond in order to shift your consciousness to the highest level? What do you need to go through of experiences in order to shift your consciousness to the highest level?"

You understand here that it is not our goal to have you grasp the highest, absolute truth and understanding of the universe. It is not our goal to make you supreme spiritual intellectuals who have an absolute linear time line for how the universe unfolded. Our goal is to shift your consciousness in a total way, in an intuitive, all-encompassing way, in an experiential way. This is our goal, this is what we look at.

This has many ramifications, which we will talk about. I want you to keep in mind for today that it is important for you to make this shift where you are willing to look beyond your comfortability, your linear mind. You must be willing to consider, not so much "What *understanding* do I need," but "What inner *experience*, what kind of a high experience, a shifting experience, maybe even a shocking experience, do I need in order to come up to my fullest potential in this embodiment. What do I need to give up in order to get there?"

These are the questions that you might consider between now and tomorrow. You might talk about this, if you feel like it, and help each other to gain a different perspective on this. You can look at a group like this and you can look at yourself and you can say that you are all studying the same teaching, you have applied the teaching so there is a common bond between you. On the other hand, you come from different nations, different cultures, different backgrounds and the one thing you can help each other grasp and experience is that people do not look at things the same way.

Not being threatened by differences

What you could help yourselves with, in a group like this, is to come to realize that it does not matter that other people look at things a different way than you do. You can come to the point where you no longer feel threatened by other people being different because you realize that the way you look at life on earth is all a product of what is in your four lower bodies. What is in your four lower bodies is not who you really are. Therefore, why would you be so attached to the contents of your four lower bodies that it prevents you from being and expressing who you really are? Are the contents of your four lower bodies really so important to you that you are willing to give up being who you really are in order to defend those concepts, those selves that are ultimately unreal? Naturally, the highest potential for your Divine plan is that you give up these limitations, these identifications, this outer mind, these emotional patterns, these physical habits. You give them up because you want something higher. You want to express who you really are. This is, of course, something we will talk more about because it is a scary concept for many people to consider: "Well, who am I really? If I am not this outer personality that was defined as I was growing up or even in past lives, who am I? Who do I want to be?"

Different layers of Divine plans

Enough for now. As my closing words, I want to answer a question that some people have had and it is: "Does every person on earth have a Divine plan?" The answer is, in a way, yes they all do but they are, of course, very, very different, depending on their level of consciousness. Now, you may take a fallen being at the very lowest level of consciousness that is allowed on earth. Take, for example, Hitler. Did he have a Divine plan? Well, yes, he had a Divine plan because there were ascended masters who met with him, discussed the potential, the high and low potential, and created a Divine plan from our perspective so that we could hold the immaculate concept. Now, we knew, of course, that it was not necessarily a very realistic plan because Hitler was at such a low level of consciousness that, even though he was out of embodiment, he was not able to work with us and formulate this Divine plan. He was in such a state of anger, rebellion, rejection and denial that he could not work with us even between embodiments.

The lower you go towards the lowest level of consciousness, the more you find people who are unable to work with us, even when they are out of the body and therefore have some respite from their four lower bodies. They still cannot work with us. That is why we make up a plan for them based on how we look at their lifestream. The reason we make up this plan is, of course, not that *we* need it—although it does help us because there are certain beings in the ascended realm who are holding the immaculate concept for everybody in embodiment. It is mainly because if the people, when they are in embodiment, decide that they want something more, then they can more easily tune in to their Divine plan and receive some kind of impulse that can help them go higher.

As you go from the lowest level of consciousness towards the higher level of consciousness, you find that people are able to participate more in making their Divine plans. This means they have more of an awareness of it when they come into embodiment. They sense that they have a purpose.

Basically, we can say that it is not really until you go beyond the 48th level that you can more consciously participate in making your Divine plan. That is why many people at that level of consciousness and above, they have a sense, at least, that life has a purpose, that they are here for a reason, that they are here to find something, to discover something, maybe even to learn, to grow, to evolve. It is, of course, tremendously helpful for people to have this sense because it helps them tune in to their Divine plan.

Why you forget your Divine plan

Of course, the central issue with your Divine plan is that it is made with the highest level of consciousness you can reach in this lifetime, but when you come into this embodiment, you come with the lowest potential you have, with the consciousness you achieved in your last embodiment. Therefore, you cannot grasp certain aspects of your Divine plan. Because of the density of the planet and your four lower bodies, you forget many aspects of your Divine plan. At least, you forget during the first few years of your embodiment.

We can say that there is a phase on the spiritual path where the main purpose of the spiritual path is, in a sense, to recapture some awareness of your Divine plan. Many of you have already done this to a large extent because you have used the teachings we have given and the tools we have given to heal psychology, to balance karma, to overcome these blockages, to open your minds to new ideas, to increase your intuition. As I said, all of you still have certain aspects that you have become comfortable with that are blocking the next vision that you are capable of achieving, especially given the teachings you now have on avatars, which of course, all of you are or you would not be here and work on how to heal the birth trauma.

My beloved, this concludes these introductory remarks to this remarkable process that we will take you through over these next few days. With that, I express my gratitude for your being here because, of course, the fact that you are here, that so many of you have come, means that we can give forth more of a teaching than we would otherwise have been able to give. It becomes an interaction between you and us. Again, the more willing you are to give up your comfortability, the higher of a teaching we can give during these next few days. It is not so that our program for this conference is completely set in stone. As with every conference, there is a low potential and a high potential and it depends on your reaction what we can bring forth in the end. My deepest gratitude for your presence here, for your willingness to be here and for your willingness, I trust, to come up higher.

2 | INVOKING A HIGHER VISION OF MY DIVINE PLAN

In the name I AM THAT I AM, Jesus Christ, I call to all representatives of the Divine Mother, especially Mother Mary, to help me overcome all conditions in my psychology that block the vision of my Divine plan, including…

[Make personal calls.]

Part 1

1. Mother Mary, I am willing to see what I have not yet seen. Help me step outside of my emotional, mental and identity mind, so I can receive with my conscious mind the idea you want to give me right now.

> O Blessed Mary's Song of Life,
> consuming every form of strife.

As I attune to sound so fair,
each cell is healthy, I declare.

**O Mother Mary, generate,
the song that does accelerate,
my mind into a peaceful state,
God's perfect love I radiate.**

2. Mother Mary, help me see beyond the filters, barriers, beliefs, attitudes, emotions that block the ideas you are releasing, so they can reach my conscious mind.

As life's own song I ever hear,
it does consume all sense of fear.
In tune with Mother's symphony,
from all diseases I AM free.

**O Mother Mary, generate,
the song that does accelerate,
my mind into a peaceful state,
God's perfect love I radiate.**

3. Mother Mary, help me avoid having the higher levels of my mind block or filter out your concepts from reaching my conscious mind. Help me connect to your ideas so they can have an impact. I want to absorb your ideas, connect to them, grasp them.

In Mother's love I do transcend,
and all my struggles hereby end.
For when with Mother's eye I see,
no imperfection touches me.

**O Mother Mary, generate,
the song that does accelerate,
my mind into a peaceful state,
God's perfect love I radiate.**

4. Mother Mary, I am willing to go beyond *understanding* and truly connect to the idea so that it shifts my consciousness. Help me stop being focused in the mental mind so I can have an intuitive experience of the idea.

I see that healing must begin
by finding Living Christ within.
For as I see with single eye,
each cell the light does amplify.

**O Mother Mary, generate,
the song that does accelerate,
my mind into a peaceful state,
God's perfect love I radiate.**

5. Mother Mary, help me neutralize the mental mind's desire to understand an idea, to categorize and label it so that it can be put it the database where the mind feels like it has the idea under control.

In Mother's music I am free,
from memories of a lesser me.
My vision in a perfect state,
that all my cells regenerate.

**O Mother Mary, generate,
the song that does accelerate,
my mind into a peaceful state,
God's perfect love I radiate.**

6. Mother Mary, I recognize that if my ego and my mental mind feel they have a spiritual idea under control, that idea cannot shift my consciousness. What I know and understand at an intellectual level, does not shift my consciousness.

O Mother's Love, sweet melody,
from imperfections I AM free.
O Mother Mary, sound of sounds,
within my heart your love abounds.

**O Mother Mary, generate,
the song that does accelerate,
my mind into a peaceful state,
God's perfect love I radiate.**

7. Mother Mary, help me see the aspect of my mind that holds my most cherished, most fundamental, most trust-worthy ideas, the ideas I have so far not been willing or able to question. I am willing to question these ideas in order to discover my Divine plan.

Through Mother's beauty so sublime,
transcending bounds of space and time.
All cells beyond the mortal tomb,
as they are whole in Mother's womb.

**O Mother Mary, generate,
the song that does accelerate,
my mind into a peaceful state,
God's perfect love I radiate.**

8. Mother Mary, help me step up to a higher experience of my Divine plan by overcoming the focus on the linear mind and the desire to understand analytically.

In resonance with life's own song,
in life's harmonics I belong.
The blueprint of my perfect state
does every cell reconsecrate.

**O Mother Mary, generate,
the song that does accelerate,
my mind into a peaceful state,
God's perfect love I radiate.**

9. Mother Mary, I see that I cannot analyze my way out of the analytical mind. Help me open my intuitive faculties so I can experience intuitively the ideas in my identity mind.

> The tuning fork in every cell
> is now attuned to Mother's bell.
> From curse of death I AM now free,
> I claim my immortality.
>
> **O Mother Mary, generate,**
> **the song that does accelerate,**
> **my mind into a peaceful state,**
> **God's perfect love I radiate.**

Part 2

1. Mother Mary, help me shift into the spherical, intuitive mind that looks at the wholeness, looks at the bigger picture and is willing to grasp, to experience, the reality that you are not seeking to give forth one absolute, linear truth.

> O Blessed Mary's Song of Life,
> consuming every form of strife.
> As I attune to sound so fair,
> each cell is healthy, I declare.
>
> **O Mother Mary, generate,**
> **the song that does accelerate,**
> **my mind into a peaceful state,**
> **God's perfect love I radiate.**

2. Mother Mary, help me truly see that the linear mind may be able to *understand* the linear mind but it will never be able to *see* the linear mind itself from the outside. The linear mind cannot step outside itself. Help my Conscious You step outside of the linear mind, outside of my current identification.

> As life's own song I ever hear,
> it does consume all sense of fear.
> In tune with Mother's symphony,
> from all diseases I AM free.

**O Mother Mary, generate,
the song that does accelerate,
my mind into a peaceful state,
God's perfect love I radiate.**

3. Mother Mary, help me see if I know so many teachings that I have become comfortable, thinking that the ascended masters cannot surprise me anymore. Help me see the aspect of my mind that does not want you to surprise me because I have become comfortable at the level I am at.

In Mother's love I do transcend,
and all my struggles hereby end.
For when with Mother's eye I see,
no imperfection touches me.

**O Mother Mary, generate,
the song that does accelerate,
my mind into a peaceful state,
God's perfect love I radiate.**

4. Mother Mary, I want to know my Divine plan much more than I want to be comfortable. Help me realize that there are certain aspects of my Divine plan I have not seen. I am willing to see what I have not seen and to give up my comfortability in order to see this.

I see that healing must begin
by finding Living Christ within.
For as I see with single eye,
each cell the light does amplify.

**O Mother Mary, generate,
the song that does accelerate,
my mind into a peaceful state,
God's perfect love I radiate.**

5. Mother Mary, help me see how I have adapted a certain outlook, a certain attitude, a certain understanding and I do not think I need to go beyond it. I realize that if I do not go beyond it, I cannot see the aspects of my Divine plan that are still hidden from me.

In Mother's music I am free,
from memories of a lesser me.
My vision in a perfect state,
that all my cells regenerate.

O Mother Mary, generate,
the song that does accelerate,
my mind into a peaceful state,
God's perfect love I radiate.

6. Mother Mary, I ask to be shown, so that I can remember this consciously, what it is that I am too comfortable with that blocks the vision of my Divine plan. I am not holding on to that comfortability.

O Mother's Love, sweet melody,
from imperfections I AM free.
O Mother Mary, sound of sounds,
within my heart your love abounds.

O Mother Mary, generate,
the song that does accelerate,
my mind into a peaceful state,
God's perfect love I radiate.

7. Mother Mary, help me see any subtle feeling of comfortability, thinking there are certain things I do not need to change. I really want to know the hidden aspects of my Divine plan, and I am willing to become aware that they are hidden because there is some level of comfortability in my mind that is preventing me from seeing them.

Through Mother's beauty so sublime,
transcending bounds of space and time.
All cells beyond the mortal tomb,
as they are whole in Mother's womb.

O Mother Mary, generate,
the song that does accelerate,
my mind into a peaceful state,
God's perfect love I radiate.

8. Mother Mary, help me see if I have become comfortable with the linear mind and have used the teachings of the ascended masters to create a linear view of the world where I feel I have figured out how the world works.

> In resonance with life's own song,
> in life's harmonics I belong.
> The blueprint of my perfect state
> does every cell reconsecrate.
>
> **O Mother Mary, generate,**
> **the song that does accelerate,**
> **my mind into a peaceful state,**
> **God's perfect love I radiate.**

9. Mother Mary, I am willing to step up higher in order to grasp the highest potential in my Divine plan. I recognize that the goal of my Divine plan is that I reach the highest level of consciousness I have the potential to reach.

> The tuning fork in every cell
> is now attuned to Mother's bell.
> From curse of death I AM now free,
> I claim my immortality.
>
> **O Mother Mary, generate,**
> **the song that does accelerate,**
> **my mind into a peaceful state,**
> **God's perfect love I radiate.**

Part 3

1. Mother Mary, help me know if I have the potential for this to be my last embodiment, so that I can ascend either immediately after this embodiment or shortly thereafter.

> O Blessed Mary's Song of Life,
> consuming every form of strife.

As I attune to sound so fair,
each cell is healthy, I declare.

**O Mother Mary, generate,
the song that does accelerate,
my mind into a peaceful state,
God's perfect love I radiate.**

2. Mother Mary, help me see how to shift my conscious mind from the lowest consciousness to the highest. What are the prejudices, the filters and the holy cows in my four lower bodies that I need to challenge and see beyond in order to shift my consciousness? What do I need to go through of experiences in order to shift my consciousness to the highest level?

As life's own song I ever hear,
it does consume all sense of fear.
In tune with Mother's symphony,
from all diseases I AM free.

**O Mother Mary, generate,
the song that does accelerate,
my mind into a peaceful state,
God's perfect love I radiate.**

3. Mother Mary, help me see what inner experience, what kind of high experience, a shifting experience, maybe even a shocking experience, I need in order to come up to my fullest potential in this embodiment. What do I need to give up in order to get there?

In Mother's love I do transcend,
and all my struggles hereby end.
For when with Mother's eye I see,
no imperfection touches me.

**O Mother Mary, generate,
the song that does accelerate,
my mind into a peaceful state,
God's perfect love I radiate.**

4. Mother Mary, I realize that the way I look at life on earth is all a product of what is in my four lower bodies. What is in my four lower bodies is not who I really am. I am not so attached to the contents of my four lower bodies because I want to express who I really am.

> I see that healing must begin
> by finding Living Christ within.
> For as I see with single eye,
> each cell the light does amplify.
>
> **O Mother Mary, generate,**
> **the song that does accelerate,**
> **my mind into a peaceful state,**
> **God's perfect love I radiate.**

5. Mother Mary, the contents of my four lower bodies are not so important that I am willing to give up being who I really am in order to defend those concepts, those selves that are ultimately unreal.

> In Mother's music I am free,
> from memories of a lesser me.
> My vision in a perfect state,
> that all my cells regenerate.
>
> **O Mother Mary, generate,**
> **the song that does accelerate,**
> **my mind into a peaceful state,**
> **God's perfect love I radiate.**

6. Mother Mary, I realize that the highest potential for my Divine plan is that I give up these limitations, these identifications, this outer mind, these emotional patterns, these physical habits. I give them up because I want something higher, I want to express who I really am.

> O Mother's Love, sweet melody,
> from imperfections I AM free.
> O Mother Mary, sound of sounds,
> within my heart your love abounds.

> O Mother Mary, generate,
> the song that does accelerate,
> my mind into a peaceful state,
> God's perfect love I radiate.

7. Mother Mary, help me overcome the fear of considering who I really am. I see I am not this outer personality that was defined as I was growing up or even in past lives, and I am willing to consider: "Who am I? Who do I want to be?"

> Through Mother's beauty so sublime,
> transcending bounds of space and time.
> All cells beyond the mortal tomb,
> as they are whole in Mother's womb.

> O Mother Mary, generate,
> the song that does accelerate,
> my mind into a peaceful state,
> God's perfect love I radiate.

8. Mother Mary, help me recapture some awareness of my Divine plan and the highest potential for that plan.

> In resonance with life's own song,
> in life's harmonics I belong.
> The blueprint of my perfect state
> does every cell reconsecrate.

> O Mother Mary, generate,
> the song that does accelerate,
> my mind into a peaceful state,
> God's perfect love I radiate.

9. Mother Mary, help me see the aspects that I have become comfortable with that are blocking the next vision that I am capable of achieving, especially related to healing my birth trauma.

> The tuning fork in every cell
> is now attuned to Mother's bell.

From curse of death I AM now free,
I claim my immortality.

**O Mother Mary, generate,
the song that does accelerate,
my mind into a peaceful state,
God's perfect love I radiate.**

Sealing

In the name of the Divine Mother, I call to Mother Mary for the sealing of myself and all people in my circle of influence in the creative flow of the Divine Mother, the River of Life. I call for the multiplication of my calls by all representatives of the Divine Mother, so that we form the perfect figure-eight flow of "As Above, so below." Thus, I accept that this is fully manifest, because the mouth of the Lord, the Divine Mother that I AM, has spoken it. Amen.

3 | OVERCOMING THE FEAR OF BEING WRONG

I am the Ascended Master Mother Mary, and I wish to build upon the teachings I gave you in my previous discourse. I had you go through the exercise of envisioning that you were raised up to our level, looking at the earth, looking at all the different groups of people and how they were all in a certain state of consciousness. They had certain blocks in their four lower bodies that could make it difficult for us to reach their conscious minds with a message. I also had you look at yourself and how you made your Divine plan from a higher state of consciousness than you had when you came into embodiment. What I wish to move on to here is the realization that there is a fundamental difficulty in what we are doing here, in the sense that we are giving a teaching about how to discover and implement your Divine plan. We are, of course, having to give it in general terms so that it applies to many different people.

You have to recognize that when you make your Divine plan, this is a completely individual process. You are meeting with your ascended teachers and guides and we together are looking at your lifestream. We are looking at other lifestreams that you have ties to, whether karmic or other ties and we are making an individual plan for you. Now, naturally, we cannot in a discourse like this, give each of you your individual Divine plan. What you need to do is use the general teaching to discover your individual Divine plan—and how can you do this?

You can do it only from within, my beloved. Now, I know that there are many, many spiritual people in the world who have a genuine desire to know what is the purpose for their life, whether they call it a Divine plan or something else. Probably, you may have done it yourself, or you may know people who have gone to various kinds of psychics, oracles, astrologers, tarot card readers, whatever you have, in order to get somebody to give you some kind of directions that are, what we might say, unmistakable to your outer mind in the sense that you can hear them. My beloved, based on this, you could say: "Well, when we have a sponsored messenger, why don't we simply have the messenger give a reading from the ascended masters to each person for ten or fifteen minutes, telling them about their Divine plan?"

Now, aside from the time issue, this could theoretically be done. As we allow you to ask questions that we answer, we could as well give these kinds of readings for people individually. You understand, my beloved, that if we did this, it would actually defeat part of the purpose of your Divine plan. That is why we do not encourage you, when you come to this level of the spiritual path, to go to anybody and ask them to tell you what you should do, who you are, how you should behave, what is your Divine plan and your purpose, your past lives or this or that. This belongs at a certain level of spirituality.

I do not condemn anyone for going into this, but I want to point out to you that the teaching we are giving here is not for that level of spirituality. We may call it the level where people are sort of seeking some kind of excitement, some kind of interest beyond their daily lives, some kind of almost entertainment. We could call it "entertainment spirituality" but we do not want to sound negative or in any way critical because people must take what road they need to take. Hopefully, gradually, they raise their consciousness. What I am pointing out to you is that those of you who are open to this teaching, you have raised your consciousness beyond the level where you need this. Therefore, you need to recognize something very simple. As I said last night, in your current lifetime you came in at a certain level of consciousness. Now, I warned you against being too attached to the linear mind but, of course, we have given you a linear teaching that there are 144 levels of consciousness possible on earth.

3 | *Overcoming the fear of being wrong*

What it means to shift your consciousness

Let us, just for the sake of example, say that someone came in at the 67th level and they have the potential to reach the 120th level in this lifetime. This may seem like a big leap in consciousness but for many of you who are at this level of the path, it is not actually a big leap. There are some of you that might come in close to the 96th level and actually have the potential to go to the 144th level in this lifetime, not all of you but some of you. You do not need to worry about where you are at, as such. I am giving an example here that you come in at a certain level and you have the potential to rise to a higher level. The entire purpose of your Divine plan is to take you through a series of inner insights, resolution of psychology and outer experiences that facilitate this growth in consciousness, from the lowest level to the highest potential.

What does it take to actually shift your consciousness? Well, my beloved, if you had some outside personal authority reveal to you that this is your Divine plan, this is what you are supposed to do, would that shift your consciousness? It would not! Being told by some authority figure what you are supposed to do and then trying to do it, is not going to shift your consciousness. The other thing is, even if you were told that in your Divine plan you are supposed to become a nuclear scientist and make a new discovery that will change the energy production on earth, you might with the outer mind decide to study nuclear physics and have this goal in mind, but I can guarantee you that you would not be able to make the discovery.

In order to make a certain discovery, or in order to even realize what are the higher levels of your personal Divine plan, you need to shift your consciousness upwards. That is why, discovering your Divine plan is not something you can do in one step. It is a gradual process that will be ongoing for your entire lifetime. You see, my beloved, you are at the 67th level when you come in, well you may have a potential to reach the 120th level but that is not your concern when you are at the early stages of your path.

Let us say you discover the spiritual path when you are 18 and in the meantime you may have grown a little bit beyond the 67th level so you are now at the 70th level. Your main concern is not to reach the 120th level, your main concern is to reach the 71st level. Then, when you go there, to reach the 72nd level and so on. What I am saying here is something that many of you may not have thought about but which you actually all know, when you really think about it. Knowing and understanding a spiritual teaching is not the same as shifting your consciousness.

It is possible to intellectually, with the linear, analytical mind, know and understand a spiritual teaching but you have not actually shifted from the 70th to the 71st level. Only when you do shift your mind, will you be able to see and implement the next level of your Divine plan. You see what I am saying here. It is a matter of you realizing that discovering and implementing your Divine plan is an interactive process that is ongoing for your entire lifetime.

No need to panic

That is why some of you may look back at your lives and you are all wondering: "Have I followed my Divine plan, did I do something wrong, what about that relationship where I was in love with that person but the relationship never came about. Does that mean that an important aspect of my Divine plan has now been aborted because this didn't happen? Or what because I made this mistake when I was young or I didn't get this education or I didn't get that job?" You can go into almost a state of panic. You understand that it is not our purpose to give you the concept of your Divine plan in order to get you to go into a state of stress and panic about it.

You need to recognize here that you can look back at your life and you can say: "Have I followed my Divine plan?" I would say: "Have you shifted your consciousness from when you came into embodiment to your present level?" All of you have, so I would say: "Well then you have certainly followed your Divine plan." You may not have shifted your consciousness as much as you *could* do. Our whole purpose for giving you this teaching is, of course, to get you to shift your consciousness to the point where you can catch up to where you ideally would have been if you had made the maximum progress. Some of you may be lagging a little bit behind where you could have been, but you can quickly catch up by applying the teachings we are giving you. Also, do not get yourself into the expectation that if you use the teaching we are giving you (in this workbook), then one day in six months or a year, you will have the full vision of your Divine plan appear to you while angels are playing trumpets in the background.

As I said, you will not see the fullness of your Divine plan at any point in your life until you are ready to go out of embodiment. Then, you will see the last phase of it. You always see it in stages. Why is this? Because, as I said, the purpose of your Divine plan is to shift your consciousness higher. How do you shift your consciousness, my beloved?

No instant salvation

Here is something that many, many, many spiritual people have misunderstood. Many people think that in order to come up to a higher level of the spiritual path (however they explain it, however they express it in words), it is a matter of getting this understanding. Then, when you have the full understanding, when you have this absolute truth, this magnificent spiritual teaching, then "poof" you will be enlightened.

My beloved, if you look at the entire spiritual or New Age movement, the majority of the people out there are still waiting for that "poof" and it never comes. Shifting your consciousness from the 70th to the 71st level is not a matter of receiving some ultimate insight. Even if you knew and intellectually understood everything, how would you shift your consciousness? You actually shift your consciousness by using the level of consciousness you have but using it in a higher way so you transcend that level of consciousness.

Do you understand what I am saying? You cannot shift from the 70th to the 71st level by seeking some ultimate insight. You need an insight that you can grasp with the 70th level but it will take you to the next level up. It is not an ultimate insight or understanding. So many people are chasing that ultimate insight. They keep chasing it and chasing it, and they go from teacher to guru and guru to teacher and they are hoping that this person now has that ultimate insight, the 10th insight, the 11th insight, the 99th insight or whatever they go for. My beloved, that is *not* how you grow on the path.

If you knew every aspect of your Divine plan, if it was told to you, it would most likely prevent you from implementing your Divine plan because, as I said, the main aspect of your Divine plan is actually the shift in consciousness. You shift by using the knowledge and insight you have at a given level but being willing to look beyond it and then getting that intuitive insight that takes you to the higher level. It is not a matter of understanding because, as we have said before, when you *understand* something, you are looking at it from a distance. You only shift your consciousness when you actually have that intuitive, mystical, holistic, all-encompassing *experience*. What actually happens is, my beloved, that at the 70th level, you are experiencing yourself a certain way. Then, something happens that challenges the way you look at things at the 70th level. It challenges what you feel comfortable with at the 70th level. Then, when you are still willing to look at this, even though there is a certain part of your ego that is uncomfortable with the teaching, that is when you have the inner, intuitive experience where you *experience* the reality of it. As you do this, you are shifting the way you experience yourself a little bit and now you are at the 71st level. It is not an *intellectual* process, it is an *intuitive* process. It is a process of shifting your identity, not increasing your mental understanding.

The inner shifting experience

You see, my beloved, even though we have said that some people are focused in the emotional body, some people in the mental and some in the identity, it is not a matter of shifting the focus of the conscious mind. It is actually a matter of shifting your sense of identity. This is what happens even if you are focused at the physical level and you are not aware that you have an identity body. You can still go from lower to higher states of consciousness by shifting your awareness without being conscious of it. Of course, as you focus your attention more in the identity body, you become more and more conscious of when you shift your identity. That way you can make faster progress because you can consciously be willing to shift your identity, you can seek out the insights that will help you shift your identity.

My beloved, these are important things to keep in mind. When you get this book, when you start working with it, do not be too eager, do not be too fast. Take the time to consider these insights we are giving you. Consider what they mean, not just understanding them intellectually but really seeking out that shifting experience where you, from within, experience the truth of what we are saying.

My beloved, you have a very, very old tradition on this planet of having gurus, of having mystery schools. Supposedly, there is some guru or some institution and as a student you can go there. You apply yourself as a student and then the school or the guru is going to take you through a process of initiation whereby you gradually raise your consciousness. My beloved, it is entirely possible to go to even a genuine guru and a genuine mystery school and you think you are making progress because of your increase in your outer understanding, but you are not shifting the consciousness. Shifting your consciousness happens only from within, it does not happen because somebody tells you something. It does not matter if you have a genuine guru who tells you something about your state of consciousness or exposes an aspect of your ego. If you do not receive from within the confirmation, if you do not *experience* the reality of it within yourself, it will not shift your consciousness.

It is the same with all of the teachings we have given through this or other messengers. You can study them, you can understand them with the outer mind, you can be able quote them but will it shift your consciousness? Not unless you experience it from within. Not unless you are willing to, as we have told you, let the Conscious You step outside of your four lower bodies, reach for your I AM Presence, reach for your ascended teachers and experience directly that there is a higher reality than your outer mind. Only *then* do you shift.

The fear of being wrong

What I told you last night was to consider that there is something that you have become comfortable with that is preventing you from seeing the next stage of your Divine plan. Naturally, this can be all individual. Some of you have received these insights, some of you have received nothing and wonder why, but I will give you a general teaching that applies to all of you. It is not meant to override your individual insights but I am pointing out that there is a certain thing, a certain psychology, that applies to all people on earth and therefore to all spiritual people as well.

Now, my beloved, what is the one thing that you are all comfortable with? Well, you have all found some level of comfortability with the idea that if you do certain things and do not do other things, then you cannot be wrong, then you are okay, you are acceptable. There is a fear that has been programmed into all people on earth, because it is a high-density planet, that you can be wrong. Where does this come from? Where does this fear come from? Well, it naturally comes from the fallen beings who, from the moment they started embodying on this planet, have created, as we have told you about before, this entire mindset (that is the essence of duality) that there is something that is right and something that is wrong. There is only, as I talked about yesterday, one truth and therefore all the others must be wrong. This applies to so many areas of life and we have said before that the only thing that the fallen beings really had to do to pervert things on earth, was to project out the concept that there is a distinction between right and wrong. Some things are right, some things are wrong.

Once you have that dualistic, relative judgment going on in people's minds, then it automatically follows that people start developing the fear of being wrong. Now, we have given you the teaching that many of you (and here I am not talking about you here but in general), many spiritual people have come to earth as avatars. You have come here to make a positive difference. You have experienced the fallen beings who have been very, very aggressive in putting you down. What is the message they gave you? It is that you were wrong for coming to earth, you are wrong being who you are as an avatar here on earth, you are wrong expressing your real being, your real creativity here on earth. This gave you what we have called the birth trauma. In order to deal with that, in order to survive that psychologically, you created what we have said: the internal selves, the primal self. Part of the primal self of all of you is that you have decided that you do not want to constantly experience this sense of being wrong.

You have found, individually, your own ways of creating the sense that: "If I stay within certain boundaries, then I'm not wrong." This is something that, of course, goes all the way back to when you received your birth trauma but you can also look at this lifetime. You can see how you were brought up by society to have certain boundaries. You stay within certain boundaries, then you are acceptable to your native society, then you are following the norm and society will not condemn you. Other people around you and your family and environment will not condemn you if you stay within these boundaries.

What I am pointing out to you is that you all have these subtle beliefs, structures, matrices in your four lower bodies that say that: "If I stay within these boundaries, I cannot be wrong." Then, you also have this sense that as long as you stay within these boundaries, you are comfortable. You are comfortable in not being wrong according to the norms of your society but ultimately according to the standard of the fallen beings. My beloved, any society that enforces – programs into its citizens – the idea that there are some things that are wrong and some things that are right is influenced by the fallen beings.

3 | Overcoming the fear of being wrong

Questioning the uncomfortable

Now, naturally, some will take this with the linear mind and say: Does that mean I am saying nothing is right and nothing is wrong and people can do whatever they want? Well, of course not! As we have said before, any society must define certain boundaries. Obviously, it is not right to go out and kill other people. What I am talking about here is not so much the outer behavior but more an inner behavior of your beliefs, your attitudes, what you talk about. In other words, the real issue here that I want to bring to your attention is that what is programmed into these standards that all societies have is that there are certain ideas that are acceptable and certain ideas that are wrong. If you believe in these ideas, you are wrong but if you talk about these ideas you are even more wrong. If you change your life and act upon these ideas, you are really wrong.

Naturally, we are not looking at here having spiritual people go out and do all kind of things that are illegal or wrong according to a normal standard of common sense. What we are looking at here is to have you consider that there are certain ideas that it would be uncomfortable for you to question.

If you are willing to look at this individually, you can gradually come to see that, whether it was just from this lifetime or whether it goes back many lifetimes, there are certain ideas where if you were to question these, you would feel uncomfortable. One way to expose this is to read the book *My Lives* where you will see that many people feel there were certain ideas in that book that made them feel uncomfortable because they had to question their existing beliefs. There are, of course, many other examples of this. Often, our teachings do the same thing to people.

If you can identify that there is a certain idea that you do not want to question (you take for granted, you believe this is some higher truth), then I can assure you that this is part of your comfortability. It comes from the fact that if you do not question the idea, then you feel you cannot be wrong, and that makes you feel comfortable.

If you were to question this idea, you become uncomfortable because now you are afraid that you could be wrong and you could be condemned. Whatever that fear is for you individually (based on your experiences in past lives of being persecuted harshly by other people), then you are afraid to open up this "can of worms" because you never know what is going to happen.

Christhood and your Divine plan

What I wish to point out to you here is that many of you (who have walked the spiritual path for a long time and who have reached a certain level of consciousness), have reached the point where your challenge is to more consciously express the Christhood that you built into your Divine plan. What is Christhood? Well, it can be defined in many ways but as Jesus has said several times, Christhood is challenging status quo. The Christ comes into embodiment, the Living Christ in embodiment, has as its primary purpose to challenge status quo and make people realize that there is an alternative to the state of consciousness that has become a closed system. I can assure you that for all of you who are open to these teachings and who have reached a more mature level of the path, there is a certain element of Christhood that is built into your Divine plans.

You are here to challenge status quo in some way. This may not be in some ultimate way where you bring forth some new, revolutionary ideology that challenges existing ideologies. For many of you it is at the personal level where you challenge the way the people around you look at certain problems or look at certain aspects of life. It can be very individual how you are meant to do this but all of you have this as an element of your Divine plan. What I am bringing you to is the awareness that in order to actually be able to see this and in order to be able to implement it, you need to be willing to look at your fear of being wrong. You need to recognize that this is an integral part of your birth trauma, it is an integral part of your primal self. That is where, as I have said before, we have given you a lot of tools before we gave you this teaching on your Divine plan because now you can take the book *Healing Your Spiritual Traumas* and you can use that to seek to heal this fear of being wrong.

Naturally, my beloved, you have come to a point where you recognize both the existence of ascended masters and of fallen beings. You recognize that we of the ascended masters want to pull you up and set you free from all limitations. The fallen beings want to pull you down and keep you trapped in those limitations. You can begin to ask yourself: "What do I want to live the rest of my life based on?" Do you want to live based on the fear of being wrong according to the standard of the fallen beings, or the awareness that comes from understanding the ascended master teachings, which is that you are never wrong for challenging the ideas of the fallen beings. The world might say you are wrong, but we of the ascended masters certainly do not.

It is very important for you to consider this. This does not have to be something you do all at once in an ultimate way because, as I said, you are currently at a certain level of consciousness and your primary concern is to go to the next level up, which is often not such a big dramatic step. The question is, what is the fear of being wrong that you are dealing with right now? What is the one idea you could express at your current level of consciousness that would take you to a higher level and how is the fear of being wrong preventing you from expressing that idea?

Challenging ideas at the personal level

Now, my beloved, I said earlier that the Divine plan is an interactive process. As another example, say that your family has a certain view of life, a certain attitude to life. There is a particular family member who has the potential to rise higher in this lifetime but is stuck in this view of life. It is part of your Divine plan that you would help that person question this belief and go beyond it, but you are kind of afraid of doing this because you feel that other members of your family would condemn you for doing so. The question now is: "How will you rise to the next level of your Divine plan?" Can you rise to the next level of your Divine plan without expressing the higher understanding that you see, without actually giving that to the other person?

My beloved, you cannot. You cannot rise to the next level without challenging yourself. Why is that? Because, my beloved, you may say: "Well, if I express my insights, then certain members of my family will get mad at me and I'll get a negative reaction." I will tell you in a very, very direct manner that it is only by expressing your understanding and experiencing the reaction that you will be forced to shift your own perception, your own attitude. Only in dealing with this challenge, experiencing this challenge, will you be able to shift to the next level up.

You see, my beloved, it is not a matter of receiving some intellectual understanding. It is not a matter of you having an insight that is higher than your family members and then you say: "Because I have this insight, I've already shifted to a higher level of consciousness than they have." Maybe you have shifted to a higher level of consciousness than theirs but you have not shifted to the next level up, and you will not until you express your insight, experience their reaction and then deal with your internal reaction to them.

Only when you deal with this and find a way to overcome the patterns, the fears, the attachments, the emotional-mental reaction you have, only then will you shift your own consciousness to the next level. That is why, my beloved, what I am telling you here is that in order to step up and really get into consciously seeing more aspects of your Divine plan, you need to get yourself into a frame of mind where you are not afraid to take the experience even if it makes you uncomfortable, even if it makes you afraid. You are still willing to take that experience because you realize that it is only in having the experience that you are processing the hang-ups in your own psychology, coming to see them and then transcending them.

Growth requires interaction with people

We have given you so many tools, my beloved, to transcend the hang-ups in your psychology. You have enough tools to transcend them but what many of you have not realized is that you cannot sit in your private room and read books and give invocations indefinitely and then experience maximum growth from this. You can experience growth from it but you need to have the interchange between doing the spiritual work and having actual experiences where you are challenged, where you are tested, where you see a reaction in yourself.

This is, of course, where many of the people that I talked about who run to fortune tellers and psychics and read books about your life's purpose and your Divine plan, they are not willing to do that work. They want to stay where they are comfortable. Well, as we have said before, comfortability and the spiritual path are not really compatible. Certainly, also this planet is not really compatible with being comfortable. You need to make that shift where you say: "Who am I? Am I an ascended master student? Am I a person who is determined to make the maximum progress in this lifetime? Well, if I am, then I don't need to be comfortable."

It is not a matter of being comfortable. I am not saying to torture yourself but it is a matter of realizing that there is a certain element in your psychology where you want to stay where you are comfortable, you want to run away from what makes you uncomfortable. It is only by identifying that and going right into it (being willing to go into the situation and experience the reaction you have), it is only then that you will be able to see the hang-up in your psychology. You cannot see it intellectually from a distance. You need to go into it and experience it, and then you can use the tools we have given you to overcome it, to identify the self, to separate yourself from it and to let it die. This is how the process of growth works.

The spiritual path is not easy

It is a teaching that for some will be discouraging because they have, perhaps for many years on the spiritual path, been holding on to this ideal that is projected out there in the collective consciousness that spiritual progress is just an entirely easy, positive, uplifting process. My beloved, this particular idea (that the spiritual path does not require work, does not require groveling with your own psychology) is, of course, projected out there by the fallen beings in order to keep people trapped at this level where they are always looking outside themselves and they are never really looking in the mirror, looking at their own psychology.

You, of course, are beyond this or you would not have responded to this teaching. I am simply making you aware that you can consciously make a shift because you realize that regardless of what the fallen beings project at you, regardless of what other people project at you, you are never wrong for shifting your consciousness. You are never wrong for shifting your consciousness upwards.

When you fully accept that, when you fully experience the reality of that, then you can actually enter a new phase of your interaction with the ascended masters where *we* become your frame of reference, instead of the fallen beings or other people being your frame of reference—or even the selves, the separate selves, the internal spirits, being your frame of reference. You can begin to realize that we are not frustrated, we are not angry, we are not impatient, we are not looking to condemn you or criticize you.

Why the masters do not condemn us

I know very well, my beloved, that there are ascended master students who believe, and there have been ascended master organizations that had a collective culture where the teachings of the ascended masters were actually used to reinforce the sense of how you could be wrong and how you could be right. There have been ascended master organizations where people have been so concerned about dressing the right way, talking the right way, walking the right way, looking the right way, thinking the right way, feeling the right way—and condemning each other and themselves for not being right according to some outer standard.

That was what we had to work with at the time. In some cases, as we have said, we actually had to magnify people's beliefs so they became so extreme that people were finally willing to question it. My beloved, you who have the teaching you have, you can very quickly step beyond all this and realize that we of the ascended masters – the real ascended masters – are beyond duality. We do not judge you based on a standard of right and wrong. We do not criticize, we do not condemn you. We have total acceptance of you – *you* – each one of you. We accept you unconditionally for who you are. We only have one desire and it is to help you become more of who you are by shifting your identity upwards.

My beloved, I truly wish that you could look at yourself with the same unconditional acceptance with which I look at you. I know that if you apply the tools that we have given you, you can come to that point. I know you cannot come to that point by me telling you, and I am not telling you in order to make you feel bad that you cannot accept yourself, my beloved. You can see how the ego can take any teaching and make you feel: "Mother Mary says I should be accepting myself unconditionally but I can't so I must be wrong."

These are the kind of loops that you can come to identify, and you realize that this is simply a separate self. As the messenger expressed last night, there is a part of the mind that is programmed to create problems and project that you have to solve them. Well, there is also a part of the mind, the separate self, that is programmed to project that you are wrong and to use any idea that comes to you to turn this around and show: "Yeah, here is another way in which you are wrong—you are not living up to your highest potential, you are not good enough."

My beloved, you are all good enough. You are all right where you should be, because you are at the point on your path where you are ready to take the next step up and that is what we are concerned with. There is no standard we are comparing you to. Do not even begin to believe that we say that until you are at the 144th level of consciousness, you are wrong. My beloved, you are on the path. What really matters is that you continue to take one step at a time and shift upwards. We accept that you are who you are, that you are at your current level. We wish that you can accept that as well because, my beloved, there actually comes a point where you cannot go higher on the path unless you overcome the linear mind.

There also comes a point where you cannot go higher on the path until you overcome the critical mind that is always criticizing yourself.

No constructive criticism

There is a concept in the world of "constructive criticism" but, my beloved, as long as people are in a dualistic state of consciousness, there is no such thing as constructive criticism. Criticism is a vibration. It does not matter how "right" the person is in what they are pointing out. If it is still done with that level of consciousness, it is not constructive. It is the same thing with you yourselves. You may think that you have to be critical of yourself because that is how you grow. My beloved, there is a self that has a dualistic vibration of criticism and that self cannot take you higher on the path.

There comes a point where you need to step back and see that this is just a self. It is not a matter of whether the self is right or not in what it is pointing out. It is a matter of identifying that the vibration of the self is not love-based—it is fear-based. Therefore, you need to separate from that self, look at it and say: "I don't need you anymore!" You do not need to go into some judgment, you do not even need to go into a justification (as some of you are prone to do) and say: "Yeah, but it served a purpose; it helped me to grow on the path." Maybe it did, but, my beloved, what you need to do is identify it and say: "I don't need this self anymore and I am letting it die."

My beloved, this was what I wanted to give you for now. I thank you, again, for your presence, for your awareness. We, of course, look forward to giving you more teachings as you have a little chance to implement some of the ideas we have given you and to shift your consciousness to the next level up where you can receive the next teaching.

4 | INVOKING FREEDOM FROM THE FEAR OF BEING WRONG

In the name I AM THAT I AM, Jesus Christ, I call to all representatives of the Divine Mother, especially Mother Mary, to help me overcome all fear of being wrong, including…

[Make personal calls.]

Part 1

1. Mother Mary, I see that if I was told from without what my Divine plan is, it would not be constructive. The entire purpose of my Divine plan is to take me through a series of inner insights, resolution of psychology and outer experiences that facilitate my growth in consciousness, from the lowest level to the highest potential.

O Blessed Mary's Song of Life,
consuming every form of strife.

As I attune to sound so fair,
each cell is healthy, I declare.

O Mother Mary, generate,
the song that does accelerate,
my mind into a peaceful state,
God's perfect love I radiate.

2. Mother Mary, in order to realize what are the higher levels of my Divine plan, I need to shift my consciousness upwards and this is not something I can do in one step. It is a gradual process that will be ongoing for my entire lifetime.

As life's own song I ever hear,
it does consume all sense of fear.
In tune with Mother's symphony,
from all diseases I AM free.

O Mother Mary, generate,
the song that does accelerate,
my mind into a peaceful state,
God's perfect love I radiate.

3. Mother Mary, I see that knowing and understanding a spiritual teaching is not the same as shifting my consciousness. Only when I shift my mind, will I be able to see and implement the next level of my Divine plan. Discovering and implementing my Divine plan is an interactive process that is ongoing for my entire lifetime.

In Mother's love I do transcend,
and all my struggles hereby end.
For when with Mother's eye I see,
no imperfection touches me.

O Mother Mary, generate,
the song that does accelerate,
my mind into a peaceful state,
God's perfect love I radiate.

4. Mother Mary, I recognize that if I have shifted my consciousness from when I came into embodiment to my present level, then I have followed my Divine plan.

> I see that healing must begin
> by finding Living Christ within.
> For as I see with single eye,
> each cell the light does amplify.
>
> **O Mother Mary, generate,**
> **the song that does accelerate,**
> **my mind into a peaceful state,**
> **God's perfect love I radiate.**

5. Mother Mary, I accept that I will not see the fullness of my Divine plan at any point in my life. I always see it in stages because the purpose of my Divine plan is to shift my consciousness higher.

> In Mother's music I am free,
> from memories of a lesser me.
> My vision in a perfect state,
> that all my cells regenerate.
>
> **O Mother Mary, generate,**
> **the song that does accelerate,**
> **my mind into a peaceful state,**
> **God's perfect love I radiate.**

6. Mother Mary, I see that in order to come up to a higher level of the spiritual path, it is not a matter of getting understanding. I shift my consciousness by using the level of consciousness I have, but using it in a higher way so I transcend that level of consciousness.

> O Mother's Love, sweet melody,
> from imperfections I AM free.
> O Mother Mary, sound of sounds,
> within my heart your love abounds.

> O Mother Mary, generate,
> the song that does accelerate,
> my mind into a peaceful state,
> God's perfect love I radiate.

7. Mother Mary, I am not seeking some ultimate insight. I am seeking the insight that I can grasp with my present level of consciousness, but it will take me to the next level up.

> Through Mother's beauty so sublime,
> transcending bounds of space and time.
> All cells beyond the mortal tomb,
> as they are whole in Mother's womb.

> O Mother Mary, generate,
> the song that does accelerate,
> my mind into a peaceful state,
> God's perfect love I radiate.

8. Mother Mary, I see that I only shift my consciousness when I have that intuitive, mystical, holistic, all-encompassing *experience,* so I shift the way I experience myself and now I am at the next level.

> In resonance with life's own song,
> in life's harmonics I belong.
> The blueprint of my perfect state
> does every cell reconsecrate.

> O Mother Mary, generate,
> the song that does accelerate,
> my mind into a peaceful state,
> God's perfect love I radiate.

9. Mother Mary, I see that it is not a matter of shifting the focus of the conscious mind. It is a matter of shifting my sense of identity. Help me become more and more conscious of when I shift my identity. I am willing to shift my identity, and I seek the insights that will help me shift my identity.

The tuning fork in every cell
is now attuned to Mother's bell.
From curse of death I AM now free,
I claim my immortality.

O Mother Mary, generate,
the song that does accelerate,
my mind into a peaceful state,
God's perfect love I radiate.

Part 2

1. Mother Mary, I am willing to let the Conscious You step outside of my four lower bodies, reach for my I AM Presence, reach for my ascended teachers and experience directly that there is a higher reality than my outer mind. I am willing to shift.

O Blessed Mary's Song of Life,
consuming every form of strife.
As I attune to sound so fair,
each cell is healthy, I declare.

O Mother Mary, generate,
the song that does accelerate,
my mind into a peaceful state,
God's perfect love I radiate.

2. Mother Mary, help me see my comfortability with the idea that if I do certain things and do not do other things, then I cannot be wrong, then I am okay, I am acceptable.

As life's own song I ever hear,
it does consume all sense of fear.
In tune with Mother's symphony,
from all diseases I AM free.

**O Mother Mary, generate,
the song that does accelerate,
my mind into a peaceful state,
God's perfect love I radiate.**

3. Mother Mary, help me uncover the programming that I can be wrong, the mindset that there is something that is right and something that is wrong, causing me to develop the fear of being wrong.

In Mother's love I do transcend,
and all my struggles hereby end.
For when with Mother's eye I see,
no imperfection touches me.

**O Mother Mary, generate,
the song that does accelerate,
my mind into a peaceful state,
God's perfect love I radiate.**

4. Mother Mary, help me uncover the programming from the fallen beings that I was wrong for coming to earth, I am wrong for being who I am as an avatar on earth, I am wrong expressing my real being, my real creativity here on earth.

I see that healing must begin
by finding Living Christ within.
For as I see with single eye,
each cell the light does amplify.

**O Mother Mary, generate,
the song that does accelerate,
my mind into a peaceful state,
God's perfect love I radiate.**

5. Mother Mary, help me see that in order to survive the attack of the fallen beings psychologically, I created the internal selves, the primal self. Part of the primal self is that I have decided that I do not want to constantly experience this sense of being wrong.

In Mother's music I am free,
from memories of a lesser me.
My vision in a perfect state,
that all my cells regenerate.

O Mother Mary, generate,
the song that does accelerate,
my mind into a peaceful state,
God's perfect love I radiate.

6. Mother Mary, help me see how I have found my individual way of creating the sense: "If I stay within certain boundaries, then I'm not wrong."

O Mother's Love, sweet melody,
from imperfections I AM free.
O Mother Mary, sound of sounds,
within my heart your love abounds.

O Mother Mary, generate,
the song that does accelerate,
my mind into a peaceful state,
God's perfect love I radiate.

7. Mother Mary, help me uncover the sense that as long as I stay within these boundaries, I am comfortable in not being wrong according to the norms of my society, but ultimately according to the standard of the fallen beings.

Through Mother's beauty so sublime,
transcending bounds of space and time.
All cells beyond the mortal tomb,
as they are whole in Mother's womb.

O Mother Mary, generate,
the song that does accelerate,
my mind into a peaceful state,
God's perfect love I radiate.

8. Mother Mary, help me see that it would make me uncomfortable to question certain ideas because I would be afraid that I could be wrong and I could be condemned. Help me see my individual fear, based on my experiences in past lives of being persecuted harshly by other people.

> In resonance with life's own song,
> in life's harmonics I belong.
> The blueprint of my perfect state
> does every cell reconsecrate.
>
> **O Mother Mary, generate,**
> **the song that does accelerate,**
> **my mind into a peaceful state,**
> **God's perfect love I radiate.**

9. Mother Mary, help me see that I have reached a level of consciousness where my challenge is to more consciously express the Christhood that I built into my Divine plan, namely to challenge status quo.

> The tuning fork in every cell
> is now attuned to Mother's bell.
> From curse of death I AM now free,
> I claim my immortality.
>
> **O Mother Mary, generate,**
> **the song that does accelerate,**
> **my mind into a peaceful state,**
> **God's perfect love I radiate.**

Part 3

1. Mother Mary, help me see that I am here to challenge status quo in some way. I am determined to implement this, and I am willing to look at my fear of being wrong.

> O Blessed Mary's Song of Life,
> consuming every form of strife.

> As I attune to sound so fair,
> each cell is healthy, I declare.
>
> **O Mother Mary, generate,**
> **the song that does accelerate,**
> **my mind into a peaceful state,**
> **God's perfect love I radiate.**

2. Mother Mary, I recognize that this is an integral part of my birth trauma, it is an integral part of my primal self. I am willing to use the tools to heal this fear of being wrong.

> As life's own song I ever hear,
> it does consume all sense of fear.
> In tune with Mother's symphony,
> from all diseases I AM free.
>
> **O Mother Mary, generate,**
> **the song that does accelerate,**
> **my mind into a peaceful state,**
> **God's perfect love I radiate.**

3. Mother Mary, I hereby decide that I want to live the rest of my life based on the awareness that comes from understanding the ascended master teachings, which is that I am never wrong for challenging the ideas of the fallen beings. The world might say I am wrong, but the ascended masters do not.

> In Mother's love I do transcend,
> and all my struggles hereby end.
> For when with Mother's eye I see,
> no imperfection touches me.
>
> **O Mother Mary, generate,**
> **the song that does accelerate,**
> **my mind into a peaceful state,**
> **God's perfect love I radiate.**

4. Mother Mary, help me see what is the fear of being wrong that I am dealing with right now. What is the one idea I could express at my current level of consciousness that would take me to a higher level? How is the fear of being wrong preventing me from expressing that idea?

> I see that healing must begin
> by finding Living Christ within.
> For as I see with single eye,
> each cell the light does amplify.
>
> **O Mother Mary, generate,**
> **the song that does accelerate,**
> **my mind into a peaceful state,**
> **God's perfect love I radiate.**

5. Mother Mary, I see that I cannot rise to the next level of my Divine plan without expressing the higher understanding that I see, without actually giving that to another person. I cannot rise to the next level without challenging myself.

> In Mother's music I am free,
> from memories of a lesser me.
> My vision in a perfect state,
> that all my cells regenerate.
>
> **O Mother Mary, generate,**
> **the song that does accelerate,**
> **my mind into a peaceful state,**
> **God's perfect love I radiate.**

6. Mother Mary, I see that it is only by expressing my understanding, and experiencing the reaction from other people, that I will be forced to shift my own perception, my own attitude. Only in dealing with this challenge, will I be able to shift to the next level up.

> O Mother's Love, sweet melody,
> from imperfections I AM free.
> O Mother Mary, sound of sounds,
> within my heart your love abounds.

> **O Mother Mary, generate,**
> **the song that does accelerate,**
> **my mind into a peaceful state,**
> **God's perfect love I radiate.**

7. Mother Mary, I will shift only when I express my insight, experience people's reaction and then deal with my internal reaction to them. Only when I overcome the patterns, the fears, the attachments, the emotional-mental reaction I have, only then will I shift my consciousness to the next level.

> Through Mother's beauty so sublime,
> transcending bounds of space and time.
> All cells beyond the mortal tomb,
> as they are whole in Mother's womb.

> **O Mother Mary, generate,**
> **the song that does accelerate,**
> **my mind into a peaceful state,**
> **God's perfect love I radiate.**

8. Mother Mary, I am getting myself into a frame of mind where I am not afraid to take the experience, even if it makes me uncomfortable, even if it makes me afraid.

> In resonance with life's own song,
> in life's harmonics I belong.
> The blueprint of my perfect state
> does every cell reconsecrate.

> **O Mother Mary, generate,**
> **the song that does accelerate,**
> **my mind into a peaceful state,**
> **God's perfect love I radiate.**

9. Mother Mary, I am willing to take that experience because I realize that it is only in having the experience that I am processing the hang-ups in my own psychology, coming to see them and then transcending them.

The tuning fork in every cell
is now attuned to Mother's bell.
From curse of death I AM now free,
I claim my immortality.

O Mother Mary, generate,
the song that does accelerate,
my mind into a peaceful state,
God's perfect love I radiate.

Part 4

1. Mother Mary, I realize that I cannot sit in my private room and read books and give invocations indefinitely and then experience maximum growth from this. I need to have the interchange between doing the spiritual work and having actual experiences where I am challenged, where I am tested, where I see a reaction in myself.

O Blessed Mary's Song of Life,
consuming every form of strife.
As I attune to sound so fair,
each cell is healthy, I declare.

O Mother Mary, generate,
the song that does accelerate,
my mind into a peaceful state,
God's perfect love I radiate.

2. Mother Mary, I am making the shift of saying: "Who am I? Am I an ascended master student? Am I a person who is determined to make the maximum progress in this lifetime? Well, if I am, then I don't need to be comfortable."

As life's own song I ever hear,
it does consume all sense of fear.
In tune with Mother's symphony,
from all diseases I AM free.

4 | Invoking freedom from the fear of being wrong

**O Mother Mary, generate,
the song that does accelerate,
my mind into a peaceful state,
God's perfect love I radiate.**

3. Mother Mary, I realize there is a certain element in my psychology where I want to stay where I am comfortable, I want to run away from what makes me uncomfortable. I am identifying that and going right into it so I can see the hang-up in my psychology.

In Mother's love I do transcend,
and all my struggles hereby end.
For when with Mother's eye I see,
no imperfection touches me.

**O Mother Mary, generate,
the song that does accelerate,
my mind into a peaceful state,
God's perfect love I radiate.**

4. Mother Mary, I am identifying the self, separating myself from it and letting it die. I am letting go of the idea that spiritual progress is an easy, positive, uplifting process that does not require work, does not require groveling with my own psychology.

I see that healing must begin
by finding Living Christ within.
For as I see with single eye,
each cell the light does amplify.

**O Mother Mary, generate,
the song that does accelerate,
my mind into a peaceful state,
God's perfect love I radiate.**

5. Mother Mary, I realize that regardless of what the fallen beings project at me, regardless of what other people project at me, I am never wrong for shifting my consciousness upwards.

In Mother's music I am free,
from memories of a lesser me.
My vision in a perfect state,
that all my cells regenerate.

**O Mother Mary, generate,
the song that does accelerate,
my mind into a peaceful state,
God's perfect love I radiate.**

6. Mother Mary, I hereby enter a new phase of my interaction with the ascended masters where *you* are my frame of reference, instead of the fallen beings or other people being my frame of reference—or even the separate selves, the internal spirits, being my frame of reference.

O Mother's Love, sweet melody,
from imperfections I AM free.
O Mother Mary, sound of sounds,
within my heart your love abounds.

**O Mother Mary, generate,
the song that does accelerate,
my mind into a peaceful state,
God's perfect love I radiate.**

7. Mother Mary, I realize that you are the real ascended masters and you are beyond duality. You do not judge me based on a standard of right and wrong. You do not criticize, you do not condemn me. You have total acceptance of *me*. You accept me unconditionally for who I am.

Through Mother's beauty so sublime,
transcending bounds of space and time.
All cells beyond the mortal tomb,
as they are whole in Mother's womb.

**O Mother Mary, generate,
the song that does accelerate,
my mind into a peaceful state,
God's perfect love I radiate.**

8. Mother Mary, help me look at myself with the same unconditional acceptance with which you look at me. What really matters is that I continue to take one step at a time and shift upwards. You accept that I am who I am, that I am at my current level.

> In resonance with life's own song,
> in life's harmonics I belong.
> The blueprint of my perfect state
> does every cell reconsecrate.
>
> **O Mother Mary, generate,**
> **the song that does accelerate,**
> **my mind into a peaceful state,**
> **God's perfect love I radiate.**

9. Mother Mary, I see that I cannot go higher on the path unless I overcome the critical mind that is always criticizing myself. This self has a dualistic vibration of criticism and cannot take me higher on the path. I separate my Conscious You from that self, look at it and say: "I don't need you anymore! I am letting you die!"

> The tuning fork in every cell
> is now attuned to Mother's bell.
> From curse of death I AM now free,
> I claim my immortality.
>
> **O Mother Mary, generate,**
> **the song that does accelerate,**
> **my mind into a peaceful state,**
> **God's perfect love I radiate.**

Sealing

In the name of the Divine Mother, I call to Mother Mary for the sealing of myself and all people in my circle of influence in the creative flow of the Divine Mother, the River of Life. I call for the multiplication of my calls by all representatives of the Divine Mother, so that we form the perfect figure-eight flow of "As Above, so below." Thus, I accept that this is fully manifest, because the mouth of the Lord, the Divine Mother that I AM, has spoken it. Amen.

5 | YOU ARE NOT ON EARTH TO SOLVE PROBLEMS

I AM the Ascended Master MORE and it is my joy to address you and give you a teaching that may seem a little difficult and a little heavy to you. Nevertheless, it is important for your grasping of what your Divine plan is all about and how to implement it.

An unbalanced approach to your Divine plan

My beloved, Mother Mary raised the question of why we have not given more teachings on your Divine plan earlier. She, of course, partly answered the question but I want to bring out another facet. In a previous dispensation we gave more teachings on the Divine plan and we put more emphasis on it. We said that people had to balance their karma, they had a sacred labor they had to fulfill. What we saw in many cases was that when people heard about this concept, they went into a quite unbalanced reaction. Now, I am not saying this to in any way criticize anyone. What I am seeking to point out here is that many students, especially in previous decades, when they heard about the concept of a Divine plan, they became very enthusiastic about carrying it out.

There is, of course, nothing inherently wrong with enthusiasm. You need a certain amount of enthusiasm on the spiritual path. On the other hand, you have the old saying that: "The road to hell is paved with good intentions." I can also say that the vehicle that takes you to hell is fueled by overly enthusiastic intentions.

Many, many people have taken our teachings in an unbalanced way and used them to bring themselves into a state that they would see as quite positive because they are just being eager, anxious, determined, blue-ray and blue-flame and they are not letting anything stand in the way of the fulfillment of their Divine plan. In a sense, it is as if you have one of these rallies that goes through the countryside where you are supposed to get to a certain destination. These students get so eager that they jump into the rally car and they step on the accelerator and they are speeding down the road with the gravel spraying to all sides of the car, but they have not brought the map that will bring them to their destination. They are so focused on moving as fast as possible that they have not even considered where they are going and how to actually get there.

We have said before that one of the big problems with ascended master students is that you have a correct vision of *what* needs to happen, or at least that a change needs to happen, but you do not have the correct vision of the *how*—of how this can be brought about. One of the reasons we have not given more teachings about the Divine plan in this dispensation is that we have been more careful, taken more time to gradually build up to where you have the understanding and the practical tools in the form of the invocations and the books where you can actually deal with the opposition. Of course, you also have the practical tools to deal with whatever it is in your psychology that causes an unbalanced reaction. I am not specifically speaking to those of you who are here but also to many other people who might find this teaching and maybe even hear about a Divine plan for the first time.

The primal self and imbalance

It is important to be aware that when you first find an ascended master teaching, and especially when you hear about the concept of the Divine plan, (but also about the concept of a golden age and how to change the earth) it is not uncommon that people take this in an imbalanced way. What is the imbalance exactly? Well, that is to a large degree an individual matter so it depends on your psychology. What it really depends on is the primal self you created in response to the original birth trauma that you experienced, most likely in your first embodiment (sometimes it was not in the first but in one of the following).

When you experienced that trauma, there were, of course, certain feelings, certain thoughts about this. This often caused you to create a certain self that is looking for some way, so to speak, to even the score, to compensate, to set things right because of the birth trauma you received. In other words, this self is saying: "The fallen beings did this to me, I want to even the score, I want to . . . [whatever it may be individually]." You want to do something to them, with them or you want to see something happen to them that, so to speak, evens the score and you feel like they got what they deserved. This can cause some of you to become, as I said, overly enthusiastic about changing the world. In many cases, this has caused some students to go into a period where they are focused on the outer things.

One thing many people have done is, of course, to become very eager at giving decrees, giving hours and hours of decrees—in the old dispensation, going to services several times a week and giving hours of decrees there. They thought that they had to do this in order to change the world, to bind the fallen beings, to balance the karma and change the world for Saint Germain. Therefore, they had no need and no time or attention to work on their psychology. Of course, you can go back and you can say: "Well, they did this because of what was said in dictations or at least how what was said in dictations was interpreted in the organizational culture."

This is true, but again, as we have now said several times, we must look at a certain group of people at a certain time, see what they are ready for, give them that, sometimes even give them something to such an extreme that they will eventually have had enough of it and start looking beyond it. There were some people at the time who were not *ready* but some of them were not *willing* to look at their own psychology. We gave them this outer environment where they had the perfect excuse for not looking at their psychology because they had to give all these decrees.

On the other hand, there were so many things said about what decrees needed to be given that if you followed all of them, twenty-four hours a day was not enough. This was an attempt on our part to say: "Well, we can't reach them, we can't make them see what they need to see, so let us then give them so much that it eventually becomes too much and hopefully some of them, at least, will step back and find a more balanced approach." Some, indeed, did so and some did not—and that is unfortunately what we have to accept. We cannot reach everybody with any teaching.

A higher sense of proportion

My point here is that in today's age and in your dispensation, you have a different level of teaching. You have much more emphasis on your personal growth, on the resolution and healing of your psychology and these past traumas that we have recently told you about.

This means that you have the potential to take a much more balanced approach, just as Mother Mary has already mentioned. I want to go into this a little more. The true goal of the ascended masters is not to produce specific outer changes on earth. You may say: "But does that not contradict the teachings about Saint Germain's Golden Age where he wants to improve all aspects of life on earth and bring forth a higher level of civilization?" Well, *yes* and *no,* my beloved. From an outer, linear perspective it may seem to contradict but even Saint Germain has said himself that his main goal for the Golden Age is actually to raise people's consciousness, not to bring these specific outer things into manifestation. He is using the outer things as a tool for raising people's consciousness and they are not an end in themselves.

You have to recognize here that we have given you the concept that the earth is not a natural planet. We have told you that there are billions of other planets in the universe that are at the level of being natural planets and therefore not having all of the fear-based manifestations you see on earth. As Mother Mary hinted at, there are actually billions of planets that have accelerated, where the inhabitants have accelerated the planet, to a level that is so far beyond earth that most people could scarcely fathom it.

You have to recognize that we of the ascended masters, as a broad group of beings, are, of course, very well aware that most planets are at a higher level. Now, of course, those of us who have chosen to stay with earth and work with earth are not so focused on these higher planets but we know that they exist. We have interactions with the ascended masters who are working with these planets and even the ones who have the overall vision for the entire material universe and how that universe evolves.

This means that we have a sense of proportion that you do not often have on earth when you are in embodiment.

Many people on earth are very focused on earth and, of course, many people think it is the only inhabited planet. Many Christians think it must be a very important planet to God, many New Age and spiritual people think it is important because it makes *them* important because they are here and so forth and so on.

What I wish to give you is a little bit of the sense of proportion that we have as ascended masters. When you step back and look at the entire material universe, you know from science how there are billions of galaxies, billions of suns, billions of solar systems, billions of planets that could potentially have life. I tell you, what science has discovered of the so-called earth-like planets is only a fraction of the planets that have life. You are looking for planets that have the same type of life that you have on earth. There are, of course, many other types of life that are, so to speak, not carbon-based but are based on other chemical elements that are therefore not visible to the physical senses and the sense-based scientific instruments you have on earth. That is why you cannot see life on Venus even though we have told you that there is life on Venus. The same goes for many other planets throughout the universe.

When you step back, look from this broader perspective, you are clearly seeing that the vast majority of the planets are accelerating very quickly. The inhabitants there are in a positive spiral, a self-reinforcing positive spiral. As they interact with the ascended masters, as they raise their consciousness, the masters can give them more light and then they can accelerate themselves even more and this becomes a positive upward spiral. There is a relatively small number of planets that are like earth. How do we, then (when we have this broader perspective) look at earth? Of course, we look at the earth as clearly not being one of these planets that have gone into a self-reinforcing, accelerating spiral. There is an upward spiral on earth but it has not become self-reinforcing because there has not been a critical mass of the inhabitants who are in physical embodiment who have gone into raising their consciousness. Earth is largely being pulled up by the rest of the universe, by the ascended masters and by the few people in embodiment who are raising their consciousness.

Earth is a teaching device

This type of planet is a planet where we look at it largely as a teaching device for beings who cannot learn directly from within. Therefore, they need to have a planet where they can see a physical outpicturing of their state of consciousness. Grant you, most people are not aware of this, are not even open to the idea. If you told them, they would just shake their heads and think you are crazy. Nevertheless, the reality is that earth is outpicturing people's state of consciousness.

When you know this, you need to ask yourself a simple question: "If earth is outpicturing the state of consciousness of the people upon it, is there any condition on earth that is ultimately real, that has any longevity, any endurance, that has any ongoing eternal value?" The reality is that there is really nothing on earth that needs to be preserved, that we of the ascended masters want to see preserved in the long run.

Everything here is a temporary manifestation that we clearly see needs to be transcended before the earth becomes a natural planet. You may look at the earth and say: "Well, if the earth makes the change to become a natural planet, isn't there anything of the current conditions that will endure?" For many people the shocking answer would be: "Not really." There is hardly anything here that would endure in its present form when the earth becomes a natural planet again. My beloved, the primary thing that will change when the earth goes back to the state of being a natural planet is that the density of matter will decrease, the vibration of matter will be increased. This means that most of the physical conditions, including what scientists call the laws of nature, that exist right now will simply be transcended. The earth will accelerate beyond it.

With this in mind, you can gain the perspective that it is not so ultimately important to the ascended masters that a certain condition be changed, a certain physical condition. This means that you can, then, make the shift that also Mother Mary talked about and say: "Well, what am I then supposed to do as part of my Divine plan? If I made my Divine plan from a higher level of awareness than I have right now, what did I, then, incorporate in my Divine plan that I was supposed to do in the physical? What changes am I here to help bring about?"

This is, of course, a highly individual question. Even though I say that the physical conditions are not ultimately important (they are part of the entire equation of the earth), it will not be possible to move into the Golden Age or to move the earth to a natural state without bringing about many changes that are physical. This includes new ideas, new inventions, new technology, new forms of government, new forms of education, new forms of culture and art and so forth and so on. Indeed, there are many physical changes that need to happen, but I find it very, very important to give you this perspective that these changes are not ultimate, they are not final. They are steps on the way, they are stages in the transition process.

Consciousness comes before the physical

This is primarily to help you avoid going into this reaction where you think that specific physical changes and specific conditions are so ultimately important. The shift that we are seeking to help you make is that you truly integrate, you truly grasp, you truly experience, the reality that we have expressed now in many ways over these last few years, namely that consciousness comes before the physical manifestation. In other words, there is a popular belief floating around in the mass consciousness (that is partly based on Christianity) that some kind of miracle from above could change the earth. It is partly based on materialistic science that only a physical, natural law-based change can bring about new conditions.

What we seek to help you internalize and experience is the reality that everything is an outpicturing of the state of consciousness of the people on earth. Before there can be real change, before there can, in fact, be *any* change, there must be a change in consciousness. You can look back at the history of technology, for example, and you can say: "Well, but there was an actual physical process that gradually lead from this discovery to that discovery to the next discovery. One scientist built on what previous scientists had brought forth and suddenly you had the equations of Einstein and the theory of relativity and that is what lead to the development of the atomic bomb."

My beloved, what materialists do not see (because they do not want to look) is that before this physical process could even take place, there was a change in the collective consciousness. If you looked at all of the historical events that have taken place, you could see (if you could see the three higher bodies of the collective consciousness) that there was a certain shift, a certain change. You could see that this happened, whether it was a so-called positive change or a negative change. Nothing that happened in the physical was ever exclusively decided or brought about at the physical level. There was always change in the emotional, mental and identity levels before a physical change could happen. It has been this way throughout history and it will be this way in the future.

Have I shifted my consciousness?

You can, then, use this to look at yourself and your approach to the spiritual path, to the concept of your Divine plan, and you can say: "Well, the important thing is not really the physical changes that I am here to bring about. So the important thing is not really to look at what do I need to do physically." As I said, many students become so anxious about changing the world or changing other people that they forget to look at themselves. Many other students are not so focused on changing others or changing the world but they are focused on figuring out: "What do I need to do physically?" They think, as Mother Mary again hinted at, that if some guru came and told them: "You are supposed to bring forth this new invention in this area," then it would be enough that they knew this. Now, they could study the area in a linear, analytical way and they would be able to bring forth the invention. As Mother Mary said: you cannot actually do this until you have shifted your consciousness to the point where you can receive this from within. In order to do that, you may have to overcome some traumas, some wrong beliefs, some unbalanced reaction, and, then, you can receive it from within. You cannot receive it from *without*.

Again, you can look at yourself, you can look at your reaction to the entire idea of a Divine plan, and you can, when you are honest with yourself, look for any imbalances: "Am I overly enthusiastic, am I focused outside myself, am I focused on how we need to have the fallen ones judged and taken off the planet, how we need to bring forth new inventions and technology, how we need to change the political area, how we need to change other people, make them see the error of their ways, make them see the ascended master teachings and the only truth?" Again, I am not blaming you at all for having these reactions. They are, we might say, natural reactions on this unnatural planet. Nevertheless, they will not help you discover the higher levels of your Divine plan—they will actually block that discovery.

Overcoming the sense of injustice

If you can identify that you have a certain imbalance, then you can take the teachings about your birth trauma, about the primal self and you can consider how your imbalance is actually springing from this desire to even the score, to somehow compensate for the injustice, the wrong that you felt was done to you when you received that original trauma. I am not disputing that something wrong was done to you and that it was an injustice. I am just saying that you have to question (as do all people who feel they have been wronged by others), and the question is simple: "Do you want to punish those who wronged you or do you want to be free of those who wronged you and move on with your spiritual path?"

If you want to move on, then obviously you need to look at and realize: "This is simply my birth trauma creating a reaction. It created a separate self that is part of my primal self and I don't want to carry this with me for the rest of this lifetime because I know I can't carry it with me into the ascended realm. I am willing to look at it, to separate myself from it, to use the tools that the masters have given me until I come to that point where I can spontaneously let go and let that self die."

My beloved, a self that is based on a sense of injustice, a sense that something was wrong, a desire to compensate, that self can never be fulfilled. You might say: "Well but there were certain fallen beings that exposed me to this birth trauma and if those were judged and taken to the second death, then my self based on that trauma should be satisfied and should then be dissolved."

As we have told you many times, no matter what conditions could possibly happen, the self would not simply lie down and die. It would continue doing what it does. It would just look around on this planet, find some other injustice and then it would project that this also had to be compensated for, or resolved, or someone else had to be punished—because that is what the self does. It is as mindless as a computer and it will mindlessly grind away and execute its programming—just finding some outer condition that is the excuse for it.

You will not be free of it no matter what outer conditions were brought about. You will only be free of it when you recognize that the problem projected by this self can never be solved. You do not need to solve it. You simply need to come to see it as unreal and then you need to give up, you need to surrender, the desire to solve the problem—it has no solution.

It is the same as when I gave you the perspective of the earth. You can look at multiple problems, a myriad of problems, almost an infinity of problems that are present on earth. You can focus on: "I have to solve this problem, I have to decree for the solution of this problem, I have to do this, I have to do that." You can continue, for the rest of your life, focusing your attention outside yourself, on solving all of these problems.

I am not denying that the problems have a temporary existence. I am not denying that they have an impact on people on earth. You are not going to help the planet progress by solving these problems. You are going to help the planet progress by personally transcending the consciousness that projected these problems, thereby pulling up the collective consciousness so that other people can come to see that we do not have to keep fighting the Jews or the Arabs or the Palestinians or the Serbs, or the Croats or the French or the English or the Germans, or this or that. We can just walk away from it, because we will feel better, we will be happier, when we walk away from the problem even though it has not been solved.

There is no problem to be solved

You see, my beloved, there was a phase in Europe where the nation states were in a constant state of war with each other. It was often projected that there was some kind of injustice because that nation had done something wrong. You saw how, after the First World War, the Treaty of Versailles was driven by the French and the English determining that Germany had done something wrong and needed to be punished. This set the stage for the Second World War and so forth and so on.

Now, after the Second World War there was a new awareness that spread throughout Europe, which has led to the fact that there has not been a major war since then, at least in the broader part of Europe. Now, my beloved, the Second World War, when you look at it and the defeat of Germany and the division of Europe into East and West, what problem did the Second World War solve? It never solved any problem.

Why has there not been a war since then? Well, because a critical mass of people saw the absurdity of the warring consciousness that precipitated these two wars and they individually (and eventually it reached critical mass collectively) transcended it. They did it the hard way, by seeing this taken to such an extreme and precipitating the Holocaust and the mass killings that happened during the war—but they did it. That shift in consciousness is why there has not been a war. It was not that the particular problem that precipitated the First World War or the Second World War was solved because ultimately it had no solution.

Look at the events and ask yourself: "How could it have been solved?" It could not—there was no solution. That is why there ended up being a war because the problem was created by the fallen beings in such a way that there was no solution so that the problem would inevitably lead to war. It was only when enough people, whether they were conscious of this or not, came to the realization that: "There was nothing here that could be solved. We could only look forward and decide to transcend that consciousness and not get into those patterns again that had led to the war."

No problem to solve in families

It is the same at the personal level. It is the same in families. It is the same everywhere. You earlier talked about your families and how there can often be a karmic pattern, a psychological pattern, that goes back several lifetimes because these people have reincarnated over and over again. Well, one potential you could do as ascended master students was, perhaps, come to a point where you could make some of your family members see that there is no solution here, there is nothing that can be solved by changing the other family members. It is simply a matter of seeing that what is going on in the family, the dynamic in the family, is the expression of a certain state of consciousness. The only way to change things, the only way for you to be free, is to simply walk away from that consciousness, to transcend it by resolving it in yourself.

This is for many of you a part of your Divine plan when it comes to family. It is to help them see that there is no problem to solve. It is a matter of transcending consciousness, finding a different way to look at each other, to interact with each other and to allow each other to be who you are. This really requires you to change yourself to where you accept yourself and allow yourself to be who you are. Only when you allow yourself to be who you are, can you allow someone else to be who they are without feeling threatened and without wanting to change them in order to avoid dealing with your own psychology. You are getting to a point where you are comfortable because the other person is no longer pushing your buttons so you can feel you do not have to change yourself. Some of you will be able to explain these concepts in a universal way without mentioning ascended masters to your family members and help them see that it is simply a matter of making a decision: "We are no longer going to interact that way, we are no longer going to blame each other, we are no longer going to seek to change each other, we are just going to allow each other to be who we are, enjoying being together when we are together or otherwise go our separate ways."

No more compensation

My beloved, where does the unbalanced enthusiasm come from? It comes from the belief that there is a problem that absolutely must be solved. It is *imperative*, it is *ultimately important* that this problem be solved. What is the deeper psychology behind it? It is that you as a person feel stuck because there is something in you that you do not know how to change. You are either seeking to divert attention from that or you are seeking to project (your subconscious self is projecting) that if this outer problem were solved, if these other people changed, then you would not have the problem in yourself. Why have you not been able to solve this problem? Well, because you have not had the teaching on the cause of the problem, which for many of you goes all the way back to the primal self. You often feel stuck because you experience that there is an imbalance in you but you do not know how to solve it. Therefore, you are trying to solve it by changing all of these things outside yourself because you do not know how to change inside yourself. How can you know how to change the primal self if you do not even know that you have a primal self and where it came from?

This is why I say to you (who are a part of this dispensation, you who are open to these teachings, you now have those teachings, have those tools), you can (if you are willing) very quickly move beyond any imbalanced state. You can get to a point, my beloved, where you are not seeking to change the world or other people as a way to compensate for a condition inside your own psyche. You have looked at that condition, you have resolved that condition—and then what happens? When you have resolved that condition, when you have resolved that tendency to focus on changing outer things, then, all of a sudden, you now can begin to connect to your Divine plan. Now, you can suddenly see what you are actually meant to change or bring about here on earth.

The difference is that you will not be doing this from a desire to compensate for something. You will be doing it from an entirely positive reason. You are doing this because this is an expression of who you are. Ultimately, what is going to give you peace and joy about being in embodiment on a planet like this is that you are expressing who you are. You are being non-attached to the outer results, to the fruits of action because you find joy in just expressing your higher being. That is the higher potential of your Divine plan.

The creative phase of your Divine plan

There is, of course, a work phase where you may have to do certain things, have relationships with certain people, do certain things in the outer, go through certain experiences. Many of you have already sensed this intuitively, you have already done it. What we seek to help you get to is the point where you can go into the higher phase of your Divine plan: the creative phase. This is where you can begin to give your gift and express your Self, the highest potential that you wanted to express before you came into embodiment, based on the higher level of consciousness that you have the potential to reach.

This can become a positive spiral where you are at peace with being in embodiment. You do not have a deficit attitude that you are always behind, that you should always be somewhere else. There is always something that you *should* have done, that you *have not* done and there is more that you *could* do. Instead, you are at peace with being who you are, knowing that you will continue to take step by step to come up higher for the rest of this lifetime. You will get more and more comfortable, more and more creative, in expressing your creativity and more and more peaceful in enjoying the process of seeing your life unfold. This is the state we want you to reach because that is when you can actually enjoy being on this planet. My beloved, why would we not want you to enjoy being in embodiment?

Taking time to enjoy being on earth

I will tell you that there is a considerable number of ascended masters who have ascended from earth and who have looked back to the process of being in embodiment, going into whatever downward spirals we went into and then gradually, slowly, climbing out of them and coming to the point of qualifying for our ascension. We look back at this process, and we can see that we actually wish that we could have taken some more time in embodiment to actually enjoy being on this planet. We can also be realistic and see that times were different back then, the collective consciousness was denser. Therefore, there was in some cases more of an urgency that we ascend at a certain time for a variety of reasons. There simply was not the time to enjoy this.

You can see how, in Jesus' case, he ascended in a physical way shortly after the completion of his public mission. Then, he was given the dispensation to materialize another body and live in that body until the age of 81, before he went through his final, spiritual ascension at that time. In those years when he was living in Kashmir, he did enjoy being in embodiment even with the density that the planet had at the time. You will also see that in my last embodiment, including with Kuthumi, we also had some time. We had a certain spiritual attainment and non-attachment that we were actually able to enjoy being in embodiment at the time. This is not something that has really been emphasized in previous ascended master dispensations but it is the case—we had that time. The result of having this time is that you can actually come to a point where you are completely at peace with being here but you are also at peace with ascending. Whereas, if you have a more rushed time schedule, you often do not come to the point where you are at peace with being on earth.

Therefore, you can almost come to the point where you have qualified for your ascension but you are not quite at peace with ascending. You must actually spend some time resolving that last sense of un-peace before you are really at the point where you can completely leave the earth behind and move into the ascended state. Naturally, we would like those of you who have the potential to ascend after this lifetime to come to this point where you can be at peace, you can enjoy being here. You can therefore set an example that spiritual people can be at peace, can enjoy life. They do not have to withdraw from life, live in a cave, they do not have to live a certain strict, regimented life. They can actually enjoy life and express that joy and then they can be at peace with moving on. For those of you who have the potential to ascend after this lifetime, these are the higher levels of your Divine plan. This can for some of you require a conscious shift in awareness where you actually see this.

In order to see it, you may have to be willing to look at some of your attitudes to what it means to be a spiritual person and an ascended master student, what it means to reach a higher level of consciousness, what it means to express your Christhood or manifest Buddhahood. You need to do away with some of these past images that have been created of how a spiritual person is supposed to behave in a certain way.

Daring to be who you are

You need to recognize here, as Mother Mary said, that your Divine plan is completely individual. There is no way you can look at the past and look at how other spiritual people reacted in the past and say: "Oh, this has set the mold for how we should all be in the future." Jesus went through what he went through 2,000 years ago at the beginning of the Age of Pisces. You are now at the beginning of the Age of Aquarius. You are not going to qualify for your ascension by doing exactly what Jesus did because the consciousness has shifted, the requirements are different.

This is all incorporated in your Divine plan. You looked at the time you were going to embody in, you looked at your consciousness and you mapped this out. If you have the potential to ascend after this lifetime, you also have the potential to gradually come to see your Divine plan and how to express your Christhood. I am simply saying that in order to do this, you have to stop having some kind of standard for how you think you should behave, what you think you should *do* or *not do*.

Again, this is not a matter of saying that you can do anything you want and nothing is wrong or nothing is unspiritual. It is a matter of saying: "I am not going to follow the standards in the world, the standards of the fallen beings, the standards of the mass consciousness or even the standards that I have created so far in this embodiment. I am going to look at: What was it that I incorporated in my Divine plan, that I chose from a higher awareness. I am going to pull that into my conscious awareness and I am going to dare to be that way, to be the way I wanted to be before coming into embodiment—not the way other people or the fallen beings want me to be or not the way my separate selves want me to be."

In a sense, this is not necessarily a goal that you can manifest in a short period of time. It is a gradual process, as Mother Mary said, of step-by-step coming to this higher awareness. For many of you it will not come to you until later in life. It is important that you do not panic about this and that you do not get into this pattern with setting a timetable for yourself. Truly, my beloved, when you come to the higher states of consciousness towards the 144th level, when you can come to the point of beginning to make peace, then time stops being linear. All of a sudden, as the Buddha has said, time is not. Even if you came to the point of being completely at peace with being in embodiment a week before you actually laid the body off and ascended, in that week you could still radiate so much light into the collective consciousness that you could fulfill the goal of your Divine plan.

Avoid setting linear goals

You see how the linear mind always wants to do what the linear mind wants to do. When you "get" the concept of a Divine plan and that you have a goal, then the linear mind wants to say: "Yes, but this goal is far beyond me so I have to really work hard, I have to set a timetable, I have to get to this point, I have to get to that point before next week. I have to rise so high within the next year and so forth and so on." People can start in their minds creating these elaborate structures and it just works against the whole process. It suddenly turns it into a linear process, whereas, what we are trying to tell you now several times, is that it is actually a spherical, intuitive, experiential process.

It is not a matter of understanding and planning and deciding with the outer mind. It is a matter of transcending the outer mind and having those experiences that are not linear, not analytical, not based on the outer mind. It is not something the outer mind can grasp. It is often so that when you come to have an insight of: "This is the next step in my Divine plan," you cannot explain it to others, you cannot justify it. You cannot give a reason for it, even to yourself. You just know that this is the next step and this is what I am doing. You learn to flow and this is what we have called flowing with the River of Life where, when you get an insight, there is no need to justify it but also there is no opposition to implementing it. You just flow into it. Therefore, you do not need to plan ahead. Many times, it is just that a spontaneous insight is there and you right away flow into bringing it into manifestation.

Linearity can be helpful at a certain level of the path but there comes a point on the path where the gap between where you are and the ascended state cannot be crossed through a linear process. It is still gradual, it is still step-by-step but it is not a linear process where you can sit with the analytical mind and map out: "This is how I get from the 132nd to the 133rd level and all the way up to the 144th." It is much more spherical, much more intuitive and that is why there comes that point where you have to begin to see the limitations of the linear mind and begin to neutralize it consciously.

You separate yourself from it and realize that the linear mind is a tool. There is nothing inherently wrong with it, it is a tool much like the physical body. The physical body is your vehicle for interacting with earth. So is the linear mind but you do not let the limitations of the physical body determine what you can do spiritually in terms of growing in consciousness. The same with the linear mind. You do not let it limit you. Therefore, you have to come to that conscious awareness and conscious decision that you will accelerate yourself beyond the linear mind. You will stop identifying with it, you will realize that the linear mind will always do what it does, it will always compare, it will always analyze, it will always label. In many cases, you simply do not pay attention to it. You let it do its work but you just ignore it because you are looking for that spherical insight that might resolve any paradox or contradiction that the linear mind can come up with. You are also neutralizing the linear mind's desire to plan the rest of your life in minute detail. You are willing to just flow with it, trusting that as you apply yourself, as you heal your psychology and open your mind to insights, you will get those insights and when you have them, you will spontaneously implement them.

I have said more than I wanted to say, which, of course, is my nature and my joy. Even though I could go on and say much more, I will recognize the limitations of the physical octave. I thank you for being willing to experience my Presence and to allow me to experience your presences because it is my joy to interact with you. As Mother Mary said, we accept each one of you unconditionally and I do not want to in any way give you the impression (that you might have from previous dispensations) that I am the strict disciplinarian who sets conditions for when I will deal with you or that you have to come up to a certain level. Those of you who are open to these teachings, it is a joy for me to interact with you, regardless of how you see yourself.

Again, my desire, *my* desire, is that you could see yourself as I see you. That would be the gift I would be willing to give you. If you are open and willing, I may indeed be able to give you a glimpse of how I see you, if you give me a moment of your attention.

6 | INVOKING FREEDOM FROM SOLVING PROBLEMS

In the name I AM THAT I AM, Jesus Christ, I call to all representatives of the Divine Mother, especially Master MORE, to help me overcome the illusion that I am on earth to solve problems, including…

[Make personal calls.]

Part 1

1. Master MORE, help me see if I have a self that is seeking to compensate for my birth trauma by evening the score, by compensating, by setting things right. This self is saying: "The fallen beings did this to me, I want to get back at them."

> Master MORE, come to the fore,
> we will absorb your flame of MORE.

Master MORE, our will so strong,
our power centers cleared by song.

**Master MORE, your Sacred Heart,
from this we will no more depart,
we are forever in your flow,
of Diamond Will that you bestow.**

2. Master MORE, help me see if I have a desire to do something to the fallen beings, or if I want to see something happen to them that evens the score and I can feel like they got what they deserved.

Master MORE, your wisdom flows,
as our attunement ever grows.
Master MORE, we have a tie,
that helps us see through Serpent's lie.

**Master MORE, your Sacred Heart,
from this we will no more depart,
we are forever in your flow,
of Diamond Will that you bestow.**

3. Master MORE, help me see if this has caused me to become overly enthusiastic about changing the world and being focused on outer things.

Master MORE, your love so pink,
there is no purer love, we think.
Master MORE, you set us free,
from all conditionality.

**Master MORE, your Sacred Heart,
from this we will no more depart,
we are forever in your flow,
of Diamond Will that you bestow.**

4. Master MORE, help me see if I have used the desire to change the world by giving decrees and invocations as an excuse for not working on my psychology.

Master MORE, we will endure,
your discipline that makes us pure.
Master MORE, intentions true,
as we are always one with you.

Master MORE, your Sacred Heart,
from this we will no more depart,
we are forever in your flow,
of Diamond Will that you bestow.

5. Master MORE, help me fully accept that the true goal of the ascended masters is not to produce specific outer changes on earth but to raise people's consciousness. Help me use this to take a balanced approach to the path.

Master MORE, our vision raised,
the will of God is always praised.
Master MORE, creative will,
raising all life higher still.

Master MORE, your Sacred Heart,
from this we will no more depart,
we are forever in your flow,
of Diamond Will that you bestow.

6. Master MORE, I see the reality that earth is outpicturing people's state of consciousness. Therefore, there is no condition on earth that is ultimately real, that has any longevity, any endurance, that has any ongoing eternal value.

Master MORE, your peace is power,
the demons of war it will devour.
Master MORE, we serve all life,
our flames consuming war and strife.

Master MORE, your Sacred Heart,
from this we will no more depart,
we are forever in your flow,
of Diamond Will that you bestow.

7. Master MORE, help me gain clarity about what I incorporated in my Divine plan that I am supposed to do in the physical. Help me see what changes I am here to help bring about.

> Master MORE, we are so free,
> eternal bond from you we see.
> Master MORE, we find rebirth,
> in flow of your eternal mirth.

> **Master MORE, your Sacred Heart,**
> **from this we will no more depart,**
> **we are forever in your flow,**
> **of Diamond Will that you bestow.**

8. Master MORE, I know that many changes need to happen, but I also see they are not ultimate, they are not final. They are steps on the way, they are stages in the transition process.

> Master MORE, you balance all,
> the seven rays upon our call.
> Master MORE, forever MORE,
> we are the Spirit's open door.

> **Master MORE, your Sacred Heart,**
> **from this we will no more depart,**
> **we are forever in your flow,**
> **of Diamond Will that you bestow.**

9. Master MORE, help me truly integrate, truly grasp, truly experience, the reality that consciousness comes before the physical manifestation. Everything is an outpicturing of the state of consciousness, so before there can be any change, there must be a change in consciousness.

> Master MORE, your Presence here,
> filling up the inner sphere.
> Life is now a sacred flow,
> God Power we on all bestow.

> Master MORE, your Sacred Heart,
> from this we will no more depart,
> we are forever in your flow,
> of Diamond Will that you bestow.

Part 2

1. Master MORE, help me see that nothing that happened in the physical was ever exclusively decided or brought about at the physical level. There was always change in the emotional, mental and identity levels before a physical change could happen.

> Master MORE, come to the fore,
> we will absorb your flame of MORE.
> Master MORE, our will so strong,
> our power centers cleared by song.

> Master MORE, your Sacred Heart,
> from this we will no more depart,
> we are forever in your flow,
> of Diamond Will that you bestow.

2. Master MORE, help me look at my reaction to the idea of a Divine plan, and see if I am overly enthusiastic. Help me see if I am focused outside myself, focused on how to get the fallen ones judged and taken off the planet, how to bring forth new inventions and technology, how to change the political area, how to change other people.

> Master MORE, your wisdom flows,
> as our attunement ever grows.
> Master MORE, we have a tie,
> that helps us see through Serpent's lie.

> Master MORE, your Sacred Heart,
> from this we will no more depart,
> we are forever in your flow,
> of Diamond Will that you bestow.

3. Master MORE, help me see if I have an imbalance that springs from this desire to even the score, to compensate for the injustice that I felt was done to me when I received that original trauma.

> Master MORE, your love so pink,
> there is no purer love, we think.
> Master MORE, you set us free,
> from all conditionality.
>
> **Master MORE, your Sacred Heart,**
> **from this we will no more depart,**
> **we are forever in your flow,**
> **of Diamond Will that you bestow.**

4. Master MORE, I am letting go of all desire to punish those who wronged me. I want to be free of those who wronged me and move on with my spiritual path.

> Master MORE, we will endure,
> your discipline that makes us pure.
> Master MORE, intentions true,
> as we are always one with you.
>
> **Master MORE, your Sacred Heart,**
> **from this we will no more depart,**
> **we are forever in your flow,**
> **of Diamond Will that you bestow.**

5. Master MORE, I see that it was my birth trauma that created a reaction, a separate self that is part of my primal self. I don't want to carry this with me for the rest of this lifetime because I know I can't carry it with me into the ascended realm. I am willing to look at it, to separate myself from it, and I am letting that self die.

> Master MORE, our vision raised,
> the will of God is always praised.
> Master MORE, creative will,
> raising all life higher still.

**Master MORE, your Sacred Heart,
from this we will no more depart,
we are forever in your flow,
of Diamond Will that you bestow.**

6. Master MORE, I see that a self that is based on a sense of injustice can never be fulfilled. It can always find some injustice and project that this also has to be compensated for.

Master MORE, your peace is power,
the demons of war it will devour.
Master MORE, we serve all life,
our flames consuming war and strife.

**Master MORE, your Sacred Heart,
from this we will no more depart,
we are forever in your flow,
of Diamond Will that you bestow.**

7. Master MORE, I recognize that the problem projected by this self can never be solved. I do not need to solve it. I see it as unreal and I give up, I surrender, the desire to solve the problem that has no solution.

Master MORE, we are so free,
eternal bond from you we see.
Master MORE, we find rebirth,
in flow of your eternal mirth.

**Master MORE, your Sacred Heart,
from this we will no more depart,
we are forever in your flow,
of Diamond Will that you bestow.**

8. Master MORE, I see that I am not going to help the planet progress by solving outer problems. I am going to help the planet progress by personally transcending the consciousness that projected these problems, thereby pulling up the collective consciousness so that other people can be free of the problems.

Master MORE, you balance all,
the seven rays upon our call.
Master MORE, forever MORE,
we are the Spirit's open door.

**Master MORE, your Sacred Heart,
from this we will no more depart,
we are forever in your flow,
of Diamond Will that you bestow.**

9. Master MORE, I see that the dynamic in my family is the expression of a certain state of consciousness. The only way for me to be free is to walk away from that consciousness, to transcend it by resolving it in myself.

Master MORE, your Presence here,
filling up the inner sphere.
Life is now a sacred flow,
God Power we on all bestow.

**Master MORE, your Sacred Heart,
from this we will no more depart,
we are forever in your flow,
of Diamond Will that you bestow.**

Part 3

1. Master MORE, help me accept myself and allow myself to be who I am so I can allow other people to be who they are, without feeling threatened and without wanting to change them in order to avoid dealing with my own psychology.

Master MORE, come to the fore,
we will absorb your flame of MORE.
Master MORE, our will so strong,
our power centers cleared by song.

> **Master MORE, your Sacred Heart,**
> **from this we will no more depart,**
> **we are forever in your flow,**
> **of Diamond Will that you bestow.**

2. Master MORE, I am giving up the dynamic of trying to change other people so I can be comfortable, because the other person is no longer pushing my buttons so I can feel I do not have to change myself.

> Master MORE, your wisdom flows,
> as our attunement ever grows.
> Master MORE, we have a tie,
> that helps us see through Serpent's lie.

> **Master MORE, your Sacred Heart,**
> **from this we will no more depart,**
> **we are forever in your flow,**
> **of Diamond Will that you bestow.**

3. Master MORE, I am no longer going to interact with people that way, I am no longer going to blame others, I am no longer going to seek to change others. I am going to allow others to be who they are, enjoying being together or going our separate ways.

> Master MORE, your love so pink,
> there is no purer love, we think.
> Master MORE, you set us free,
> from all conditionality.

> **Master MORE, your Sacred Heart,**
> **from this we will no more depart,**
> **we are forever in your flow,**
> **of Diamond Will that you bestow.**

4. Master MORE, help me see and overcome the sense of being stuck because there is something in me that I do not know how to change, thereby seeking to divert attention from it. Help me overcome the tendency to project that if this outer problem was solved, then I would not have the problem in myself.

Master MORE, we will endure,
your discipline that makes us pure.
Master MORE, intentions true,
as we are always one with you.

**Master MORE, your Sacred Heart,
from this we will no more depart,
we are forever in your flow,
of Diamond Will that you bestow.**

5. Master MORE, help me overcome the sense of being stuck because there is an imbalance in me but I do not know how to solve it. Therefore, I am trying to solve it by changing all of these things outside myself because I do not know how to change inside myself.

Master MORE, our vision raised,
the will of God is always praised.
Master MORE, creative will,
raising all life higher still.

**Master MORE, your Sacred Heart,
from this we will no more depart,
we are forever in your flow,
of Diamond Will that you bestow.**

6. Master MORE, I am willing to move beyond any imbalanced state so I am not seeking to change the world or other people as a way to compensate for a condition inside my own psyche. I am willing to look at the condition, resolve the condition and connect to my Divine plan.

Master MORE, your peace is power,
the demons of war it will devour.
Master MORE, we serve all life,
our flames consuming war and strife.

**Master MORE, your Sacred Heart,
from this we will no more depart,
we are forever in your flow,
of Diamond Will that you bestow.**

7. Master MORE, help me see what I am actually meant to change or bring about here on earth. Help me do this because it is an expression of who I am.

> Master MORE, we are so free,
> eternal bond from you we see.
> Master MORE, we find rebirth,
> in flow of your eternal mirth.
>
> **Master MORE, your Sacred Heart,**
> **from this we will no more depart,**
> **we are forever in your flow,**
> **of Diamond Will that you bestow.**

8. Master MORE, I see that what is going to give me peace and joy about being in embodiment on earth is that I am expressing who I am. I am being non-attached to the outer results because I find joy in expressing my higher being.

> Master MORE, you balance all,
> the seven rays upon our call.
> Master MORE, forever MORE,
> we are the Spirit's open door.
>
> **Master MORE, your Sacred Heart,**
> **from this we will no more depart,**
> **we are forever in your flow,**
> **of Diamond Will that you bestow.**

9. Master MORE, help me go into the creative phase of my Divine plan and give my gift and express my Self, the highest potential that I wanted to express before I came into embodiment, based on the higher level of consciousness that I have the potential to reach.

> Master MORE, your Presence here,
> filling up the inner sphere.
> Life is now a sacred flow,
> God Power we on all bestow.

**Master MORE, your Sacred Heart,
from this we will no more depart,
we are forever in your flow,
of Diamond Will that you bestow.**

Part 4

1. Master MORE, help me create a positive spiral where I am at peace with being in embodiment. I let go of the deficit attitude that I am always behind, that I should be somewhere else, there is something that I *should* have done, that I *have not* done and there is more that I *could* do.

> Master MORE, come to the fore,
> we will absorb your flame of MORE.
> Master MORE, our will so strong,
> our power centers cleared by song.

> **Master MORE, your Sacred Heart,
> from this we will no more depart,
> we are forever in your flow,
> of Diamond Will that you bestow.**

2. Master MORE, help me be at peace with being who I am, knowing that I will continue to take one step at a time and come up higher for the rest of this lifetime. Help me be more creative in expressing my creativity and more peaceful in enjoying the process of seeing my life unfold.

> Master MORE, your wisdom flows,
> as our attunement ever grows.
> Master MORE, we have a tie,
> that helps us see through Serpent's lie.

> **Master MORE, your Sacred Heart,
> from this we will no more depart,
> we are forever in your flow,
> of Diamond Will that you bestow.**

6 | Invoking freedom from solving problems

3. Master MORE, I do want to enjoy being in embodiment on earth. I want to be at peace with being here but also be at peace with ascending. Help me resolve any sense of un-peace so I can come to the point where I can completely leave the earth behind and move into the ascended state—if it is in my Divine plan to ascend after this lifetime.

> Master MORE, your love so pink,
> there is no purer love, we think.
> Master MORE, you set us free,
> from all conditionality.
>
> **Master MORE, your Sacred Heart,**
> **from this we will no more depart,**
> **we are forever in your flow,**
> **of Diamond Will that you bestow.**

4. Master MORE, help me be at peace and enjoy being here so I can set an example that spiritual people can be at peace. We can enjoy life and express that joy and then be at peace with moving on.

> Master MORE, we will endure,
> your discipline that makes us pure.
> Master MORE, intentions true,
> as we are always one with you.
>
> **Master MORE, your Sacred Heart,**
> **from this we will no more depart,**
> **we are forever in your flow,**
> **of Diamond Will that you bestow.**

5. Master MORE, help me make this conscious shift in awareness. I am willing to look at my attitudes to what it means to be a spiritual person and an ascended master student, what it means to reach a higher level of consciousness, what it means to express my Christhood or manifest Buddhahood. I let go of all past images of how a spiritual person is supposed to behave in a certain way.

> Master MORE, our vision raised,
> the will of God is always praised.

Master MORE, creative will,
raising all life higher still.

**Master MORE, your Sacred Heart,
from this we will no more depart,
we are forever in your flow,
of Diamond Will that you bestow.**

6. Master MORE, I am not going to follow the standards in the world, the standards of the fallen beings, the standards of the mass consciousness or even the standards that I have created so far in this embodiment. I am going to look at what I incorporated in my Divine plan. I am going to pull that into my conscious awareness, and I am going to dare to be that way, to be the way I wanted to be before coming into embodiment—not the way other people or the fallen beings want me to be and not the way my separate selves want me to be.

Master MORE, your peace is power,
the demons of war it will devour.
Master MORE, we serve all life,
our flames consuming war and strife.

**Master MORE, your Sacred Heart,
from this we will no more depart,
we are forever in your flow,
of Diamond Will that you bestow.**

7. Master MORE, I see that my Divine plan is an intuitive, not a linear process. It is not a matter of understanding and planning and deciding with the outer mind. It is a matter of transcending the outer mind and having those experiences that are not linear, not analytical, not based on the outer mind.

Master MORE, we are so free,
eternal bond from you we see.
Master MORE, we find rebirth,
in flow of your eternal mirth.

> **Master MORE, your Sacred Heart,**
> **from this we will no more depart,**
> **we are forever in your flow,**
> **of Diamond Will that you bestow.**

8. Master MORE, help me know what is the next step in my Divine plan. Help me flow with my Divine plan so that when I get an insight, there is no need to justify it and there is no opposition to implementing it. I just flow into it so that when a spontaneous insight is there, I right away flow into bringing it into manifestation.

> Master MORE, you balance all,
> the seven rays upon our call.
> Master MORE, forever MORE,
> we are the Spirit's open door.

> **Master MORE, your Sacred Heart,**
> **from this we will no more depart,**
> **we are forever in your flow,**
> **of Diamond Will that you bestow.**

9. Master MORE, I make the conscious decision that I am accelerating myself beyond the linear mind. I will stop identifying with the linear mind and look for that spherical insight that might resolve any paradox or contradiction that the linear mind can come up with. I am neutralizing the linear mind's desire to plan the rest of my life in minute detail. I am willing to flow with it, trusting that as I apply myself, as I heal my psychology and open my mind to insights, I *will* get those insights. When I have them, I will spontaneously implement them.

> Master MORE, your Presence here,
> filling up the inner sphere.
> Life is now a sacred flow,
> God Power we on all bestow.

> **Master MORE, your Sacred Heart,**
> **from this we will no more depart,**
> **we are forever in your flow,**
> **of Diamond Will that you bestow.**

Sealing

In the name of the Divine Mother, I call to Mother Mary for the sealing of myself and all people in my circle of influence in the creative flow of the Divine Mother, the River of Life. I call for the multiplication of my calls by all representatives of the Divine Mother, so that we form the perfect figure-eight flow of "As Above, so below." Thus, I accept that this is fully manifest, because the mouth of the Lord, the Divine Mother that I AM, has spoken it. Amen.

7 | CHRISTHOOD AND YOUR DIVINE PLAN

I AM the Ascended Master Jesus Christ. I wish to speak to you about the topic of Christhood, how it relates to your Divine plan. We have given you teachings about what we might call the work phase of your Divine plan. When you come into embodiment (when you are a mature spiritual student), you know that there is some work that needs to be done in terms of balancing karma, receiving insights, having experiences that shift your consciousness. As a more mature spiritual student you are often planning to get this work phase out of the way early in your life so that you can move through it fairly quickly, then move into other phases of your Divine plan.

Getting the work phase out of the way

It is quite common to see people who in the early decades of their lives are very busy, absorbed in relationships, having children, building a career, working—all of these things. It is as if you might call it an obsessive compulsive disorder where they feel that they just have to do all of these things and have to do them at once. It is not so obsessive after all because it is simply this desire to move through this so that you can have the clarity of mind, perhaps the opportunity in your outer situation, to focus more on the other phases.

One of the ways, for most of you, you deal with balancing karma is through relationships. That is why you often see that people get married fairly young, they have children fairly young. Maybe you have more than one relationship. They can be very intense relationships. This is something you want to move through. You have a great desire to move through it, even though you do not understand this consciously.

For many people there comes another phase, which is often where you discover a spiritual teaching. You become aware there is a spiritual path and you begin to walk that path. You have many people who are also very, very eager at applying themselves. Whatever the spiritual teaching is, they study eagerly, practice whatever tools and techniques are given. You can almost say that it is an obsessive compulsive manner. It is because this is what you need to do in order to rise to a higher level of consciousness, a higher level of your Divine plan.

No need for regrets

One conclusion you can draw from this knowledge is that there is absolutely no reason for any of you to have any kind of regret or negative feelings about what you have gone through in your lives. You can look back at your lives and you might judge with the outer mind that many of the things you went through were not spiritual. They were not harmonious, they were too intense. You might look back and have some regrets and say: "I wish I hadn't done that."

My beloved, why did you do what you did? Because it was part of your Divine plan to go through that experience. Whatever it was for you individually, you needed that experience in order to work through what we have called the work phase of your Divine plan. We can also call this the preparatory phase where you are preparing yourself for the more creative phase of your Divine plan. You simply realize, as we have said, that you have the potential to reach a certain level of consciousness in this embodiment, but you come into embodiment with a lower level of consciousness. Then, you want to shift your consciousness as quickly as possible so you can go up towards the higher levels. Only when you get to those higher levels, can you begin to actually see the more creative aspects of your Divine plan.

What we have said is that you cannot really shift your consciousness in a theoretical and intellectual way. You need to have certain experiences in order to shift your consciousness. Why did you do what you did? Because you knew subconsciously that you needed that experience. You wanted to have it as quickly as possible in order for you to shift your consciousness.

My beloved, whatever experiences you have had, did shift your consciousness in some way. I know that most of you will look back at your lives and you will say: "But there were some experiences that were so difficult that I went into a negative spiral and for years I was depressed or disturbed or stressed about this."

Shifting out of having regrets

Yes, my beloved, but when you are willing to look back, use the tools we have given you, you can actually overcome this, go through the shift you were meant to have as a result of that experience. Then, my beloved, when you shift, the experience no longer matters. I realize there can be energy accumulated in your four lower bodies from a traumatic experience. However, you have the tools to transform that, thus you can let go of it. Many times, my beloved, you do not realize that when you had these experiences, you reacted to them with the level of consciousness you had at the time.

Now, that you have raised your consciousness, you look back at that experience with some regret. Perhaps with the feeling that as the spiritual student you would like to be, you should not have done this. My beloved, that sense of regret (blaming yourself or feeling ashamed) comes from an internal self that is often a part of this conglomerate of the primal self.

If you can identify that you are looking back at your past with regret or other negative feelings, then you should know that this is an internal self. It is a separate self and it may actually be created partly because of a spiritual teaching you had. For some reason, you interpreted it so you created the self that is blaming the self, feeling ashamed, feeling like you are not good enough, feeling (as some of you might feel) that a real spiritual person could not possibly have done that—but *you* did. The fact that you did it means that now you have lost the opportunity forever. You can never make up for it in this lifetime, therefore your lifetime was wasted. There is nothing you can do about it other than sit down in a dark room, crying for the rest of your life.

My beloved, I am making fun of this but people who have this sense that they did something so bad that they could not possibly really be spiritual often feel they could not possibly approach the ascended masters, for we would surely condemn you as you condemn yourself. How many times have we told you now that we do not look at you as you look at yourself? We do not condemn you as you condemn yourself.

What I want to say here is this: "Do not ever, my beloved, assume that an ascended master would condemn you for anything you have done." We have only one desire—to set you free. We are willing to help you be free of anything from your past.

Christhood and forgiveness

This is one of the aspects of Christhood. When you begin to have what we have called Christ discernment, you can actually come to a point where you experience that you can be forgiven, be redeemed. You can overcome, you can rise above, anything that has happened here on earth. I can tell you that there are actually many Christians, even some fundamentalist Christians, who have understood this well, even better than many New Age or even ascended master students. It is partly because these Christians do not have the concept that because you are walking a path, it is up to you to see things in your psychology and let them go. Nevertheless, they have experienced the reality that Christ can redeem them from any sin. They have accepted this.

You, on the other hand, have taken a higher level of responsibility for yourselves, which is good. But you have to realize there is a separate self in you that has taken this higher responsibility and turned it into a negative by getting you to think you should always be perfect. There are certain things you should not have done, from which you cannot be forgiven or redeemed. In other words, you can never rise above it.

Of course, this self is based on the fact that from the moment the fallen beings began to embody on this planet, they have projected into the collective consciousness that there are certain choices you can make with your free will that you can never overcome by making other choices. Again, we have told you now several times that free will is such that you can make any choice you want at any time. Meaning, you can at any time make a choice that completely replaces a previous choice. You can never make a choice of which you cannot escape the consequences by making another choice. Now, I know very well that immediately there will be a part of your being that says that here in the physical octave, you can make choices when you are young that have consequences that you cannot change by just making another choice.

Material conditions cannot prevent a shift in consciousness

Yes, my beloved, that is true. However, how many times have we told you that there is no material condition that you can take with you into the ascended realm? Therefore, there is no material condition that can keep you from ascending. There is, for that matter, no material condition that can keep you from moving on to the highest potential of your Divine plan because there is really no material condition that can prevent you from shifting your consciousness. It is shifting your consciousness that brings you to the point that you can ascend.

This brings you to the point you can move into the higher phases of your Divine plan. It is all about shifting consciousness. You recognize that on the one hand, because of the density of the material realm, there are certain mechanics here. There are certain things you can do. There are consequences that can remain for the rest of your life—that is perfectly true. This cannot limit your growth in consciousness. That is what you begin to experience when you begin to have that Christ discernment and you open yourself up to really grasping, experiencing, that aspect of Christ: Christ the redeemer, as the Christians call it. You might call it something else. You might call it the Christ that can lift you above anything from your past. The Christ that can make you new, as even Paul says you become a new being in Christ.

This is an important shift that you can make where you realize there are fallen beings on the planet. They are very aggressive at preventing you from reaching the higher stages of your Divine plan, especially manifesting Christhood. Their primary tool is the projection that you can make choices you can never rise above. This is an absolute lie that goes totally against the concept of free will. Therefore, you need to make that discernment. Here, my beloved, we move into another aspect of Christhood, or Christ discernment, that many people in the world have not actually seen.

You do not need an external savior

This, again, is because the fallen beings have done everything they could to abort my mission, as I started it 2,000 years ago. They have done everything they could to make people misunderstand the concept of the Christ. They have, with the creation of the Catholic church and forward, projected this image that Christ is the savior who comes to save you as an external force. Therefore, you do not have the power within yourself, or the ability within yourself, to raise your own consciousness to the point where you can ascend.

It is a complete turning around of the message I actually gave. It is a complete perversion. Therefore, it is, as I have said before, that most Christian churches today are clearly based on the lies of anti-christ (from their very foundation but that is a side issue).

What I want to bring forth here is this: There is nothing you cannot overcome from the past when you realize that Christ is not an external savior. Christ is not outside of you; Christ can only come inside of you. If you want to see Christ as a savior, Christ is the *internal* savior. Therefore, my beloved, you need to recognize that you can truly overcome everything from your past—if you are willing to look at yourself and see that separate self in you that is attached to the past.

For example, many of you who are on the spiritual path and who have taken responsibility for yourselves, you have an internal self that says you should be a certain way as a spiritual student. My beloved, there is a very, very aggressive consciousness in the world (again created by the fallen beings, going back thousands of years and even beyond) that wants to define these boundaries, these judgments, these standards for how people should be. Part of Christhood is to come to realize that you cannot reach the higher stages of your Divine plan by living up to these internal standards that you have created for yourself.

We have talked about the *external* standards that are put upon you from society, but I am now talking about the *internal* standards that you have created, most likely over many lifetimes as a spiritual person. You need to look at this and you need to look at how this fits in with the teaching we have given about the birth trauma and the primal self and how you reacted when you received that birth trauma. There was something you decided: "I never want to experience this again." Therefore, you created this self that reasoned that it was something you did that caused the fallen beings

7 | Christhood and your Divine plan

to persecute you—and if you never do that again, you might never be persecuted that way again.

Your internal standards

This then leads on to creating a standard for how you should be. Ever since then, my beloved, there has been a self in you that in any situation you are in here on earth (anytime you come into embodiment, during your childhood and youth) is very active in scanning the society you are in, evaluating the society you are in, finding out what the taboos are, what the norms, what the standards are. Then, it defines a framework, a model, a standard for what you *should* do and what you *should not* do. Then, it projects that if you live up to this, you are safe, you are okay, you are acceptable.

This is what most of you, in fact I should say *all* of you, have done at some point. Although some of you have started to overcome it, all of you have taken this and transferred it to when you found the spiritual path. We can see, when we look back at ascended master dispensations, how many of the students took an ascended master teaching and used it to create another standard for what they should or should not do.

My beloved, you will recognize here that this is a reactionary standard. You are reacting to conditions in the material world. This is understandable but what is the purpose of the coming of Christ? Is it to submit to the conditions in the world, as the fallen beings want the Christ to do? Or is it to give people a visible, undeniable frame of reference that there is something beyond the conditions in the material world? Naturally, it is the latter. However, this is a very delicate balance and discernment to find because when the Christ takes incarnation, as it says in the Bible, the Christ comes into the material world.

The incarnation of Christ

Now, I wish to make just a few remarks about the concept of the incarnation of Christ. The Christians have, of course, again made a mess of it by saying that I, 2,000 years ago, was the only incarnation of Christ. Up there in heaven is some universal, absolute Christ that then took incarnation in my human form. The reality we have given you, both in this latest book about *My Lives* but also in other teachings, is that there is a universal

Christ consciousness but it is not so that the universal Christ consciousness can just take incarnation any time it wants. It requires that there is a human being in embodiment who raises his or her consciousness to the level where suddenly the universal Christ mind can begin to shine through that person.

You have the potential that Christ can take incarnation in you when you reach that level of consciousness. This is important for several reasons. Most of all, because it demonstrates that when the Christ (so to speak) takes incarnation or begins to express itself in this world, it is not doing so completely independently of the conditions in this world. When I appeared 2,000 years ago in Israel, I took incarnation as a child in that embodiment. I grew up in that environment, I absorbed much of that environment and many of the things I said were, of course, adapted to the beliefs that people had, the worldview they had at the time. There is a balance to find, where the Christ does not come into the world to give people an absolute teaching because they would not be able to connect to it. The Christ adapts, as you see in the story of the man who was thirsting and instead of giving him some spiritual dissertation, I gave him a cup of cold water.

This is the principle, we have said, that the Christ comes in to meet people where they are at in consciousness and give them something that can lift them to the next step up, thereby (hopefully) setting them on the path that is ongoing and ultimately will lead them to the ascension. On the one hand, you can see that the Christ that expresses itself in the world (takes incarnation), does adapt to conditions in the world to some degree.

The question that you all need to wrestle with individually is: "How much do I adapt and how much do I go beyond?" When you begin to reach the levels of your Divine plan where you are ready to express your Christhood (begin to express your Christhood), then expressing your Christhood is not adapting to the conditions of this world. It is demonstrating that it is possible to transcend those conditions.

You understand what I am saying. How can you demonstrate to other people that it is possible to transcend a certain level of consciousness? Well, you must first take on that level of consciousness. That is why you take embodiment in a certain family, in a certain nation, in a certain culture. You immerse yourself in it for a time. Then, when you are ready to start expressing your Christhood, you go beyond it. It is not the immersion in the culture that is expressing Christhood but it is going beyond it. Now, of course, again, you are not here to go so far beyond it that people cannot relate to you. You are here to demonstrate that it is possible to go beyond, that there is something beyond.

Christhood is individual

What is Christhood? It is very individual. That is why one of the worst things you can do for yourself is to look at my life and use that to create a standard for how a Christed being should behave. Many people have done this. The Christians have obviously done this but many ascended master students have done the same thing. You have seen ascended master organizations where everybody was so focused on judging themselves and each other, based on whether they lived up to this standard that they thought the ascended masters had defined.

There is no standard for Christhood. That is what you need to grasp before you can really start expressing your Christhood. This is all individual. You have embodied in a specific situation, you have taken on certain conditions, a certain collective consciousness of your family, nation and so forth. Expressing your Christhood means demonstrating that there is something higher than that standard. In the beginning, it will not be very much higher, it will be a little bit higher so that the people can still relate to you.

Now, as you move further, you might go higher and higher. You might get to a point where the people you grew up with can no longer relate to what you actually know and understand about life and that is a different matter. What I am trying to show you here is that many of you have this far-flung idealistic, romantic view of what it means to express Christhood. In reality, in the beginning stages, Christhood is a very practical thing related to everyday conditions in your environment. It can just be a certain way to do things better, a certain way to look at things in a different way, to not take certain things so seriously, not take yourself or life so seriously. For example, you can be more joyful than other people or not be so obsessive-compulsive about a certain aspect of your culture, such as hating those other people over there on the other side of the border, or on the other side of the street, or whatever may be the case.

You can demonstrate that there is a different way, and this is an aspect of your Christhood in the beginning. Many of you can look back at your lives and see: "But haven't I done this for most of my life?" And you are right—you have. Many of you have already done this. I simply wish to make you aware of it and acknowledge that this was an expression of your Christhood. When you recognize that you have already expressed your Christhood, then it becomes easier to accept that you can actually be the Christ in action. You can actually express Christhood on earth and it does not have to be some far-flung thing, as the idealistic view that the Christians have created of my life.

Now, if you take the book about *My Lives* and if you take what I have said in other dictations and answers, you will see that my life really was not anywhere near the ideal that the Christians have created. I have said before that you could very well reason that at the end of my life, it had been a total failure. What had I actually accomplished on the outer? I had not even attracted any disciples who could really grasp the message that I came to bring.

I am not hereby trying to put it down, but I am trying to bridge the gap that many of you have in your minds. You have this internal self that is so absolutely obsessive-compulsive about pointing out your shortcomings and your mistakes that you tend to believe the projection that because you have made all these mistakes, you could not possibly be the Christ in this embodiment. I am trying to show you that being the Christ is a process. It starts out small and then it can gradually grow. You need to recognize that it does not happen just like that. It only happens by you taking one step at a time and gradually beginning to acknowledge that you do have the ability to be the open door for the Christ.

Your Divine plan and free will

Now, my beloved, what does it, then, mean to be the Christ? What does it mean to fulfill your Divine plan? Again, there is a consciousness in the world, created by the fallen beings, that wants to take every idea, every concept and reduce it to a linear standard that can be categorized and labeled by the analytical mind.

One of you brought up that when he was going to this conference, people asked him: "So what is the teaching you are following?" He could not give a name because we have deliberately not given you a name. It is an example of how people, without knowing it, have been influenced by the consciousness of the fallen beings so that they always want to label something. They always want to name it so that it can be categorized and now it is supposed to follow the standard. Of course, this is what the fallen beings have attempted to do with Christ, but the reality of Christ is that Christ never follows any standards.

Is there a standard for how you should express your Christhood in your particular situation? No, there is not. However, that leads to the next question. What is it that is defined in your Divine plan about Christhood? Is your Divine plan like a standard for how you should conduct yourself in this lifetime and thereby also for how you should express your Christhood?

How does free will enter into your Divine plan? Is your Divine plan like a straight-jacket? In the beginning years of your life, you do not have awareness of your Divine plan so you can pretty much do whatever you want. Then, at some point you are supposed to come into awareness of your Divine plan and then the only choice you have left is: "Do I put on the straight-jacket or don't I?" If you choose to put on the straight-jacket of your Divine plan, then the rest of your life is on a mechanical track because now you are just following the Divine plan that was spelled out for you. *That,* of course, is not what your Divine plan is about.

Now, we have, first of all, said you choose your Divine plan. Over the decades where we have given the concept of a Divine plan, we have seen many students interpret this to mean that your Divine plan was created by some divine being who is therefore seeking to force it upon you so you become a marionette. This is why there are some fallen beings who have created this idea that you only gain free will by rebelling against God. There are certain fallen beings that claim that it was only when they rebelled and refused to ascend that they gained truly free will. This, of course, is an illusion because how free is your will when you are reacting against something else? It is exactly as free as when you are seeking to conform to something else. Your will is only free when you choose from within.

Without going into a deeper philosophical discussion here, the reality is that your Divine plan does not spell out in minute detail how you should live your entire life. We have said that you will never actually have a clear vision of the totality of your Divine plan, you will only see this in stages—and why is that? Well, because if there was this very detailed Divine plan and if you saw the whole thing, then it would be like a mechanical path. You would just take step after step after step and follow it. The reality is that your Divine plan is made, as we have said, first of all, to raise your consciousness, and how do you raise your consciousness? By approaching a situation with the consciousness you have right now and then making a choice to reach beyond that consciousness in order to deal with a particular problem. When you reach beyond and experience that there is a higher way to look at the issue, that is when you have raised your consciousness to the next step. Your Divine plan specifies that you should get into a certain situation where you experience a certain condition. Your Divine plan does not specify how you should react to that condition. *That* is your choice.

Transcending your perception

Now, my beloved, be careful here. Many of you have imagined that your Divine plan specifies certain outer conditions. For example, you are meant to meet a certain person and marry that person and have X amount of children. Many of you have, based on this, thought that if you do not meet that person (or if you meet that person and choose not to marry them), you are failing to fulfill your Divine plan. Your Divine plan is not that way, it is not that specific. Your Divine plan is about your shift in consciousness.

When it comes to all of the outer conditions, you have many choices. Now, in the early stages, in the work stage of your Divine plan, there are many times where you have karma with a certain person and the quickest way to resolve that karma is to be in a relationship with that person. Therefore, you could say: "Well, I have actually chosen that I want to be in that relationship so when I am down here in embodiment, that is what I was meant to do." Nevertheless, you still have a wide range of choices as to how you deal with that situation: How long you stay in the relationship, how you react to the relationship and so forth. When you get beyond this work stage, where you are not so much dealing with karmic conditions, you are beginning to go into the creative phase of your Divine plan.

All of a sudden, you have many more options. This means that there is not just, for example, one occupation, one kind of job or career you could have. Even if you choose a certain career, there is not just one way you can conduct this. It is not like your life is on a track. Your Divine plan does not put your life on a track that limits your options. You always have many choices, many options, for how you do things and what you do.

My beloved, what I am saying here applies to those who are spiritual students who are at the higher levels. Naturally, there are many, many people at lower levels of consciousness who are more involved in karmic circumstances. Therefore, their choices from past lives have created consequences that limit the options they have in this life. You could go to a certain level of consciousness and see that there are people who have very few conscious choices they can make. Is this just because of the outer

7 | Christhood and your Divine plan

conditions or is it because their consciousness is so limited that they are not willing to reach beyond their perception of the world?

What I am saying here to you is that you also have a certain perception of the world and in order to have more freedom, more choices, you need to transcend it. What is it that is holding you back? What is it that makes it sometimes feel like your Divine plan is a straight-jacket or your life is totally determined by outer conditions? It is that you have a certain self that has a certain perception and that perception revolves around how you look at and react to your outer circumstances.

What is another aspect of Christhood? It is that you come to the realization that you are not here to be a slave of outer circumstances. You are here to transcend them and this does not mean that if you have children, you abandon your children and go off and sit in a cave in the Himalayas. It means that you transcend the view, the approach, the reactions you have to having children so that you can find a higher way to look at this where you are not so trapped in the current pattern.

How to truly change your life

This raises another important topic where many of you are wondering: "How can I actually change my life? How can I have better conditions? I would like to do this, I would like to do that. I would like to have more money or a better job because I actually would like to have freedom to travel and meet people and see different cultures and this and that." (This is a wish that many of you actually have.)

We now come to the topic of how can you change your outer circumstances to facilitate the vision you have or the desires you have. This is a very complex topic that I will not give you the final discourse on because Saint Germain has something to say about this also and other masters as well. What I will give you is that Christ discernment goes two ways.

First of all, Christ discernment can give you a vision that in your Divine plan is the possibility that you can manifest a higher physical circumstance than you have right know, a situation where you have more freedom. This is a vision of what *can* happen but, on the other hand, the omega aspect of this is that Christ discernment can also give you the vision that sometimes the desires or the vision you have is actually based on your primal self. As Master MORE said, your primal self has this compensatory mechanism that can often give spiritual people a desire to escape certain conditions.

That reaction actually comes from the primal self. One aspect of this is clearly that when you came as an avatar to this planet, you came with a positive attitude of wanting to bring positive change. Then, you felt rejected by the fallen beings, put down by the fallen beings. Then, you created the primal self and ever since you have felt: "I can't be myself on this planet, I can't be who I am, I can't express whatever I want, I can't just be creative because I always have to look at what reaction will I get. What will other people do or say or think? How will they reject me? What will they do to me?"

You still have the desire to express yourself and then you have a mechanism that prevents you from expressing yourself. What Christ discernment can do for you is that it can help you see that this sense that you cannot be yourself on earth comes from the primal self. It is because the primal self is like a computer. It is not self-aware, it cannot think whether it is right or wrong. The primal self is based on the perception that it is external conditions on earth that prevent you from being who you are, from expressing yourself. In reality, when you have Christ discernment, you see that it is not the external conditions that are preventing you from being yourself. It is the primal self that is preventing you from being yourself.

When you first came to earth, perhaps a very long time ago, you had a certain level of awareness. Even though it might have been higher than most people on earth had at the time, it was not the ultimate. Even if you came from a natural planet, it was not the ultimate level of awareness. Since then, you have grown in awareness even though you may not consciously realize this. You have, and that is why we have said you can go back, re-experience your birth trauma and now react to it differently. That is how you can dismiss the primal self, and we have given you the tools to do this.

When you do this, then what actually starts happening is that now you start gradually questioning all these barriers (that you have in your four lower bodies) that say you cannot be yourself, you cannot express yourself. Then, you can begin to actually consider and tune in to: "Who am I really? What is my spiritual individuality in my I AM Presence? What does it mean to express that here on earth?" Suddenly, my beloved, when you begin to accept and experience that you can actually be yourself on earth, you overcome this desire for escape, this desire to always be somebody else or somewhere else. This is the desire of thinking: "When certain outer conditions change and are the way I think they should be, then I can be myself."

No ideal conditions for Christhood

My beloved, we have said before that there is a consciousness that makes you think that when you have the ideal outer conditions, *then* you can be the Christ. The Christ is not meant to have ideal outer conditions because the Christ is meant to demonstrate that there is something higher than whatever conditions it experiences. There are no ideal conditions for expressing Christhood. If you are sitting there, waiting for certain outer conditions before you can express Christhood or be yourself, then you will be waiting for the rest of this lifetime—and for however many succeeding lifetimes you need before it clicks and you realize: "Oh, I am supposed to start where I am at and express Christhood at this level and that's how I get to a higher level."

That is how your outer conditions change. Your outer conditions will begin to change when you decide that you will start where you are and dare to express something of your higher self right here, right now. This is what this messenger decided in 2002. That is why, gradually, his outer conditions have changed to where he has the time and the freedom to focus on doing what he is doing instead of having to work, go to a job and so forth and so on.

Similar things can happen for many of you. Not necessarily in the same way but certainly in such a way that outer conditions gradually begin to change to where you are not feeling that they are restricting you from being who you are and expressing what you are here to express. That is how it can be when you get to the higher levels of your Divine plan but what does it require to get to that level?

It requires that you make the shift in consciousness, my beloved. You recognize that, as I said it 2,000 years ago: "I can of my own self do nothing but with God all things are possible." This was the expression I used back then, so let me re-phrase it based on the teachings we have given you: "With my outer self and the power in my outer self I cannot change my outer conditions, but by reconnecting to the Christ in me, by acknowledging the Christ in me, *then* it is possible to change my outer conditions."

What does it require to reconnect to the Christ in you, to begin to express your Christhood? It requires, my beloved, a conscious decision that: "I will not be a slave of my external conditions. I will be the open door, I will express myself regardless of what my outer conditions are. I will do something right now, I will multiply the talents I have been given, I will multiply the situation I am in right now." Then, when you take that first small step, the law is absolutely unfailing. There will be a multiplication from the spiritual realm. As you continue to do this, gradually your outer conditions can begin to shift.

Now, there may be some of you who also realize that actually there are certain outer conditions that you are not meant to change because you are meant to express that there is a higher way to deal with those conditions. It is not just a matter of getting away from certain conditions that are now bothering you because those conditions might be part of your Christhood. It might be part of your Divine plan to actually express Christhood in those conditions so that other people can see that they can be transcended.

Again, there is a delicate discernment. It is also so, my beloved, that as you rise higher, as you overcome the compensatory mechanisms (the attachments, as we have also called it), you have more options. You may, for instance, choose at a certain point: "No, I don't want to deal with that condition anymore, I have had enough of that experience." Or: "I don't want to deal with that kind of people anymore. I have demonstrated that there is an alternative to their state of consciousness and I don't want to keep doing that for the rest of my life. I want to move on to something else."

You have, my beloved, many, many options. It is not so that there is only one way to fulfill your Divine plan and if you do not do it, you will fail. It is not all-or-nothing. It is not black-or-white.

You cannot fail in your Divine plan

As long as you are willing to shift your consciousness, my beloved, you cannot fail in executing your Divine plan because the core of it is your shift in consciousness to the highest possible level. This is not set in stone. Before you come into embodiment, when you make your Divine plan, you are making an assessment, based on the consciousness you had in your last embodiment, of what is most realistic that you can rise to in this lifetime. If you are willing, if you really apply yourself, apply the teachings we have given, you can rise higher. Many of you can rise higher than the level that is defined in your Divine plan.

There are some of you who, in your Divine plan, did not define that you could rise to the 144th level in this lifetime. Some of you actually *can*, if you really apply yourself and go beyond because what does it require to shift your consciousness? It just requires a willingness to see something you have not seen before, a willingness to make the decision that you are not bound by this level of consciousness, a willingness to step outside. You use the Conscious You's ability to step outside of its four lower bodies and see: "I am not this; I am more than this." There is no limit put upon you from the ascended realm nor in your Divine plan of how far you can take that process if you are willing to shift.

There is, however, the limit that you need a certain continuity so you cannot shift just like that, to a level that is too far beyond where you are at. You cannot skip steps. There are spiritual students who become very impatient and they want to be enlightened *now*, in five minutes, but it cannot be done now. You have to go through all of the 144 levels of consciousness. You cannot skip from the 120th to the 133rd level. It is not possible. You will lose your sense of identity, your sense of continuity and it can actually lead to mental illness and schizophrenia. What you need to recognize here is that you need to go through the steps, for there is really no limitation to how fast you can do this if you are willing.

My beloved, naturally, I could go on for a very long time, giving you more and more teachings about this. We have already given you many teachings that you can study and that you can apply with the perspective I have given you on your Divine plan and Christhood. The real key here is to come to the point where you recognize: "I am not defined by anything on earth. I am a spiritual being." The Conscious You is what we have called pure awareness to indicate that you are not defined by anything that has form. That is why you can transcend any form, including the forms in your primal self and your separate selves. This is the core of Christhood, and you have complete free will as to how you will implement it and apply it in this lifetime.

8 | INVOKING CHRIST DISCERNMENT ABOUT MY DIVINE PLAN

In the name I AM THAT I AM, Jesus Christ, I call to all representatives of the Divine Mother, especially Jesus, to help me develop Christ discernment and see what it is in myself that prevents the unfoldment of my Divine plan, including…

[Make personal calls.]

Part 1

1. Jesus, help me overcome any kind of regret or negative feelings about what I have gone through in my life. Help me look back at my life without judging with the outer mind that many of the things I went through were not spiritual.

> O Jesus, blessed brother mine,
> I walk the path that you outline,

a great example to us all,
I follow now your inner call.

O Jesus, let the Fire of Joy,
consume the devil's subtle ploy,
transfigured is our planet earth,
the golden age is given birth.

2. Jesus, help me see that what I did was part of my Divine plan because I needed that experience in order to work through the work phase, where I am preparing myself for the more creative phase of my Divine plan.

O Jesus, open inner sight,
the ego wants to prove it's right,
but this I will no longer do,
I want to be all one with you.

O Jesus, let the Fire of Joy,
consume the devil's subtle ploy,
transfigured is our planet earth,
the golden age is given birth.

3. Jesus, help me realize that I come into embodiment with a lower level of consciousness than my potential. Help me shift my consciousness as quickly as possible, so I can go up towards the higher levels and see the more creative aspects of my Divine plan.

O Jesus, I now clearly see,
the Key of Knowledge given me,
my Christ self I hereby embrace,
as you fill up my inner space.

O Jesus, let the Fire of Joy,
consume the devil's subtle ploy,
transfigured is our planet earth,
the golden age is given birth.

4. Jesus, help me accept that I cannot really shift my consciousness in a theoretical way. I need to have certain experiences in order to shift, so I did what I did because I knew subconsciously that I needed that experience. I wanted to have it as quickly as possible in order to shift my consciousness.

> O Jesus, show me serpent's lie,
> expose the beam in my own eye,
> as Christ discernment you me give,
> in oneness I forever live.
>
> **O Jesus, let the Fire of Joy,**
> **consume the devil's subtle ploy,**
> **transfigured is our planet earth,**
> **the golden age is given birth.**

5. Jesus, help me see that when I had a difficult experience, I reacted to it with the level of consciousness I had at the time. Now, that I have raised my consciousness, I look back at that experience with some regret. This sense of regret comes from an internal self that is part of the primal self.

> O Jesus, I am truly meek,
> and thus I turn the other cheek,
> when the accuser attacks me,
> I go within and merge with thee.
>
> **O Jesus, let the Fire of Joy,**
> **consume the devil's subtle ploy,**
> **transfigured is our planet earth,**
> **the golden age is given birth.**

6. Jesus, help me see if I created this self partly because of a spiritual teaching. I interpreted the teaching so I created the self that is blaming myself, feeling ashamed, feeling like I am not good enough, feeling that a real spiritual person could not possibly have done what I did.

> O Jesus, ego I let die,
> surrender ev'ry earthly tie,
> the dead can bury what is dead,
> I choose to walk with you instead.

> O Jesus, let the Fire of Joy,
> consume the devil's subtle ploy,
> transfigured is our planet earth,
> the golden age is given birth.

7. Jesus, help me truly accept that the ascended masters do not look at me as I look at myself. You do not condemn me as I condemn myself, and therefore I can always approach you because you only want to set me free.

> O Jesus, help me rise above,
> the devil's test through higher love,
> show me separate self unreal,
> my formless self you do reveal.

> **O Jesus, let the Fire of Joy,**
> **consume the devil's subtle ploy,**
> **transfigured is our planet earth,**
> **the golden age is given birth.**

8. Jesus, help me attain the Christ discernment of experiencing that I am forgiven and redeemed, thus I can overcome anything that has happened here on earth.

> O Jesus, what is that to me,
> I just let go and follow thee,
> with this I do pass ev'ry test,
> to find with you eternal rest.

> **O Jesus, let the Fire of Joy,**
> **consume the devil's subtle ploy,**
> **transfigured is our planet earth,**
> **the golden age is given birth.**

9. Jesus, help me see that I have taken a high level of responsibility for myself, but there is a separate self that has taken this and turned it into a negative by getting me to think I should always be perfect.

> O Jesus, fiery master mine,
> my heart now melting into thine,

I love with heart and mind and soul,
the God who is my highest goal.

**O Jesus, let the Fire of Joy,
consume the devil's subtle ploy,
transfigured is our planet earth,
the golden age is given birth.**

Part 2

1. Jesus, help me see that the fallen beings have projected that there are certain choices I can make that I can never overcome by making other choices. In reality, I can always make a choice that completely replaces a previous choice.

O Jesus, blessed brother mine,
I walk the path that you outline,
a great example to us all,
I follow now your inner call.

**O Jesus, let the Fire of Joy,
consume the devil's subtle ploy,
transfigured is our planet earth,
the golden age is given birth.**

2. Jesus, help me internalize that there is no material condition that can keep me from ascending or from moving on to the highest potential of my Divine plan. The reason being that there is no material condition that can prevent me from shifting my consciousness.

O Jesus, open inner sight,
the ego wants to prove it's right,
but this I will no longer do,
I want to be all one with you.

**O Jesus, let the Fire of Joy,
consume the devil's subtle ploy,
transfigured is our planet earth,
the golden age is given birth.**

3. Jesus, help me accept that even though there are consequences that can remain for the rest of my life, this cannot limit my growth in consciousness. Help me really grasp and experience Christ the redeemer, the Christ that can make me a new being.

> O Jesus, I now clearly see,
> the Key of Knowledge given me,
> my Christ self I hereby embrace,
> as you fill up my inner space.

**O Jesus, let the Fire of Joy,
consume the devil's subtle ploy,
transfigured is our planet earth,
the golden age is given birth.**

4. Jesus, help me experience that there is nothing I cannot overcome from the past, when I realize that Christ is not outside of me; Christ can only come inside of me. I can overcome everything from my past by being willing to look at myself and see the separate self in me that is attached to the past.

> O Jesus, show me serpent's lie,
> expose the beam in my own eye,
> as Christ discernment you me give,
> in oneness I forever live.

**O Jesus, let the Fire of Joy,
consume the devil's subtle ploy,
transfigured is our planet earth,
the golden age is given birth.**

5. Jesus, help me see the internal self that says I should be a certain way as a spiritual student. I realize that I cannot reach the higher stages of my Divine plan by living up to these internal standards that I have created for myself.

> O Jesus, I am truly meek,
> and thus I turn the other cheek,
> when the accuser attacks me,
> I go within and merge with thee.

> **O Jesus, let the Fire of Joy,**
> **consume the devil's subtle ploy,**
> **transfigured is our planet earth,**
> **the golden age is given birth.**

6. Jesus, help me see this and how it fits in with the teaching about the birth trauma and the primal self and how I reacted when I received that birth trauma. Help me see how I decided: "I never want to experience this again." Therefore, I created this self that reasoned that if I never do certain things again, I should never be persecuted again.

> O Jesus, ego I let die,
> surrender ev'ry earthly tie,
> the dead can bury what is dead,
> I choose to walk with you instead.

> **O Jesus, let the Fire of Joy,**
> **consume the devil's subtle ploy,**
> **transfigured is our planet earth,**
> **the golden age is given birth.**

7. Jesus, help me see the self that in any situation is very active in evaluating the society I am in, finding out what the taboos are, what the standards are. Then, it defines a standard for what I *should* do and what I *should not* do. Then, it projects that if I live up to this, I am safe.

> O Jesus, help me rise above,
> the devil's test through higher love,

show me separate self unreal,
my formless self you do reveal.

**O Jesus, let the Fire of Joy,
consume the devil's subtle ploy,
transfigured is our planet earth,
the golden age is given birth.**

8. Jesus, help me see if I have taken an ascended master teaching and used it to create another standard for what I should or should not do. Help me see that this is a reactionary standard.

O Jesus, what is that to me,
I just let go and follow thee,
with this I do pass ev'ry test,
to find with you eternal rest.

**O Jesus, let the Fire of Joy,
consume the devil's subtle ploy,
transfigured is our planet earth,
the golden age is given birth.**

9. Jesus, help me see that the purpose of the coming of Christ is to give people a visible, undeniable frame of reference that there is something beyond the conditions in the material world.

O Jesus, fiery master mine,
my heart now melting into thine,
I love with heart and mind and soul,
the God who is my highest goal.

**O Jesus, let the Fire of Joy,
consume the devil's subtle ploy,
transfigured is our planet earth,
the golden age is given birth.**

Part 3

1. Jesus, help me accept that I have the potential that Christ can take incarnation in me when I reach a certain level of consciousness.

> O Jesus, blessed brother mine,
> I walk the path that you outline,
> a great example to us all,
> I follow now your inner call.
>
> **O Jesus, let the Fire of Joy,**
> **consume the devil's subtle ploy,**
> **transfigured is our planet earth,**
> **the golden age is given birth.**

2. Jesus, help me see that when the Christ begins to express itself in this world, it is not doing so completely independently of the conditions in this world. The Christ does not come into the world to give people an absolute teaching but seeks to help people take the next step up.

> O Jesus, open inner sight,
> the ego wants to prove it's right,
> but this I will no longer do,
> I want to be all one with you.
>
> **O Jesus, let the Fire of Joy,**
> **consume the devil's subtle ploy,**
> **transfigured is our planet earth,**
> **the golden age is given birth.**

3. Jesus, help me resolve the question on a personal level of how much I adapt and how much I go beyond. I see that expressing my Christhood is not adapting to the conditions of this world. It is demonstrating that it is possible to transcend those conditions.

> O Jesus, I now clearly see,
> the Key of Knowledge given me,

my Christ self I hereby embrace,
as you fill up my inner space.

**O Jesus, let the Fire of Joy,
consume the devil's subtle ploy,
transfigured is our planet earth,
the golden age is given birth.**

4. Jesus, help me see that in order to demonstrate to other people that it is possible to transcend a certain level of consciousness, I must first take on that level of consciousness. I must immerse myself in a certain culture and then go beyond it, so I demonstrate that it is possible to go beyond.

O Jesus, show me serpent's lie,
expose the beam in my own eye,
as Christ discernment you me give,
in oneness I forever live.

**O Jesus, let the Fire of Joy,
consume the devil's subtle ploy,
transfigured is our planet earth,
the golden age is given birth.**

5. Jesus, help me see that Christhood is very individual. That is why I cannot create a standard for how a Christed being should behave. I have embodied in a specific situation in order to demonstrate that there is something higher than that standard.

O Jesus, I am truly meek,
and thus I turn the other cheek,
when the accuser attacks me,
I go within and merge with thee.

**O Jesus, let the Fire of Joy,
consume the devil's subtle ploy,
transfigured is our planet earth,
the golden age is given birth.**

8 | *Invoking Christ discernment about my Divine plan*

6. Jesus, help me see that the beginning stages of Christhood is a very practical thing, related to everyday conditions in my environment and not taking myself or life so seriously.

> O Jesus, ego I let die,
> surrender ev'ry earthly tie,
> the dead can bury what is dead,
> I choose to walk with you instead.
>
> **O Jesus, let the Fire of Joy,**
> **consume the devil's subtle ploy,**
> **transfigured is our planet earth,**
> **the golden age is given birth.**

7. Jesus, help me be aware of and acknowledge that I have already expressed my Christhood in many situations. Help me accept that I can actually be the Christ in action. I can actually express Christhood on earth and it does not have to be in some far-flung idealistic way.

> O Jesus, help me rise above,
> the devil's test through higher love,
> show me separate self unreal,
> my formless self you do reveal.
>
> **O Jesus, let the Fire of Joy,**
> **consume the devil's subtle ploy,**
> **transfigured is our planet earth,**
> **the golden age is given birth.**

8. Jesus, help me see the internal self that is obsessive-compulsive about pointing out my shortcomings and mistakes. Help me overcome the projection that because I have made all these mistakes, I could not possibly be the Christ in this embodiment.

> O Jesus, what is that to me,
> I just let go and follow thee,
> with this I do pass ev'ry test,
> to find with you eternal rest.

**O Jesus, let the Fire of Joy,
consume the devil's subtle ploy,
transfigured is our planet earth,
the golden age is given birth.**

9. Jesus, help me accept that being the Christ is a process. It starts out small and then it gradually grows. It happens by me taking one step at a time and gradually beginning to acknowledge that I do have the ability to be the open door for the Christ.

O Jesus, fiery master mine,
my heart now melting into thine,
I love with heart and mind and soul,
the God who is my highest goal.

**O Jesus, let the Fire of Joy,
consume the devil's subtle ploy,
transfigured is our planet earth,
the golden age is given birth.**

Part 4

1. Jesus, help me accept that there is no standard for how I should express my Christhood in my particular situation. Even my Divine plan is not a standard for how I should express my Christhood.

O Jesus, blessed brother mine,
I walk the path that you outline,
a great example to us all,
I follow now your inner call.

**O Jesus, let the Fire of Joy,
consume the devil's subtle ploy,
transfigured is our planet earth,
the golden age is given birth.**

2. Jesus, help me accept that my Divine plan is not like a straight-jacket that puts my life on a mechanical track. My Divine plan is made to raise my consciousness. I raise my consciousness by approaching a situation with the consciousness I have right now, and then making a choice to reach beyond that consciousness in order to deal with a particular problem.

> O Jesus, open inner sight,
> the ego wants to prove it's right,
> but this I will no longer do,
> I want to be all one with you.

> **O Jesus, let the Fire of Joy,**
> **consume the devil's subtle ploy,**
> **transfigured is our planet earth,**
> **the golden age is given birth.**

3. Jesus, help me see that when I reach beyond and experience that there is a higher way to look at an issue, then I have raised my consciousness to the next level. My Divine plan does not specify how I should react to conditions.

> O Jesus, I now clearly see,
> the Key of Knowledge given me,
> my Christ self I hereby embrace,
> as you fill up my inner space.

> **O Jesus, let the Fire of Joy,**
> **consume the devil's subtle ploy,**
> **transfigured is our planet earth,**
> **the golden age is given birth.**

4. Jesus, help me see that my Divine plan does not put my life on a track that limits my options. I always have many choices, many options, for how I do things and what I do.

> O Jesus, show me serpent's lie,
> expose the beam in my own eye,
> as Christ discernment you me give,
> in oneness I forever live.

> O Jesus, let the Fire of Joy,
> consume the devil's subtle ploy,
> transfigured is our planet earth,
> the golden age is given birth.

5. Jesus, help me see that I have a certain perception of the world and in order to have more freedom, more choices, I need to transcend it. What is holding me back is a self that has a certain perception, and that perception revolves around how I look at and react to my outer circumstances.

> O Jesus, I am truly meek,
> and thus I turn the other cheek,
> when the accuser attacks me,
> I go within and merge with thee.

> O Jesus, let the Fire of Joy,
> consume the devil's subtle ploy,
> transfigured is our planet earth,
> the golden age is given birth.

6. Jesus, help me see that another aspect of Christhood is that I come to the realization that I am not here to be a slave of outer circumstances. I am here to transcend them, and this means that I find a higher way to look at my life where I am not so trapped in the current pattern.

> O Jesus, ego I let die,
> surrender ev'ry earthly tie,
> the dead can bury what is dead,
> I choose to walk with you instead.

> O Jesus, let the Fire of Joy,
> consume the devil's subtle ploy,
> transfigured is our planet earth,
> the golden age is given birth.

7. Jesus, help me have the Christ discernment to see that in my Divine plan is the possibility that I can manifest a higher physical circumstance than I have right know, a situation where I have more freedom.

O Jesus, help me rise above,
the devil's test through higher love,
show me separate self unreal,
my formless self you do reveal.

**O Jesus, let the Fire of Joy,
consume the devil's subtle ploy,
transfigured is our planet earth,
the golden age is given birth.**

8. Jesus, help me have the Christ discernment to see that sometimes the desires or the vision I have is actually based on my primal self. My primal self has this compensatory mechanism that can give me a desire to escape certain conditions.

O Jesus, what is that to me,
I just let go and follow thee,
with this I do pass ev'ry test,
to find with you eternal rest.

**O Jesus, let the Fire of Joy,
consume the devil's subtle ploy,
transfigured is our planet earth,
the golden age is given birth.**

9. Jesus, help me see the primal self that feels: "I can't be myself on this planet, I can't be who I am, I can't express whatever I want, I can't just be creative because I always have to look at what reaction I will get. What will other people do or say or think? How will they reject me? What will they do to me?"

O Jesus, fiery master mine,
my heart now melting into thine,
I love with heart and mind and soul,
the God who is my highest goal.

**O Jesus, let the Fire of Joy,
consume the devil's subtle ploy,
transfigured is our planet earth,
the golden age is given birth.**

Part 5

1. Jesus, help me see that I still have the desire to express myself, and then I have a mechanism that prevents me from expressing myself. Help me see that the sense that I cannot be myself on earth comes from the primal self.

> O Jesus, blessed brother mine,
> I walk the path that you outline,
> a great example to us all,
> I follow now your inner call.
>
> **O Jesus, let the Fire of Joy,
> consume the devil's subtle ploy,
> transfigured is our planet earth,
> the golden age is given birth.**

2. Jesus, help me overcome the primal self's perception that it is external conditions on earth that prevents me from being who I am and expressing myself. Help me have the Christ discernment to see that it is not the external conditions that are preventing me from being myself. It is the primal self that is preventing me from being myself.

> O Jesus, open inner sight,
> the ego wants to prove it's right,
> but this I will no longer do,
> I want to be all one with you.
>
> **O Jesus, let the Fire of Joy,
> consume the devil's subtle ploy,
> transfigured is our planet earth,
> the golden age is given birth.**

8 | Invoking Christ discernment about my Divine plan

3. Jesus, help me question the barriers that say I cannot be myself, I cannot express myself. Help me tune in to my spiritual individuality in my I AM Presence and see what it means to express that here on earth.

> O Jesus, I now clearly see,
> the Key of Knowledge given me,
> my Christ self I hereby embrace,
> as you fill up my inner space.
>
> **O Jesus, let the Fire of Joy,**
> **consume the devil's subtle ploy,**
> **transfigured is our planet earth,**
> **the golden age is given birth.**

4. Jesus, help me accept and experience that I can actually be myself on earth, and thereby overcome the desire for escape, the desire to be somebody else or somewhere else. Help me let go of the illusion that: "When certain outer conditions change and are the way I think they should be, then I can be myself."

> O Jesus, show me serpent's lie,
> expose the beam in my own eye,
> as Christ discernment you me give,
> in oneness I forever live.
>
> **O Jesus, let the Fire of Joy,**
> **consume the devil's subtle ploy,**
> **transfigured is our planet earth,**
> **the golden age is given birth.**

5. Jesus, help me accept that the Christ is not meant to have ideal outer conditions, because the Christ is meant to demonstrate that there is something higher than whatever conditions it experiences. There are no ideal conditions for expressing Christhood.

> O Jesus, I am truly meek,
> and thus I turn the other cheek,
> when the accuser attacks me,
> I go within and merge with thee.

**O Jesus, let the Fire of Joy,
consume the devil's subtle ploy,
transfigured is our planet earth,
the golden age is given birth.**

6. Jesus, help me stop waiting for certain outer conditions before I can express Christhood or be myself. Help me realize: "Oh, I am supposed to start where I am and express Christhood at this level—and that's how I get to a higher level."

O Jesus, ego I let die,
surrender ev'ry earthly tie,
the dead can bury what is dead,
I choose to walk with you instead.

**O Jesus, let the Fire of Joy,
consume the devil's subtle ploy,
transfigured is our planet earth,
the golden age is given birth.**

7. Jesus, help me accept that my outer conditions will begin to change when I decide that I will start where I am and dare to express something of my higher self right here, right now.

O Jesus, help me rise above,
the devil's test through higher love,
show me separate self unreal,
my formless self you do reveal.

**O Jesus, let the Fire of Joy,
consume the devil's subtle ploy,
transfigured is our planet earth,
the golden age is given birth.**

8. Jesus, help me move into the state of mind that allows my outer conditions to change to where I am not feeling that they are restricting me from being who I am and expressing what I am here to express.

O Jesus, what is that to me,
I just let go and follow thee,
with this I do pass ev'ry test,
to find with you eternal rest.

**O Jesus, let the Fire of Joy,
consume the devil's subtle ploy,
transfigured is our planet earth,
the golden age is given birth.**

9. Jesus, help me see that in order to get to the higher levels of my Divine plan, I need to make a shift in consciousness and recognize that with my outer self and the power in my outer self I cannot change my outer conditions, but by reconnecting to the Christ in me, by acknowledging the Christ in me, *then* it is possible to change my outer conditions.

O Jesus, fiery master mine,
my heart now melting into thine,
I love with heart and mind and soul,
the God who is my highest goal.

**O Jesus, let the Fire of Joy,
consume the devil's subtle ploy,
transfigured is our planet earth,
the golden age is given birth.**

Part 6

1. Jesus, help me see that in order to reconnect to the Christ in me, I need to make the conscious decision that: "I will not be a slave of my external conditions. I will be the open door, I will express myself regardless of what my outer conditions are. I will do *something* right now, I will multiply the talents I have been given, I will multiply the situation I am in right now."

O Jesus, blessed brother mine,
I walk the path that you outline,

a great example to us all,
I follow now your inner call.

O Jesus, let the Fire of Joy,
consume the devil's subtle ploy,
transfigured is our planet earth,
the golden age is given birth.

2. Jesus, help me accept that when I take that first small step, the law is absolutely unfailing. There will be a multiplication from the spiritual realm and as I continue, my outer conditions will begin to shift.

O Jesus, open inner sight,
the ego wants to prove it's right,
but this I will no longer do,
I want to be all one with you.

O Jesus, let the Fire of Joy,
consume the devil's subtle ploy,
transfigured is our planet earth,
the golden age is given birth.

3. Jesus, help me see if there are certain outer conditions that I am not meant to change because I am meant to express that there is a higher way to deal with those conditions. It is part of my Divine plan to express Christhood in those conditions so that other people can see that they can be transcended.

O Jesus, I now clearly see,
the Key of Knowledge given me,
my Christ self I hereby embrace,
as you fill up my inner space.

O Jesus, let the Fire of Joy,
consume the devil's subtle ploy,
transfigured is our planet earth,
the golden age is given birth.

8 | Invoking Christ discernment about my Divine plan

4. Jesus, help me accept that as long as I am willing to shift my consciousness, I cannot fail in executing my Divine plan because the core of it is my shift in consciousness to the highest possible level.

O Jesus, show me serpent's lie,
expose the beam in my own eye,
as Christ discernment you me give,
in oneness I forever live.

O Jesus, let the Fire of Joy,
consume the devil's subtle ploy,
transfigured is our planet earth,
the golden age is given birth.

5. Jesus, help me see if it is in my Divine plan that I can rise to the 144th level in this lifetime.

O Jesus, I am truly meek,
and thus I turn the other cheek,
when the accuser attacks me,
I go within and merge with thee.

O Jesus, let the Fire of Joy,
consume the devil's subtle ploy,
transfigured is our planet earth,
the golden age is given birth.

6. Jesus, help me experience that shifting my consciousness requires a willingness to see something I have not seen before, a willingness to make the decision that I am not bound by this level of consciousness, I am willing to step outside.

O Jesus, ego I let die,
surrender ev'ry earthly tie,
the dead can bury what is dead,
I choose to walk with you instead.

**O Jesus, let the Fire of Joy,
consume the devil's subtle ploy,
transfigured is our planet earth,
the golden age is given birth.**

7. Jesus, help me learn how to use the Conscious You's ability to step outside of its four lower bodies and see: "I am not this; I am more than this."

O Jesus, help me rise above,
the devil's test through higher love,
show me separate self unreal,
my formless self you do reveal.

**O Jesus, let the Fire of Joy,
consume the devil's subtle ploy,
transfigured is our planet earth,
the golden age is given birth.**

8. Jesus, help me accept that there is no limit put upon me from the ascended realm nor in my Divine plan of how far I can take that process if I am willing to shift. I do need to go through the steps, but there is no limitation to how fast I can do this if I am willing.

O Jesus, what is that to me,
I just let go and follow thee,
with this I do pass ev'ry test,
to find with you eternal rest.

**O Jesus, let the Fire of Joy,
consume the devil's subtle ploy,
transfigured is our planet earth,
the golden age is given birth.**

9. Jesus, I now recognize: "I am not defined by anything on earth. I am a spiritual being. My Conscious You is not defined by anything that has form. I can transcend any form, including the forms in my primal self and my separate selves. This is the core of Christhood, and I have complete free will as to how I will implement it and apply it in this lifetime."

O Jesus, fiery master mine,
my heart now melting into thine,
I love with heart and mind and soul,
the God who is my highest goal.

**O Jesus, let the Fire of Joy,
consume the devil's subtle ploy,
transfigured is our planet earth,
the golden age is given birth.**

Sealing

In the name of the Divine Mother, I call to Mother Mary for the sealing of myself and all people in my circle of influence in the creative flow of the Divine Mother, the River of Life. I call for the multiplication of my calls by all representatives of the Divine Mother, so that we form the perfect figure-eight flow of "As Above, so below." Thus, I accept that this is fully manifest, because the mouth of the Lord, the Divine Mother that I AM, has spoken it. Amen.

9 | THE REVOLUTIONARY ASPECT OF YOUR DIVINE PLAN

I AM the Ascended Master Saint Germain. What I wish to discourse with you on is the concept of *evolution* versus *revolution*. Now, the previous masters have attempted to give you the concept that your Divine plan is not some far-flung, unattainable goal that is beyond your reach. Certainly, this is a very important concept for you to internalize.

Evolutionary and revolutionary phases

You need to recognize that there is an evolutionary *aspect* of your Divine plan, an evolutionary *phase* of your Divine plan. We have talked about the work phase of your Divine plan, we have said that there is a certain phase where you are starting to go into expressing your Christhood but you do this in the situation you are in, you do this in small increments and small steps. This is what we will call the *evolutionary* phase of your Divine plan. In a sense, this evolutionary phase will continue for the rest of your lifetime. There will always be an evolutionary element of your Divine plan.

Nevertheless, what you need to recognize is that there comes a point where you begin to go on to the higher stages of Christhood, the higher stages of the path. There are certain points, certain key points in your life, where you cannot get to the next level up in an evolutionary way by taking smaller steps. You cannot even get to the next level by being in the evolutionary state of consciousness.

It is necessary to know this at those levels—not at the lower levels where you do not need to worry about this. Let me step back a minute and say that for many of you, for many of you who will find this teaching, you are still in the evolutionary phase. What I will give you here will not apply to you now. It may not apply to you for some years but there will come a point, if you are an advanced lifestream who has the potential to manifest a high level of consciousness in this embodiment, where you cannot go further by taking these small steps.

In a sense, there is a contradiction in what I am telling you because, naturally, we have given you the concept of the 144 levels. We have said you cannot skip steps so even if you are at the 123rd level, your next level up is the 124th and in a way the step from the 123rd to the 124th is not such a big dramatic step—it is not really a "revolutionary" change.

What I wish to give you here is the concept that you are still walking the path, going through the different levels of consciousness, but my beloved, running parallel with this gradual, evolutionary path, there is the potential that you can go through a shift in consciousness, a shift in attitude, a shift in the way you look at life. This brings you from the level you were at before, to a level that is so decisively higher that it really must be seen as a revolutionary step.

Many of you have experienced such shifts in consciousness. Many of you can see that there was a time where you had no spiritual teaching. Then, you found your first spiritual teaching and it was a dramatic shift that brought you up higher and it changed the way you look at life. You may see that you have had other steps like this where you suddenly had an insight, you suddenly experienced something that was a revolutionary, a more dramatic shift in consciousness.

Being balanced about a revolutionary shift

What I am giving you here is that there comes, at the higher levels, a point where you need to actually recognize that parallel to the evolutionary change, there can be the necessity that you go through a more dramatic, a more revolutionary shift in consciousness. This can only be brought about if you are willing to make such a shift, if you are making the decision to open yourself to the insight that you are now ready for.

You cannot do this until you are ready. That is why I need to, again, look back at previous ascended master dispensations and point out to you, how there were many, many students that would say that they went through a revolutionary change in consciousness and perspective. Now, they became what Master MORE called "very determined, very blue-flame, very blue-ray, don't let anything stand in your way, mow down the opposition and any other people who stand in your way and just walk towards that goal."

There is, of course, the joke that was told in previous dispensations where El Morya and Kuthumi were given the task to go up to a mountain and get a message from a spiritual master. El Morya walked straight up the mountain, got the message and walked straight down. Kuthumi took his time, looked at the birds, smelled the flowers, but when they came down El Morya had forgotten the message and Kuthumi had retained it. This is the same thing with many of the spiritual students because it is possible, my beloved, to go through a revolutionary shift in awareness but you still have so much of the primal self, so many separate selves, left that you do not interpret the experience correctly.

What I am saying here is that there were many students in the previous dispensations who did have a genuine mystical, spiritual experience. They saw a higher state of consciousness, but then their outer minds interpreted this in an unbalanced way. They took on this very unbalanced reaction and now they became what they would call "determined" but what in reality was "blind." They put on blinders and they were looking only at that one goal. They were actually, in a way, saying to their intuition, to their Christ self, to the ascended masters: "Don't bother me now, I have the vision of where I need to go, don't disturb me by giving me any other insights. I don't need you until I get to the goal." Of course, they could not get to the goal without getting the insights but they had pushed that out of their minds.

Seeing your higher potential

What I need you to recognize here is that when I am talking about a "revolutionary shift," this cannot happen until you have used the teachings about the primal self and many other teachings we have given on the ego and traumas and you have healed your psychology to a certain level. There is a need, when you have received this healing, to recognize that you have come to a level where it is no longer the right step for you to make an incremental change, but where it can be necessary to make a decisive shift in the way you look at life. Of course, this applies to many things. It can apply especially to: What does it mean for you to be the Christ in action? What is the highest potential of your Divine plan that you can bring forth?

Now, to use a practical example here, this messenger first heard about the teachings of the ascended masters in 1984. He followed a previous ascended master dispensation, studied the teachings, applied the teachings, took all kinds of courses, went to psychologists, worked on his psychology. Then, in 2002 he came to the realization that he had followed the path partly based on a human ambition of doing something important, making a decisive difference, feeling that his life was worthwhile. This was, in essence, part of his primal self, part of his birth trauma but not all of it.

It was part of what all of you might feel because you came to earth to make a positive difference and you have not been able to make that difference so you have this inner frustration. He saw this, and then he was able to realize that he needed to make a decisive, dramatic shift to let that go, to let go of that ambition, to surrender it completely. He was able to do this and that is when he, then, felt the Presence of Jesus who asked him if he wanted to start the website where people could ask questions and get the answers from Jesus.

If you look at the messenger's history, from 1984 to 2002 he had grown in an evolutionary way. Gradually, step-by-step, he made quite a bit of progress in that amount of years but it was still increment by increment. In his world view, he had up until that point never seen himself as having the potential to be a messenger for the ascended masters. He had never been dissatisfied with the previous messenger, never been envious of the previous messenger, never had any thought that he could do better or that she was doing wrong. He was just taking advantage of the teaching. He saw himself as an ascended master student and that he would continue to grow incrementally based on using the ascended master teachings that he had.

What I am saying here is that the step for him to move from being an ascended master student to an ascended master messenger was not an evolutionary step. It required a revolutionary shift in consciousness. This is not to say that all of you are now going to think that you have to do the same and become messengers for the ascended masters. What I am saying is that for many of you, you have the potential (at some point in your life, maybe not now, maybe not until later), but you have the potential as part of your Divine plan that you can step up to a higher way of looking at life, looking at yourself, and accepting the higher potential you can bring forth. You cannot do this in an evolutionary way.

It is not so, my beloved, that all ascended master students are meant to gradually evolve until they become ascended master messengers. An ascended master student can incrementally evolve until you are ready to ascend. Even though I would say that in order to really be ready to ascend, you also have to go through a number of revolutionary shifts in consciousness. There is no evolutionary path that leads increment by increment from being a student to being a messenger, it requires a revolutionary shift. Likewise, many of you will need to come to that point where you sense: "There is something more. I can't see it right now—why can't I see it?"

It is because you have not made the decision that you are willing to see it, no matter what it is and no matter what changes it requires of you. Once you have this revolutionary shift, certain things might have to change. There is always the ego that fears change, there is always the dark forces who want to keep you within certain boundaries and you have to overcome that gravitational pull. There is also the primal self that does not want you to step outside of the boundaries where it feels you are safe.

Being willing to no longer be safe

You have to come to that point where you are willing to no longer be safe. My beloved, you can be on the spiritual path and you can have the concept that there is a path that leads from lower to higher levels of consciousness. You can evolutionarily grow until you become able to express some aspect of your Christhood. If you take the *My Lives* book, it describes how Jesus, before his public mission in Palestine, went through an evolutionary process that prepared him for that mission. Yet if you look at it, there came that point that is described (of course there was a more complex psychological shift), but there is in the Bible the account of the wedding in Cana. He was sitting there, realizing that it was time for him to step up but he was resisting it and Mother Mary had to step in and give him that final impetus that it was time.

That was when Jesus went through the revolutionary shift, of actually accepting himself as the Living Christ in embodiment. Some of you can come to that point also where you accept this. I can assure you, it is a *revolutionary* shift. It is not just another increment up, it is a leap, like they call it the quantum leap. You understand, my beloved, that there was a time where scientists believed that the world was a continuous whole where there was gradual changes in the energy levels of these subatomic particles. Then, Max Planck received an intuitive insight and saw that they do not change in infinitely small increments. There is a minimum leap that they must make—called the quantum leap. It is the same thing here, there is an evolutionary aspect of the path to Christhood but you cannot forever be approaching the goal, as we have said before in the allegory of Zeno's paradox where you always go to the halfway point, and to the halfway point and never get there.

You cannot become the Living Christ by getting gradually closer and closer. There comes a point where you have to make a decision and accept that you have manifested a level of Christhood, you have reached the level of Christhood. Then, from that moment on, you look at yourself and your role in the world differently. It may not be this romantic change that people project out there.

This is what previous ascended master students did not understand. They sometimes thought that when they had gone through a dramatic experience, they had suddenly become the Christ in action. It was now their role to go around and discipline all other people and tell them what they were doing wrong. That is not what I am talking about, I am talking about a more delicate shift that is not brought about by an outer ambition. These students of previous dispensations often had an outer ambition, a human ambition, of being someone important, having an important role, an important position. They were looking for this outer position, this outer recognition but the Living Christ does not look for this.

Shifting how you look at the material world

There comes that point where you need to recognize that you have the potential to be the open door to bring forth something new, something decisively new, in the field, perhaps, where you have expertise, but maybe even in an entirely different field where you do not have any previous experience or expertise. When this is in your Divine plan, you need to tune in to this. One of the shifts that those of you who have the potential to reach higher levels of consciousness need to make, is in how you look at the material world, how you look at the physical octave. My beloved, we have talked about how, in your birth trauma, you went into an entirely reactionary pattern. This means, among many other things, that you look at matter as something solid that cannot be changed with the mind. My beloved, how did Jesus turn the water into wine? Well, it was not Jesus the outer person, it was because he became an open door for the energies of God. The point here is this: The energies of God can change matter. When you reach a certain level of Christhood, you become the open door for these energies—if you can make that revolutionary shift and accept that matter can be changed by mind! All of the fallen beings, all of the demons, many human beings would scream loudly that this is a lie, that this cannot be done. It is one of the last defences that the fallen beings have, to make people think that there are many conditions in matter that human beings do not have the power to change.

This is a revolutionary step and some of you have it as part of your Divine plan to make that step, whatever that means for you individually. Again, I do not wish to put any ambition out there that your egos can take and inflate. There are certainly some of you who have the potential to bring forth new ideas, new technologies that are at a much higher level than what you have today, that are what I have called "non-force-based technology." These kinds of technologies will seem like magic compared to what you have today. It will seem like science fiction, like it is impossible, because it is beyond what you currently see as the laws of nature. Others have the potential to be healers. Others have the potential to bring forth ideas in every area of life that are revolutionary.

You cannot bring forth a revolutionary idea if you are in an evolutionary state of mind. You need to make that shift and open yourself to actually be the open door for some revolutionary insight, technology, idea, even attitude and belief or way of looking at life. Many of you can feel, if you are honest, a certain resistance in you towards this idea. It comes from the primal self or another separate self that will tell you that this is dangerous, that this is impossible, that this cannot happen, that you should not do it because you will become prideful, or any number of other ideas that they will project into your mind.

You need to look at this individually and ask yourself: "What is the mechanism behind it? What is the belief behind it? What is the limitation that this belief is based upon?" Then, you need to use your Christ discernment, you need to do the work to resolve this self, separate yourself from it. You also need to use your Christ discernment to open yourself to where you actually experience the reality of what you can bring forth. I used this messenger as an example and said it was not an evolutionary change for him to start doing the website with Jesus, it was based on an actual experience. You have to, first of all, be willing to have that experience by being willing to let go of your beliefs, your attitude, your view of yourself, your view of the world. Then, you have to be willing to implement the new view and to do so in a way that is neither prideful, nor the opposite of prideful where you put yourself down.

Finding balance beyond pride and false humility

You have to find a very delicate balance where there is no human ambition that can make you prideful, as we have seen in previous dispensations. Neither is there that human self-denial that puts you down, as we have also seen in previous dispensations. In other words, there were students who held themselves back from expressing Christhood. There were students who were over-eager and instead of expressing Christhood they expressed the ambitions of the ego and thought it was Christhood.

You need to find that balance because this is what we have taught you gradually, very gradually. We have brought you towards this ability to discern and walk that balance, that narrow path instead of the broad way. This is truly within the reach of those of you who have this as a potential in your Divine plans. Many of you are not at that point yet, but all of you can benefit from at least keeping these concepts in your mind. Some of you might find that when you feel you are at that point, it can help you to listen to this dictation and to go beyond the words in the dictation to follow the vibration in the words and follow it to the Being that I AM, Saint Germain, and the love I have for you.

Then, when you lock in to and experience that love, you can experience the reality that the love that I bring can make matter sing. That is when you can also begin to experience that the light of God, the love of God, can shift matter because it can make matter sing a different tune than the tune of the fallen beings!

When you get to that level, some of you will be able to realize that you are actually here to express an aspect of your Christhood where you are being the open door for sending out a vibration that makes matter sing! It makes the atoms and molecules of physical matter start to accelerate at a higher level. Thereby, you can play an entirely different role in raising the collective consciousness and bringing forth the golden age.

Your Divine plan and the golden age

The golden age cannot be forced upon humanity so there must be those in embodiment who are electrodes for bringing about a shift in the collective whereby people can consciously come to accept that there is something higher. When the first people started dreaming about creating a flying machine, the vast majority of human beings could not accept that this was even possible. When the first airplanes had been created and demonstrated, there very quickly happened a revolutionary shift in the collective consciousness. Suddenly, more and more people began to accept that it is actually possible to fly through the air.

There are many more such shifts that need to happen as we move into the golden age, before I can actually release the ideas and the technology that will make the golden age physical. There must first be awareness and acceptance before there can be physical manifestation. There must be a critical mass of human beings who accept the higher potential before it can actually be manifest. Many of you have it as part of your Divine plan to be electrodes for this. That is why the invocation you have been giving talks about whether you can help bring about a change by taking direct action or by making the calls. "Making the calls" is a symbol for what I am talking about here where you recognize that you can be an electrode for releasing and sending out an energy that can raise the collective consciousness, that can make matter sing, that can bring about this shift.

Some of you can see that perhaps you are at an age, perhaps you do not have the education, where you can go into a scientific field and bring forth a new technology through direct actions. This is not what is realistic for you in this life, but if you feel strongly about a new form of technology, or a new form of education, or a new form of culture and art, then, if you cannot take direct physical action to bring it about, you can take direct spiritual action by making the calls. You can open yourself to become an electrode for this energy that can bring about the shift in the collective consciousness and even the shift in physical matter. Certainly, it can bring the shift in the emotional realm, the mental realm, the identity realm so that people can shift their consciousness and begin to accept the potential, as not just a potential but as something that can actually happen. It is not science fiction, it is not some far-flung Utopian dream that might be manifest in the distant future. It could actually be manifested now, and when a critical mass come to that acceptance, well, then the technology will be manifest within a very short period of time, as you have already seen has happened many times throughout history.

We can always go higher

The shift I want you to make here, all of you (all spiritual students, whether you are at this level or that level), is that you recognize that there has at any moment in time been a collective consciousness that thought: "Oh, we have reached the ultimate level, we can't possibly go any higher." You see right now, how there is a collective consciousness that: "We have reached some ultimate level and maybe there is new technological solutions but they are all going to be within the framework of what we have right now, it's going to be improvements, incremental improvements of what we have now."

You who are the spiritual students, you who have a love for my golden age, I am asking you to make a revolutionary shift in consciousness where you realize that what you have right now does not set the limitations for what can be brought forth in the future! We cannot make manifest the golden age that I envision by making evolutionary changes to what we have right now. We need certain revolutionary shifts and *you* can make that shift in consciousness and accept that this is fully possible, that I am capable, I already have the ideas. When enough people accept it, then it can be made physical, and you will make yourself one of the people who accept this. Therefore, you will forget about the naysayers and the doomsday prophets and those who think nothing can change.

You will accept that change is the order of the day and the decade and the millennium and the era, for I, Saint Germain, am decreeing it and you are accepting my decree! By the interaction between me in the spiritual realm and you in physical embodiment, the alpha and the omega flow, the figure-eight flow, then, it cannot fail to manifest! It is only a matter of how long it takes before a critical mass of people can accept it.

I am asking *you* to shift so that at least *you* are accepting it and *you* are making a contribution to making it a manifest reality. Will *you* make this shift? Then, I thank you for being willing to follow me and allow this

Word, this release, to make your matter sing! Tune in now and sense how the matter of your four lower bodies is singing a new tune.

10 | INVOKING THE REVOLUTIONARY ASPECT OF MY DIVINE PLAN

In the name I AM THAT I AM, Jesus Christ, I call to all representatives of the Divine Mother, especially Saint Germain, to help me see the revolutionary aspects of my Divine plan, including…

[Make personal calls.]

Part 1

1. Saint Germain, help me recognize if I am facing one of these key points in my life, where I cannot get to the next level up in an evolutionary way by taking smaller steps. I cannot get to the next level by being in the evolutionary state of consciousness.

> O Saint Germain, you do inspire,
> my vision raised forever higher,

with you I form a figure-eight,
your Golden Age I co-create.

O Saint Germain, what love you bring,
it truly makes all matter sing,
your violet flame does all restore,
with you we are becoming more.

2. Saint Germain, help me recognize the potential that I can go through a shift in consciousness, a shift in attitude, a shift in the way I look at life that brings me to a level that is so decisively higher that it is a revolutionary step.

O Saint Germain, what Freedom Flame,
released when we recite your name,
acceleration is your gift,
our planet it will surely lift.

O Saint Germain, what love you bring,
it truly makes all matter sing,
your violet flame does all restore,
with you we are becoming more.

3. Saint Germain, help me recognize that parallel to the evolutionary change, there is the necessity that I go through a more dramatic, a more revolutionary shift in consciousness. I am willing to make such a shift. I am making the decision to open myself to the insight that I am now ready for.

O Saint Germain, in love we claim,
our right to bring your violet flame,
from you Above, to us below,
it is an all-transforming flow.

O Saint Germain, what love you bring,
it truly makes all matter sing,
your violet flame does all restore,
with you we are becoming more.

4. Saint Germain, help me avoid interpreting a genuine mystical, spiritual experience in an unbalanced way. Help me avoid the unbalanced reaction of putting on blinders and becoming fixated on one goal.

O Saint Germain, I love you so,
my aura filled with violet glow,
my chakras filled with violet fire,
I am your cosmic amplifier.

**O Saint Germain, what love you bring,
it truly makes all matter sing,
your violet flame does all restore,
with you we are becoming more.**

5. Saint Germain, help me recognize that a revolutionary shift cannot happen until I have used the teachings about the primal self and have healed my psychology to a certain level.

O Saint Germain, I am now free,
your violet flame is therapy,
transform all hang-ups in my mind,
as inner peace I surely find.

**O Saint Germain, what love you bring,
it truly makes all matter sing,
your violet flame does all restore,
with you we are becoming more.**

6. Saint Germain, help me recognize when I have received enough healing and it is necessary to make a decisive shift in the way I look at life. Help me see what it means for me to be the Christ in action and what is the highest potential of my Divine plan.

O Saint Germain, my body pure,
your violet flame for all is cure,
consume the cause of all disease,
and therefore I am all at ease.

**O Saint Germain, what love you bring,
it truly makes all matter sing,
your violet flame does all restore,
with you we are becoming more.**

7. Saint Germain, help me see if I have followed the path partly based on a human ambition of doing something important, making a decisive difference, and feeling that my life has been worthwhile.

O Saint Germain, I'm karma-free,
the past no longer burdens me,
a brand new opportunity,
I am in Christic unity.

**O Saint Germain, what love you bring,
it truly makes all matter sing,
your violet flame does all restore,
with you we are becoming more.**

8. Saint Germain, help me see if I came to earth to make a positive difference, and I have not been able to make that difference so I have this inner frustration.

O Saint Germain, we are now one,
I am for you a violet sun,
as we transform this planet earth,
your Golden Age is given birth.

**O Saint Germain, what love you bring,
it truly makes all matter sing,
your violet flame does all restore,
with you we are becoming more.**

9. Saint Germain, help me make a decisive shift to let go of that ambition, to surrender it completely.

O Saint Germain, the earth is free,
from burden of duality,

in oneness we bring what is best,
your Golden Age is manifest.

**O Saint Germain, what love you bring,
it truly makes all matter sing,
your violet flame does all restore,
with you we are becoming more.**

Part 2

1. Saint Germain, help me recognize the potential, as part of my Divine plan, that I can step up to a higher way of looking at life, looking at myself, and accepting the higher potential I can bring forth. I see that I cannot do this in an evolutionary way.

O Saint Germain, you do inspire,
my vision raised forever higher,
with you I form a figure-eight,
your Golden Age I co-create.

**O Saint Germain, what love you bring,
it truly makes all matter sing,
your violet flame does all restore,
with you we are becoming more.**

2. Saint Germain, help me recognize that if I sense there is a higher form of service, but I cannot see it, it is because I have not made the decision that I am willing to see it, no matter what it is and no matter what changes it requires of me.

O Saint Germain, what Freedom Flame,
released when we recite your name,
acceleration is your gift,
our planet it will surely lift.

> O Saint Germain, what love you bring,
> it truly makes all matter sing,
> your violet flame does all restore,
> with you we are becoming more.

3. Saint Germain, I am willing to no longer be safe. I am willing to go through the revolutionary shift of actually accepting myself as the Living Christ in embodiment.

> O Saint Germain, in love we claim,
> our right to bring your violet flame,
> from you Above, to us below,
> it is an all-transforming flow.

> O Saint Germain, what love you bring,
> it truly makes all matter sing,
> your violet flame does all restore,
> with you we are becoming more.

4. Saint Germain, help me see that although there is an evolutionary aspect of the path to Christhood, I cannot forever be approaching the goal. I cannot become the Living Christ by getting gradually closer and closer. There comes a point where I have to make a decision and accept that I have manifested a level of Christhood.

> O Saint Germain, I love you so,
> my aura filled with violet glow,
> my chakras filled with violet fire,
> I am your cosmic amplifier.

> O Saint Germain, what love you bring,
> it truly makes all matter sing,
> your violet flame does all restore,
> with you we are becoming more.

5. Saint Germain, help me see and surrender any outer ambition, any human ambition, of being someone important, having an important role, an important position. I give up looking for this outer position, this outer recognition because I see that the Living Christ does not look for this.

O Saint Germain, I am now free,
your violet flame is therapy,
transform all hang-ups in my mind,
as inner peace I surely find.

**O Saint Germain, what love you bring,
it truly makes all matter sing,
your violet flame does all restore,
with you we are becoming more.**

6. Saint Germain, help me recognize that I have the potential to be the open door to bring forth something decisively new in a certain field. Help me tune in to this.

O Saint Germain, my body pure,
your violet flame for all is cure,
consume the cause of all disease,
and therefore I am all at ease.

**O Saint Germain, what love you bring,
it truly makes all matter sing,
your violet flame does all restore,
with you we are becoming more.**

7. Saint Germain, help me make a recolutionary shift in how I look at the material world. Help me overcome the illusion that matter is something solid that cannot be changed with the mind.

O Saint Germain, I'm karma-free,
the past no longer burdens me,
a brand new opportunity,
I am in Christic unity.

**O Saint Germain, what love you bring,
it truly makes all matter sing,
your violet flame does all restore,
with you we are becoming more.**

8. Saint Germain, help me internalize that the energies of God can change matter. When I reach a certain level of Christhood, I become the open door for these energies. Help me make that revolutionary shift and accept that matter can be changed by mind!

> O Saint Germain, we are now one,
> I am for you a violet sun,
> as we transform this planet earth,
> your Golden Age is given birth.
>
> **O Saint Germain, what love you bring,**
> **it truly makes all matter sing,**
> **your violet flame does all restore,**
> **with you we are becoming more.**

9. Saint Germain, help me see if this revolutionary step is part of my Divine plan and what that means for me individually. Help me see if I have the potential to bring forth new ideas in any field, such as new technologies that are not force-based.

> O Saint Germain, the earth is free,
> from burden of duality,
> in oneness we bring what is best,
> your Golden Age is manifest.
>
> **O Saint Germain, what love you bring,**
> **it truly makes all matter sing,**
> **your violet flame does all restore,**
> **with you we are becoming more.**

Part 3

1. Saint Germain, help me see that I cannot bring forth a revolutionary idea if I am in an evolutionary state of mind. Help me make the shift and open myself to be the open door for some revolutionary insight, technology, idea, even attitude and belief or way of looking at life.

O Saint Germain, you do inspire,
my vision raised forever higher,
with you I form a figure-eight,
your Golden Age I co-create.

**O Saint Germain, what love you bring,
it truly makes all matter sing,
your violet flame does all restore,
with you we are becoming more.**

2. Saint Germain, help me see any resistance in me towards this idea. Help me see the primal self or another separate self that says this is dangerous, that this is impossible, that this cannot happen, that I should not do it because I will become prideful, or other excuses.

O Saint Germain, what Freedom Flame,
released when we recite your name,
acceleration is your gift,
our planet it will surely lift.

**O Saint Germain, what love you bring,
it truly makes all matter sing,
your violet flame does all restore,
with you we are becoming more.**

3. Saint Germain, help me see the mechanism behind it, the belief behind it and the limitation that this belief is based upon. Help me use my Christ discernment to resolve this self, separate myself from it and let it die.

O Saint Germain, in love we claim,
our right to bring your violet flame,
from you Above, to us below,
it is an all-transforming flow.

**O Saint Germain, what love you bring,
it truly makes all matter sing,
your violet flame does all restore,
with you we are becoming more.**

4. Saint Germain, help me use my Christ discernment to open myself to actually experiencing the reality of what I can bring forth. I am willing to have that experience and I am willing to let go of my beliefs, my attitude, my view of myself, my view of the world.

> O Saint Germain, I love you so,
> my aura filled with violet glow,
> my chakras filled with violet fire,
> I am your cosmic amplifier.
>
> **O Saint Germain, what love you bring,**
> **it truly makes all matter sing,**
> **your violet flame does all restore,**
> **with you we are becoming more.**

5. Saint Germain, I am willing to implement the new view and to do so in a way that is neither prideful, nor the opposite of prideful where I put myself down. Help me find the balance where there is no human ambition that can make me prideful, neither is there human self-denial that puts me down.

> O Saint Germain, I am now free,
> your violet flame is therapy,
> transform all hang-ups in my mind,
> as inner peace I surely find.
>
> **O Saint Germain, what love you bring,**
> **it truly makes all matter sing,**
> **your violet flame does all restore,**
> **with you we are becoming more.**

6. Saint Germain, help me follow your vibration to the Being that you are and the love you have for me. Help me lock in to and experience that love, experience the reality that the love that you bring can make matter sing.

> O Saint Germain, my body pure,
> your violet flame for all is cure,
> consume the cause of all disease,
> and therefore I am all at ease.

10 | Invoking the revolutionary aspect of my Divine plan

**O Saint Germain, what love you bring,
it truly makes all matter sing,
your violet flame does all restore,
with you we are becoming more.**

7. Saint Germain, help me experience that the light of God, the love of God, can shift matter because it can make matter sing a different tune than the tune of the fallen beings!

O Saint Germain, I'm karma-free,
the past no longer burdens me,
a brand new opportunity,
I am in Christic unity.

**O Saint Germain, what love you bring,
it truly makes all matter sing,
your violet flame does all restore,
with you we are becoming more.**

8. Saint Germain, help me realize that I am here to express an aspect of my Christhood where I am being the open door for sending out a vibration that makes matter sing! It makes the atoms and molecules of physical matter start to accelerate to a higher level.

O Saint Germain, we are now one,
I am for you a violet sun,
as we transform this planet earth,
your Golden Age is given birth.

**O Saint Germain, what love you bring,
it truly makes all matter sing,
your violet flame does all restore,
with you we are becoming more.**

9. Saint Germain, help me play an entirely different role in bringing forth the golden age by being an electrode for bringing about a shift in the collective whereby people can consciously come to accept that there is something higher.

O Saint Germain, the earth is free,
from burden of duality,
in oneness we bring what is best,
your Golden Age is manifest.

**O Saint Germain, what love you bring,
it truly makes all matter sing,
your violet flame does all restore,
with you we are becoming more.**

Part 4

1. Saint Germain, help me be part of the many shifts that need to happen as we move into the golden age, so you can release the ideas and the technology that will make the golden age physical.

O Saint Germain, you do inspire,
my vision raised forever higher,
with you I form a figure-eight,
your Golden Age I co-create.

**O Saint Germain, what love you bring,
it truly makes all matter sing,
your violet flame does all restore,
with you we are becoming more.**

2. Saint Germain, help me see that there must first be awareness and acceptance before there can be physical manifestation. There must be a critical mass of human beings who accept the higher potential before it can actually be manifest. I am willing to be an electrode for this.

O Saint Germain, what Freedom Flame,
released when we recite your name,
acceleration is your gift,
our planet it will surely lift.

> **O Saint Germain, what love you bring,**
> **it truly makes all matter sing,**
> **your violet flame does all restore,**
> **with you we are becoming more.**

3. Saint Germain, help me see whether I can help bring about a change by taking direct action or by making the calls. Help me recognize that I can be an electrode for releasing and sending out an energy that can raise the collective consciousness, that can make matter sing, that can bring about this shift.

> O Saint Germain, in love we claim,
> our right to bring your violet flame,
> from you Above, to us below,
> it is an all-transforming flow.

> **O Saint Germain, what love you bring,**
> **it truly makes all matter sing,**
> **your violet flame does all restore,**
> **with you we are becoming more.**

4. Saint Germain, help me see that even if I cannot take direct physical action to bring about a change, I can take direct spiritual action by making the calls and opening myself to become an electrode for this energy that can bring about the shift in the collective consciousness and even the shift in physical matter.

> O Saint Germain, I love you so,
> my aura filled with violet glow,
> my chakras filled with violet fire,
> I am your cosmic amplifier.

> **O Saint Germain, what love you bring,**
> **it truly makes all matter sing,**
> **your violet flame does all restore,**
> **with you we are becoming more.**

5. Saint Germain, help me be an electrode for bringing about a shift in the emotional realm, the mental realm, the identity realm, so that people can shift their consciousness and begin to accept the potential, as not just the potential but as something that can actually happen.

> O Saint Germain, I am now free,
> your violet flame is therapy,
> transform all hang-ups in my mind,
> as inner peace I surely find.
>
> **O Saint Germain, what love you bring,**
> **it truly makes all matter sing,**
> **your violet flame does all restore,**
> **with you we are becoming more.**

6. Saint Germain, help me accept that your Golden Age is not science fiction, it is not some far-flung Utopian dream that might be manifest in the distant future. When a critical mass come to accept it, then the technology will be manifest within a very short period of time.

> O Saint Germain, my body pure,
> your violet flame for all is cure,
> consume the cause of all disease,
> and therefore I am all at ease.
>
> **O Saint Germain, what love you bring,**
> **it truly makes all matter sing,**
> **your violet flame does all restore,**
> **with you we are becoming more.**

7. Saint Germain, help me recognize that there has at any moment in time been a collective consciousness that thought: "Oh, we have reached the ultimate level, we can't possibly go any higher."

> O Saint Germain, I'm karma-free,
> the past no longer burdens me,
> a brand new opportunity,
> I am in Christic unity.

**O Saint Germain, what love you bring,
it truly makes all matter sing,
your violet flame does all restore,
with you we are becoming more.**

8. Saint Germain, I have a love for your Golden Age, and I am making a revolutionary shift in consciousness where I realize that what I have right now does not set the limitations for what can be brought forth in the future! I make a revolutionary shift in consciousness and accept that this is fully possible, that you are capable, you already have the ideas.

O Saint Germain, we are now one,
I am for you a violet sun,
as we transform this planet earth,
your Golden Age is given birth.

**O Saint Germain, what love you bring,
it truly makes all matter sing,
your violet flame does all restore,
with you we are becoming more.**

9. Saint Germain, I am making myself one of the people who accepts this. I accept that change is the order of the day for you, Saint Germain, are decreeing it and I am accepting your decree! By the interaction between you in the spiritual realm and me in physical embodiment, it cannot fail to manifest! I am accepting it and I am making a contribution to making it a manifest reality. I sense how the matter of my four lower bodies is singing a new tune.

O Saint Germain, the earth is free,
from burden of duality,
in oneness we bring what is best,
your Golden Age is manifest.

**O Saint Germain, what love you bring,
it truly makes all matter sing,
your violet flame does all restore,
with you we are becoming more.**

Sealing

In the name of the Divine Mother, I call to Mother Mary for the sealing of myself and all people in my circle of influence in the creative flow of the Divine Mother, the River of Life. I call for the multiplication of my calls by all representatives of the Divine Mother, so that we form the perfect figure-eight flow of "As Above, so below." Thus, I accept that this is fully manifest, because the mouth of the Lord, the Divine Mother that I AM, has spoken it. Amen.

11 | CONSCIOUS VERSUS UNCONSCIOUS CHOICES

I AM the Ascended Master the Great Divine Director, or as I prefer to say these days, the Divine Director, for truly "Divine direction" is beyond all divisions and dualities. What is the meaning of making the distinction between great and less than great?

Conscious and unconscious stages of your Divine plan

Now, my beloved, we have given you dictations up until this point that have brought forth various aspects of your Divine plan. Lastly, you have heard that there comes these points where, in order to step up to a higher level of Christhood, you need to make certain decisions. In order to open yourself to a revolutionary change, you need to make certain decisions.

Well, in a sense your Divine plan, at least at the higher stages, is all about the decisions you make. Now, we have said that there is a *work* phase of your Divine plan, there is a *creative* phase of your Divine plan, there is an *evolutionary* stage of your Divine plan, there is a *revolutionary* stage. In order to confuse you even more, and bring you into a state of magnificent confusion hopefully, I would like to introduce the concept that there is a *conscious* phase of your Divine plan and an *unconscious* phase.

With that I mean that if you look back at your lives, you can see that you have often been brought into situations where you could say that you did not make a conscious choice to go into that situation. It sort of just happened based on circumstances and you did not have a conscious realization of why you needed to do this and how that was a part of your Divine plan. Yet, it is still part of your Divine plan because you needed the experience. You might say: "Well, in that phase of my Divine plan, I am not consciously choosing what I am doing and I am not knowingly making these choices. I'm not knowing what the options are and what the consequences are." You could say: "Am I actually choosing at that stage?" The reality is, of course, that you *are*, you are always choosing. All people on earth are constantly making choices.

You can go to people who are in a very low state of consciousness where it might seem like their lives are in a constant state of turmoil. There are always external conditions that are seemingly forcing these people to do this or that, or that are forcing them to remain paralyzed and seemingly powerless. You can say: "Well, how are these people choosing?" You may not be choosing in the immediate situation, but your situation is still a result of choices you have made in the past. Even in the immediate situation, though you are not choosing to manifest certain circumstances, you are still choosing how to respond or not respond to them.

When you move from the unconscious phase into the conscious phase, it is not so that you suddenly begin to make choices, but you may actually experience that you are suddenly beginning to make choices. The reason for this is that you are becoming more conscious of the choices you are constantly making. When you follow our teachings and apply them, in the beginning you are becoming more conscious of your reactions. You are beginning to be aware that when you are in a certain situation, you are triggered by the situation into a certain reactionary pattern. Then, you start noticing this and you start becoming aware that in certain situations (or when you are around certain people), you always react this particular way. Then, of course, we have given you the tools to ask the question: "Well, doesn't that show that I have a reactionary pattern and the reactionary pattern comes from some kind of internal spirit or some kind of self, perhaps it even goes all the way back to my primal self where I started this phase of reacting to the conditions on earth?" You can use the tools, then, to increase your awareness of what is behind this reactionary pattern. When you see what is behind it, you can free yourself from it and now you no longer react that way.

Of course, every time you overcome one of these reactionary patterns, you expand your awareness, you can see another aspect, another facet, of your Divine plan. All of a sudden, you can make more conscious decisions because instead of being triggered into a reaction by some subconscious pattern, you no longer have that pattern. Therefore, you can choose: "How do I want to react in this situation, how do I want to react to these people? Do I actually want to react to certain types of people or do I want to select them out of my life?"

Creativity is based on choices

What you realize here is that, as you may move into the creative phase of your Divine plan, what is creativity based on? It is based on making choices! My beloved, you have a very old discussion that has been going on among philosophers and artists as to "what is the source of creativity?" Well, my beloved, you might say (and many artists, writers, painters would say) that they receive inspiration. In the old days, they talked about muses that were seen as non-material beings that would come in and almost like a fairy or an angel, land on the shoulder of the writer and inspire him or her to write. Of course, many writers have felt a genuine flow of inspiration through them, even a genuine flow of the Spirit. In some cases, it has indeed been a higher Spirit, just as you are now experiencing the flow of a higher Spirit through this messenger's consciousness that he is not producing with his consciousness.

You could say that if you are creative, is there not some flow of energy through your Being that is the source of this creativity? Well, of course there is—this is what we have called co-creation. You recognize that you are not being truly creative only by using the energies that are already in the material realm and the abilities that you have in your lower mind. You are being truly creative by connecting to something higher than your self, being the open door for that and thereby having the energy flow into your four lower bodies and be expressed in the physical octave. Of course, this flow of the Spirit, if you want to call it that, or flow of inspiration, is an integral part of all creativity.

Nevertheless, where many artists or philosophers fail to have the full understanding of creativity is that they think this is something that either happens or does not happen and there is nothing you can do about it. You have a concept among writers about "writers block," as they call it, where they sometimes cannot write for weeks, months or years. There is the panic of sitting in front of a white sheet of paper where you can write anything, but suddenly your mind goes into a state of paralysis and you cannot write *anything*.

What I wish to bring to your attention is that creativity requires decisions on your part. It is not a passive experience where you passively wait for the inspiration to strike. You can do much to open yourself up to the flow of the Spirit. It has been said that: "The Holy Spirit bloweth where it listeth" (John 3:8) and this is to indicate that you cannot, with the outer mind, control the flow of the Spirit. You cannot with the outer mind and a human ambition force the flow of the Spirit. If, my beloved, you seek to force the flow, then you will not tune in to the Spirit, the Holy Spirit, the spiritual realm, the ascended masters. You will tune in to lower spirits in the lower identity, the mental or even the emotional realm.

Throughout history, some writers and artists have been attuned to these lower realms and have had a certain flow of this lower spirit through them that has allowed them to, in some cases, bring forth enormous volumes of writings and information or enormous amounts of paintings or music or whatever. This is not what we call true creativity because it is not co-creation. It is not co-creating with the spiritual realm—it is co-creating with a lower realm that is still in this world.

You cannot force the Holy Spirit but nevertheless you cannot receive it either by passively sitting around and waiting. You find that middle way, that straight and narrow path, where you are resolving your personal traumas, overcoming the inner spirits, the inner selves, and this increases the openness in your mind. You also have to become more conscious of the fact that you have to choose to become the open door, you have to choose "to be" the open door in specific situations. This requires you to make that conscious decision. It can be many different conscious decisions where you are actually, as other masters have said this morning, you are willing to be the Christ in a particular situation. You are willing to acknowledge that you have this ability, you are willing to reach for some revolutionary idea, or even just for an idea that is a step higher than your current level of consciousness or the consciousness of the people around you.

You have to make that decision to open your mind. Then, when you have cleared the mind, the four lower bodies, so that there is room for an idea to penetrate, when you make the conscious decision that you are willing to be the open door, *then* the Holy Spirit will flow through you. "The Holy Spirit bloweth where it listeth" means that anytime there is an opening, the Holy Spirit will flow through it because there is so much that we want to express from the spiritual realm that we are not sitting up here being picky and saying: "Ah, that person is not worthy to be an open door." As soon as there is an open door, we express something through that person that is appropriate for the situation, for the person's level of consciousness and so on.

You see, my beloved, it is not so, as there sometimes is an idea among ascended master students, that some people are worthy to be instruments for the Holy Spirit and others are not. Some people may not be *open,* some people may not be *willing* consciously, but all are worthy once you apply yourself. It is not an exclusive club here.

The initiation of the Piscean Age

There is often a very old consciousness even among spiritual students, but it goes all the way back to actually the challenge of the Piscean Age, where you saw what happened to Jesus. He came to give an example that all people can put on the Christ consciousness. The fallen beings then created the Catholic church and created the image that he was the exclusive incarnation of Christ, thereby saying that nobody else could do it. Why did people actually believe this? Why did so many people stay in the Catholic church, often reincarnating again and again in the Catholic church? Why do so many Christians still believe in this?

Well, it is, of course, because they have not met and passed the initiation of the Piscean Age, which is to overcome the idolatry created by the fallen beings that only certain people are worthy. You need to come to the recognition here that free will is free will and self-awareness is self-awareness. All self-aware beings (and that means all human beings in embodiment on earth) have a spark of the Creator's consciousness. There is not one spark of the Creator's consciousness that can be more worthy than another. You are all inherently worthy by the fact that you have self-awareness. The question can be: "What is your attainment, your background, what is the openness and the healing you have in your four lower bodies?" This is not a matter of *worthiness*—it is a matter of *openness* to receive the Spirit.

In the Piscean Age, you have this challenge to overcome the false image created by the fallen beings that there is a division between the haves and the have-nots, those who are worthy and those who are not, the noble class and the peasants and what have you—so many of these divisions. Of course, you can see it in spiritual movements where there is often an idolatry of the guru, thinking the guru is somehow special and has something that other people do not have—or why else would he or she be a guru or messenger. You are a guru or messenger, a true guru or messenger, because you have walked the path yourself and you have healed your four lower bodies to the point where you can receive something from above. It still does not make you more worthy than others, it just means you are further along on the path. All of you are equally worthy, all of you have an equal potential to raise your consciousness, heal your four lower bodies, become the open doors.

Respecting your own free will

When you do this, you will feel the Spirit flow through you, as many of you, indeed, already have in some measure. What I want to bring out at this stage is that you have to make a decision, actually many decisions, but you have to make the decision that you are willing to be the open door, that you are willing to receive something and you are willing to express it—whatever the reaction may be from other people. I understand very well, *we* all understand, that before you can come to that point where you say: "I am going to express this, come what may," you may need a certain healing of your psychology. You certainly may need to look at and separate yourself from that primal self, created when you were brutally put down by the fallen beings in your first embodiment and decided that you would never run that risk again. There can be a period where you have to overcome this fear so you are willing to run the risk.

My beloved, as you start looking at the primal self and start separating yourself from it, you will feel how that fear of the consequences, that sense of risk, falls away. You can get to the point where you realize that you have no compensatory mechanism, you have no desire to punish the fallen beings. Neither do you have a desire to be accepted or acknowledged by other human beings because you no longer have that insecurity in yourself that made you want to be accepted by others. You can come to the point where you recognize that you have absolute respect for free will. When you have respect for the free will of other people, it means that when you say something that is an expression of a higher idea, then if you respect their free will, you set other people free to respond or not respond in any way they want.

You can also realize that as you have respect for the free will of others (which most of you have), you need to have equal respect for your own free will and that means you have to decide that your choices are independent of other people's choices. Just because someone does not accept you or reject you, you will not go into a negative reaction about what you did. You will not say: "Oh, I am never going to say anything again." You do not have to have a negative reaction, and you do not need to feel rejected by other people if they do not accept what you are saying.

You can come to a point, my beloved, where it is not a matter of you being in this dualistic state of mind where, when you express something, you think that there has to be a certain reaction and the reaction will be either positive or negative. You can come to a point where you are not even thinking about what the reaction might be. Beforehand, you are setting other people free to react however they want because you know you have set yourself free to not respond negatively to their reactions.

You can come to the point where you are not expressing yourself because you want to save the world, change other people or be validated by other people. You are expressing yourself because this is an expression of who you are, your higher Being, and that is what gives you the supreme joy on earth.

My beloved, I can assure you that when you come to this point, where you consciously are aware that you have a connection to your I AM Presence, there is a flow from your I AM Presence and what is coming through you is an expression of your spiritual individuality. It is filtered through the individuality you have down here but it still has a certain element of purity that it is an expression of your true individuality. Then, you will experience a much greater joy than you have ever experienced by acting through the lower self alone. There is really no activity you could have (that is based on the lower self) that would give you the same joy and the sense of fulfilment that you get when you feel the flow of the Spirit and you know you are co-creating.

A reward in itself

That is why, when you get to this point, the activity of expressing your higher Being is a reward in itself. Therefore, as Jesus said: "Do you want your reward in heaven or your reward on earth?" You realize that this is the reward in heaven and it is higher than any reward you could get on earth. Therefore, you can set other people free. You can set yourself free, and eventually you can come to being in a state of perpetual openness with the Spirit. You are not judging, evaluating or analyzing, you are just expressing whatever comes to you.

Now, I know that some people will immediately say: "Well, does that mean that these people will do anything they want?" Yes, it does mean they will do anything "they" want but not anything their egos want. When people say: "Oh, he thinks he can do anything he wants," they often mean that these are ego-based people who think they can do anything their ego wants regardless of the consequences for others. Naturally, when you are acting from your higher self and your higher self is in a state of oneness, it does not do something that hurts other people. It will do something that will disturb or provoke other people because that might be the only way to have a chance of awakening them.

Of course, again, you can say, does your I AM Presence sit up there and say: "Aha, I know exactly how to push this person's buttons." No, it does not. It just expresses itself and that expression is so different from the person's level of consciousness that the person experiences it as a provocation. The I AM Presence is not deliberately seeking to provoke, it is just expressing itself. That is why you can come to a point where, even when people are provoked, become angry or reject you, you are not disturbed by it. You allow them to have their reaction but you do not let this detract you from being the open door the next time.

What does it, then, take to come to this point where you are the open door and you are expressing an element of your higher being, and therefore expressing the more creative aspects of your Divine plan, the higher potential of your Divine plan? Well, again, it is a matter of making choices and making more and more conscious choices. What I submit to you is that you actually come to a point where you need to go through a phase where you become more and more conscious of the fact that you are selecting out, you are selecting away.

Selecting out from your life

Many of you have already done this in order to be on the spiritual path but you can be more conscious of this. You get a sense that a certain activity you might have participated in or certain people that you might have spent time with are actually a distraction. Now, I know that you can go back with the linear mind and say: "Well, didn't Jesus tell us that we need to come to a point where we look back at our lives and we have no regrets? Because whatever we needed to go through was an experience we needed to have." Yes, my beloved, that is true—when you look back. But that, of course, does not mean that because you do not need to have regrets about what you did previously, you need to continue to do the same thing for the rest of your life.

What I am saying is that when you step into this phase of becoming more conscious, you need to be aware that this planet is a very diversified planet. There are many, many activities on this planet. Some of them can be very exciting, but other activities are deliberately defined by the fallen beings for one purpose only and that is to distract people from spiritual growth or their Divine plan. There are many, many activities on earth that most people think are normal, genuine or even creative experiences or activities but their only purpose is, *really,* to serve as a distraction that sucks your energy and your attention into doing something that may be fun, that may be rewarding or that may even seem to be beneficial and altruistic. But for you, it is a distraction that takes you away from focusing your attention on your Divine plan and the more creative aspects of it.

Naturally, all of you have already selected many things out because you felt this was not helpful for your spiritual growth. There are many more activities and attitudes that you can select out as you become more and more conscious and make more and more conscious choices. We have said you will never see the totality of your Divine plan because it is something that actually is determined as you make choices. Nevertheless, you will begin (as you open yourself up to this, even as you work with this concept of what is a distraction, what is not a distraction), you will get more of a sense of focus.

Gradually, you will gain a more and more clear focus on what is your particular role to bring forth in this lifetime. Then, you get more of a sense that: "Oh, this activity is actually not supporting what I'm here to do. It's actually taking my awareness and energy away from it." You realize suddenly and spontaneously: "Now is the time to select it away." This spontaneous realization does not come until you consciously decide that you are willing to consider which activities are just a distraction and which are actually part of your Divine plan.

This has many ramifications, and in a sense you could say that for the rest of your life, until you ascend, you are going to select certain things out that are no longer compatible with the level of consciousness you have risen to. I simply want you to be aware of the need to have this openness, to once in a while step back, look at life and see: "What is it I am really here to do?"

Selecting out spiritual activities

Now, many of you have, as part of your path, gone into various activities that you might consider to be spiritual, beneficial or so forth and so on. I am in no way blaming you for having gone into them, but many of you will find that there comes a point where you realize you no longer need this. This is not really why you are here, this is not what you are here to bring forth.

You see, when you look at the spiritual or New Age field, so many people are curiosity seekers. They go into all kinds of, as other masters have said, aura readers, fortune tellers, astrologers, tarot card readers and this and that—past life readers, psychics, whatever have you. There is a whole phenomenon out there that is actually presented as spiritual activities but the main purpose of most of it is simply to distract spiritual people from their spiritual goals and their Divine plans. Again, you could say for some of you, you might have an awareness of certain past lifetimes or you might have a curiosity about past lifetimes but is it really essential for your Divine plan that you spend your time and energy on trying to find out who you were in a past life?

There could be many other activities to which this applies. Many spiritual people have had a phase where they went through, be it astrology, be it numerology, be it any other kind of things, but ultimately there can come this point where you realize: "I no longer need this, I no longer need this at my present level of consciousness." Then, you can focus more and more on the essential things.

The intent to change other people

Then there is, of course, another temptation that is out there because those of you who came as avatars, you came with a desire to change the earth for the better. Now, as this messenger has realized after he received these latest teachings on the primal self, this desire to change the earth for the better was actually what he needed to overcome by coming to earth. He had not overcome this on a natural planet and so he chose to go down to earth, which is so difficult to change, in order to give himself an extreme opportunity to overcome this desire to change others—and to change *anything* for that matter.

You realize, my beloved, that there is a fundamental difference between having an intention of changing other people and then being an open door for your I AM Presence expressing itself through you. This is subtle to understand because, naturally, the ascended masters would like to see change on earth, would like to see this planet rise to a level where people are not suffering but are consciously growing spiritually. We are beyond the dualistic level of consciousness and therefore we do not have this dualistic intent, based on the epic mindset, of bringing forth some important change. There is a difference in the sense that we have total respect for free will.

Those of you who came to earth with this lower intent, you may say it was a benevolent intent and I will not dispute that. It *was* benevolent, but not in an ultimate way because you were *not* non-attached. You came here with this intent and it is, in a subtle way, a part of the epic mindset. It is not the extreme way that you see in the fallen beings where you were willing to kill other people in order to further this ultimate cause. You did not believe that the end justifies the means, as the fallen beings do. Nevertheless, you still thought that it was okay for you to sort of push people in gentle ways in order to get them to overcome suffering. This is actually what you needed to overcome here on earth.

You realize that there are many, many causes out there that are defined so that they can attract the attention of spiritual people. When you become aware that there is a spiritual side to life, there is a spiritual path, there is the potential for manifesting a golden age, then, again, you are tying in to that desire that brought you to the planet. You are therefore reasoning with your outer mind: "Sure I'm here to change planet earth, I'm here to bring about a positive change. How can I do it? Oh there is *this* cause; there is *that* cause, there is the *next* cause."

Many of you have had a phase where there were so many things you wanted to do to improve conditions on earth that you actually wore yourself out. You scattered your attention because there were so many causes you wanted to help promote. You realize, my beloved, that this is not what can take you to the higher levels of your Divine plan because none of you are here to solve every problem on earth. None of you can do this! When you are in physical embodiment, you have the limitations of time and space. Each day still only has 24 hours. You need to sleep some of those hours. You still only have a certain amount of waking hours, a certain amount of attention, a certain amount of energy that you can put on something.

What I am saying is that it is perfectly fine that, as you are at the beginning stages of the path, you get very enthusiastic and you want to help with this, that and the next thing—and so you take on too much. As you begin to move into this more conscious phase of your Divine plan, the more creative phase, you need to take a look at even the causes that are out there. You can say: "They are not distractions created by the fallen beings, they are worthy causes." Perhaps, there are some people that have it as part of their Divine plan to pursue those causes but you need to consider: "Is it the higher levels of my Divine plan that *I* devote my energy to these causes?" When you begin to honestly consider this, and you are willing to select out the ones that are not a part of your higher Divine plan, then you will begin to gain a more clear vision of what is your focus, what is your speciality, what is the area where you can bring forth change.

Then, you can gradually begin to select away all of these other activities that are not contributing to that. You will then find that your mind will become more and more attuned, more and more focused, more and more aligned, more and more in harmony with your I AM Presence. Therefore, you will feel a greater and greater sense of joy, a sense of determination. It is not really an outer will, it is simply a spontaneous desire to focus on this area and to bring this forth.

Focus without imbalance

This, my beloved, should not be construed to mean that you become the kind of person, like you see in the concept of the mad professor, who is constantly sitting in his laboratory, writing down formulas on the blackboard and constantly trying to make this equation and he is ignoring everything else and cannot do any other activity. You can still, as we have said, live a relatively normal, active life in society. You are doing what you need to do, perhaps to make a living, raise your children, whatever this may be.

It is just that in your mind, you know that there is a certain activity that is the main focus. You may also know that raising your children is part of your Divine plan. Beyond that you may also have a certain area you need to study because you have the potential to bring forth some new ideas.

11 | Conscious versus unconscious choices

Well, these are not incompatible. You just realize that this is part of my Divine plan, maybe my job and my career is part of my Divine plan. My family and children are part of my Divine plan and then I have this area of study. My beloved, doing this course or doing that course or running here or running there, this is not part of your Divine plan so you can select these things out.

Now, again, there is a balance to be found. You cannot always be focused on one thing. Well, as you grow higher and higher in consciousness, you *can* become more and more focused, but you still need to have some time to relax, to do something different.

As this messenger was reminded earlier today, the Buddha reaches the stage of enlightenment, he goes into nirvana, he comes back out of nirvana and then he goes out and creates an ashram and he starts teaching and many students come to him and he is teaching. Now, this is the Buddha who has supposedly reached enlightenment, but nevertheless the Buddha taught for nine months of the year and then for three months of the year he was in seclusion, in meditation. In other words, he was doing something different, he was relaxing from the teaching activity. Again, you need to be realistic and recognize that no matter how focused you are, in order to live a relatively active, normal life, you need to have time also to do something that is simply relaxing. You are getting your mind off the other activities in your life because, at least until you reach the very highest levels of awareness, the mind needs a break.

In fact, I would say that even at the 144th level of awareness, the mind cannot be focused on the same thing all the time. You need to step away, you need to have a break. For example, scientists can for weeks have been focusing on a specific problem they are trying to solve in physics, writing down the formulas and this and that. Then, their minds get so tired that they give up and go fishing and while they are standing there fishing, all of a sudden the solution comes to them in an intuitive flash.

There needs to be that alpha and omega where, for a time, your mind is focused but then you need to go into the omega and relax and do something different. Some of you can find that balance where sometimes you are focused on your work, other times you are relaxing with the family so that becomes part of bringing up your children. Others might need other activities where you go out in nature and do something different that simply gets your mind off the concentration. Select out the activities that are not part of your Divine plan but do not become fanatical or rigid where you suddenly start to think, as some ascended master students have done, that you need to be either reading the teachings or giving decrees in all of your waking hours.

Living an active life in society

You see many, many people who have found the spiritual path and suddenly they have decided to go on some kind of meditation retreat where they sit and meditate all of the waking hours that they can. You have the concept of people in India who go into a cave in the Himalayas and sit there in solitude for a long time. For some people, this can be valid, but do not use this to construe that this is valid for all people.

As we have said, many of you in this lifetime have volunteered, and made part of your Divine plans, to demonstrate how to walk the spiritual path while living an active life in society. We are not talking about here that you withdraw from society, withdraw from your family or withdraw from other activities. We are saying there are many activities in the world and in your lives that are basically distractions. They may be worthy causes but they are not what you are here to focus on.

As you go higher, you need to keep in mind that you will begin to gain a more and more selective vision of what is your focus in this lifetime, what it was that you chose to focus on. Then, you just select away the activities that are not compatible with that, but still maintain a normal lifestyle as it is for you or perhaps changing your lifestyle to some degree in order to weed out these activities that are draining your energies and your attention.

My beloved, you look at the world and there are many ways of measuring what people have. For example: "What is a rich person? Is it one who has a lot of money, a lot of physical property? Is it one who has a lot of talents? Is it one who has a lot of time?" Well, I would say it is one who has attention, attention left over to focus on what is important for that person to bring forth. Be mindful of the fact that there are many activities in the world that are pulling on your attention but keep it more and more focused on what is the focus of your Divine plan.

With this, I have given you what I wish to give you in this instalment and I thank you for your attention to me.

12 | INVOKING AWARENESS OF MY CHOICES

In the name I AM THAT I AM, Jesus Christ, I call to all representatives of the Divine Mother, especially the Divine Director, to help me gain a greater awareness of how I make choices and what options I actually have, including...

[Make personal calls.]

Part 1

1. Divine Director, help me become more conscious of the choices I am making.

> Divine Director, I now see,
> the world is unreality,
> in my heart I now truly feel,
> the Spirit is all that is real.

**Divine Director, send the light,
from blindness clear my inner sight,
my vision free, my vision clear,
your guidance is forever here.**

2. Divine Director, help me become more conscious of my reactions and see when I am triggered by a situation into a certain reactionary pattern.

Divine Director, vision give,
in clarity I want to live,
I now behold my plan Divine,
the plan that is uniquely mine.

**Divine Director, send the light,
from blindness clear my inner sight,
my vision free, my vision clear,
your guidance is forever here.**

3. Divine Director, help me see any reactionary pattern that comes from an internal spirit, a self, perhaps from my primal self.

Divine Director, show in me,
the ego games, and set me free,
help me escape the ego's cage,
to help bring in the golden age.

**Divine Director, send the light,
from blindness clear my inner sight,
my vision free, my vision clear,
your guidance is forever here.**

4. Divine Director, help me increase my awareness of what is behind this reactionary pattern and free myself from it so I no longer react that way.

Divine Director, I'm with you,
my vision one, no longer two,
as karma's veil you do disperse,
I see a whole new universe.

> Divine Director, send the light,
> from blindness clear my inner sight,
> my vision free, my vision clear,
> your guidance is forever here.

5. Divine Director, I realize that when I overcome these reactionary patterns, I can see new aspects of my Divine plan. I can make more conscious decisions about how I want to react in a situation, how I want to react to certain people.

> Divine Director, I go up,
> electric light now fills my cup,
> consume in me all shadows old,
> bestow on me a vision bold.

> Divine Director, send the light,
> from blindness clear my inner sight,
> my vision free, my vision clear,
> your guidance is forever here.

6. Divine Director, help me internalize that creativity is based on making choices! I am not being truly creative only by using the energies that are already in the material realm and the abilities that I have in my lower mind. I am being truly creative by connecting to something higher than my self, being the open door for the flow of the Spirit.

> Divine Director, heart of gold,
> my sacred labor I unfold,
> o blessed Guru, I now see,
> where my own plan is taking me.

> Divine Director, send the light,
> from blindness clear my inner sight,
> my vision free, my vision clear,
> your guidance is forever here.

7. Divine Director, help me see that this flow is not something that either happens or does not happen. Creativity requires decisions on my part. I can do much to open myself to the flow of the Spirit.

Divine Director, by your grace,
in grander scheme I find my place,
my individual flame I see,
uniqueness God has given me.

**Divine Director, send the light,
from blindness clear my inner sight,
my vision free, my vision clear,
your guidance is forever here.**

8. Divine Director, help me see that I cannot force the Holy Spirit, but I cannot receive it by passively waiting. Help me find the middle way where I am resolving my personal traumas and increasing the openness in my mind.

Divine Director, vision one,
I see that I AM God's own Sun,
with your direction so Divine,
I am now letting my light shine.

**Divine Director, send the light,
from blindness clear my inner sight,
my vision free, my vision clear,
your guidance is forever here.**

9. Divine Director, help me become more conscious of the fact that I have to choose to become the open door. I have to choose "to be" the open door in specific situations. This requires me to make a conscious decision that I am willing to be the Christ in a particular situation.

Divine Director, what a gift,
to be a part of Spirit's lift,
to raise mankind out of the night,
to bask in Spirit's loving sight.

**Divine Director, send the light,
from blindness clear my inner sight,
my vision free, my vision clear,
your guidance is forever here.**

Part 2

1. Divine Director, I am willing to acknowledge that I have a certain ability, I am willing to reach for a revolutionary idea, or an idea that is a step higher than my current level of consciousness or the consciousness of the people around me.

> Divine Director, I now see,
> the world is unreality,
> in my heart I now truly feel,
> the Spirit is all that is real.
>
> **Divine Director, send the light,**
> **from blindness clear my inner sight,**
> **my vision free, my vision clear,**
> **your guidance is forever here.**

2. Divine Director, I am making the conscious decision to open my mind to be the open door. I know that the Holy Spirit *will* flow through me when there is an opening.

> Divine Director, vision give,
> in clarity I want to live,
> I now behold my plan Divine,
> the plan that is uniquely mine.
>
> **Divine Director, send the light,**
> **from blindness clear my inner sight,**
> **my vision free, my vision clear,**
> **your guidance is forever here.**

3. Divine Director, help me overcome the illusion that some people are worthy to be instruments for the Holy Spirit and others are not. I am *open*, and I am *willing* and I am *worthy* once I apply myself.

> Divine Director, show in me,
> the ego games, and set me free,

help me escape the ego's cage,
to help bring in the golden age.

**Divine Director, send the light,
from blindness clear my inner sight,
my vision free, my vision clear,
your guidance is forever here.**

4. Divine Director, help me pass the initiation of the Piscean Age and overcome the idolatry created by the fallen beings that only certain people are worthy.

Divine Director, I'm with you,
my vision one, no longer two,
as karma's veil you do disperse,
I see a whole new universe.

**Divine Director, send the light,
from blindness clear my inner sight,
my vision free, my vision clear,
your guidance is forever here.**

5. Divine Director, help me fully accept that I am inherently worthy by the fact that I have self-awareness. It is not a matter of *worthiness*—it is a matter of *openness* to receive the Spirit.

Divine Director, I go up,
electric light now fills my cup,
consume in me all shadows old,
bestow on me a vision bold.

**Divine Director, send the light,
from blindness clear my inner sight,
my vision free, my vision clear,
your guidance is forever here.**

6. Divine Director, I am making the decision that I am willing to be the open door, that I am willing to receive something and I am willing to express it—whatever the reaction may be from other people.

Divine Director, heart of gold,
my sacred labor I unfold,
o blessed Guru, I now see,
where my own plan is taking me.

**Divine Director, send the light,
from blindness clear my inner sight,
my vision free, my vision clear,
your guidance is forever here.**

7. Divine Director, help me go through the healing of my psychology and look at and separate myself from that primal self. Help me overcome my primal fear so I am willing to run the risk of expressing something new.

Divine Director, by your grace,
in grander scheme I find my place,
my individual flame I see,
uniqueness God has given me.

**Divine Director, send the light,
from blindness clear my inner sight,
my vision free, my vision clear,
your guidance is forever here.**

8. Divine Director, help me look at and separate myself from the primal self so that my fear of the consequences, my sense of risk, falls away.

Divine Director, vision one,
I see that I AM God's own Sun,
with your direction so Divine,
I am now letting my light shine.

**Divine Director, send the light,
from blindness clear my inner sight,
my vision free, my vision clear,
your guidance is forever here.**

9. Divine Director, help me reach the point where I have no compensatory mechanism, I have no desire to punish the fallen beings. Neither do I have a desire to be accepted or acknowledged by other human beings because I no longer have any insecurity in myself.

> Divine Director, what a gift,
> to be a part of Spirit's lift,
> to raise mankind out of the night,
> to bask in Spirit's loving sight.
>
> **Divine Director, send the light,**
> **from blindness clear my inner sight,**
> **my vision free, my vision clear,**
> **your guidance is forever here.**

Part 3

1. Divine Director, help me recognize that I have absolute respect for free will. When I have respect for the free will of other people, it means that when I say something that is an expression of a higher idea, then if I respect their free will, I set other people free to respond or not respond in any way they want.

> Divine Director, I now see,
> the world is unreality,
> in my heart I now truly feel,
> the Spirit is all that is real.
>
> **Divine Director, send the light,**
> **from blindness clear my inner sight,**
> **my vision free, my vision clear,**
> **your guidance is forever here.**

2. Divine Director, help me realize that as I have respect for the free will of others, I need to have equal respect for my own free will. I hereby decide that my choices are independent of other people's choices.

Divine Director, vision give,
in clarity I want to live,
I now behold my plan Divine,
the plan that is uniquely mine.

**Divine Director, send the light,
from blindness clear my inner sight,
my vision free, my vision clear,
your guidance is forever here.**

3. Divine Director, if someone rejects me, I will not go into a negative reaction about what I did. I do not have to have a negative reaction, and I do not need to feel rejected by other people.

Divine Director, show in me,
the ego games, and set me free,
help me escape the ego's cage,
to help bring in the golden age.

**Divine Director, send the light,
from blindness clear my inner sight,
my vision free, my vision clear,
your guidance is forever here.**

4. Divine Director, help me overcome the dualistic state of mind where, when I express something, I think there has to be a certain reaction and the reaction will be either positive or negative. Help me come to a point where I am not even thinking about what the reaction might be. I am setting other people free to react however they want, because I know I have set myself free from any reactions to them.

Divine Director, I'm with you,
my vision one, no longer two,
as karma's veil you do disperse,
I see a whole new universe.

> **Divine Director, send the light,
> from blindness clear my inner sight,
> my vision free, my vision clear,
> your guidance is forever here.**

5. Divine Director, help me come to the point where I am not expressing myself because I want to save the world, change other people or be validated by other people. I am expressing myself because this is an expression of who I am, my higher being, and that is what gives me the supreme joy on earth.

> Divine Director, I go up,
> electric light now fills my cup,
> consume in me all shadows old,
> bestow on me a vision bold.

> **Divine Director, send the light,
> from blindness clear my inner sight,
> my vision free, my vision clear,
> your guidance is forever here.**

6. Divine Director, help me become consciously aware that I have a connection to my I AM Presence. There is a flow from my I AM Presence and what is coming through me is an expression of my spiritual individuality.

> Divine Director, heart of gold,
> my sacred labor I unfold,
> o blessed Guru, I now see,
> where my own plan is taking me.

> **Divine Director, send the light,
> from blindness clear my inner sight,
> my vision free, my vision clear,
> your guidance is forever here.**

7. Divine Director, help me experience a greater joy than I have ever experienced by acting through the lower self alone. Help me experience that there is no activity that can give me the same joy and sense of fulfilment that I get when I feel the flow of the Spirit and I know I am co-creating.

> Divine Director, by your grace,
> in grander scheme I find my place,
> my individual flame I see,
> uniqueness God has given me.
>
> **Divine Director, send the light,**
> **from blindness clear my inner sight,**
> **my vision free, my vision clear,**
> **your guidance is forever here.**

8. Divine Director, help me get to the point where the activity of expressing my higher being is a reward in itself. Help me set other people free, set myself free, and come to be in a state of perpetual openness with the Spirit.

> Divine Director, vision one,
> I see that I AM God's own Sun,
> with your direction so Divine,
> I am now letting my light shine.
>
> **Divine Director, send the light,**
> **from blindness clear my inner sight,**
> **my vision free, my vision clear,**
> **your guidance is forever here.**

9. Divine Director, I see that being the open door is a matter of making choices and making more conscious choices. Help me become more conscious of the need to select out, to select away.

> Divine Director, what a gift,
> to be a part of Spirit's lift,
> to raise mankind out of the night,
> to bask in Spirit's loving sight.
>
> **Divine Director, send the light,**
> **from blindness clear my inner sight,**
> **my vision free, my vision clear,**
> **your guidance is forever here.**

Part 4

1. Divine Director, help me sense that a certain activity or certain people are a distraction. Help me identify the activities that are deliberately defined by the fallen beings to distract me from my Divine plan.

> Divine Director, I now see,
> the world is unreality,
> in my heart I now truly feel,
> the Spirit is all that is real.
>
> **Divine Director, send the light,**
> **from blindness clear my inner sight,**
> **my vision free, my vision clear,**
> **your guidance is forever here.**

2. Divine Director, help me identify the activities that seem fun, rewarding or even beneficial and altruistic, but for me, it is a distraction that takes me away from focusing my attention on my Divine plan and the more creative aspects of it.

> Divine Director, vision give,
> in clarity I want to live,
> I now behold my plan Divine,
> the plan that is uniquely mine.
>
> **Divine Director, send the light,**
> **from blindness clear my inner sight,**
> **my vision free, my vision clear,**
> **your guidance is forever here.**

3. Divine Director, help me get a more clear focus on what it is my role to bring forth in this lifetime. Help me sense what activities are not supporting what I am here to do and spontaneously select them away.

> Divine Director, show in me,
> the ego games, and set me free,

> help me escape the ego's cage,
> to help bring in the golden age.
>
> **Divine Director, send the light,**
> **from blindness clear my inner sight,**
> **my vision free, my vision clear,**
> **your guidance is forever here.**

4. Divine Director, I hereby consciously decide that I am willing to consider which activities are just a distraction and which are part of my Divine plan.

> Divine Director, I'm with you,
> my vision one, no longer two,
> as karma's veil you do disperse,
> I see a whole new universe.
>
> **Divine Director, send the light,**
> **from blindness clear my inner sight,**
> **my vision free, my vision clear,**
> **your guidance is forever here.**

5. Divine Director, help me see that many activities are presented as spiritual activities but the main purpose of most of it is to distract people from their spiritual goals and their Divine plans.

> Divine Director, I go up,
> electric light now fills my cup,
> consume in me all shadows old,
> bestow on me a vision bold.
>
> **Divine Director, send the light,**
> **from blindness clear my inner sight,**
> **my vision free, my vision clear,**
> **your guidance is forever here.**

6. Divine Director, help me see if the desire to change the earth for the better is actually what I needed to overcome by coming to earth. Help me overcome the desire to change others—even to change *anything*.

Divine Director, heart of gold,
my sacred labor I unfold,
o blessed Guru, I now see,
where my own plan is taking me.

**Divine Director, send the light,
from blindness clear my inner sight,
my vision free, my vision clear,
your guidance is forever here.**

7. Divine Director, help me realize the fundamental difference between having an intention of changing other people and then being an open door for my I AM Presence expressing itself through me. Help me have total respect for free will.

Divine Director, by your grace,
in grander scheme I find my place,
my individual flame I see,
uniqueness God has given me.

**Divine Director, send the light,
from blindness clear my inner sight,
my vision free, my vision clear,
your guidance is forever here.**

8. Divine Director, help me see where I have an attachment to changing things and how this, in a subtle way, is part of the epic mindset because I am willing to push people in order to get them to overcome suffering.

Divine Director, vision one,
I see that I AM God's own Sun,
with your direction so Divine,
I am now letting my light shine.

**Divine Director, send the light,
from blindness clear my inner sight,
my vision free, my vision clear,
your guidance is forever here.**

12 | Invoking awareness of my choices

9. Divine Director, help me realize that many causes are defined so that they can attract the attention of spiritual people. Help me see if my desire to improve conditions on earth is wearing myself out and scattering my attention.

> Divine Director, what a gift,
> to be a part of Spirit's lift,
> to raise mankind out of the night,
> to bask in Spirit's loving sight.
>
> **Divine Director, send the light,**
> **from blindness clear my inner sight,**
> **my vision free, my vision clear,**
> **your guidance is forever here.**

Part 5

1. Divine Director, help me move into the more conscious phase of my Divine plan and look at even the worthy causes in the world and see whether they are part of the higher levels of my Divine plan.

> Divine Director, I now see,
> the world is unreality,
> in my heart I now truly feel,
> the Spirit is all that is real.
>
> **Divine Director, send the light,**
> **from blindness clear my inner sight,**
> **my vision free, my vision clear,**
> **your guidance is forever here.**

2. Divine Director, I am willing to select out the causes that are not a part of my higher Divine plan. Help me gain a more clear vision of what is my focus, what is my specialty, what is the area where I can bring forth change.

> Divine Director, vision give,
> in clarity I want to live,

> I now behold my plan Divine,
> the plan that is uniquely mine.
>
> **Divine Director, send the light,**
> **from blindness clear my inner sight,**
> **my vision free, my vision clear,**
> **your guidance is forever here.**

3. Divine Director, help me select away all activities that are not contributing to my specialty. Help me attune my mind and become more aligned, more in harmony with my I AM Presence. Help me feel the joy and determination so it is not an outer will, but a spontaneous desire to focus on this area and to bring this forth.

> Divine Director, show in me,
> the ego games, and set me free,
> help me escape the ego's cage,
> to help bring in the golden age.
>
> **Divine Director, send the light,**
> **from blindness clear my inner sight,**
> **my vision free, my vision clear,**
> **your guidance is forever here.**

4. Divine Director, help me live a relatively normal, active life in society while in my mind knowing that there is a certain activity that is the main focus. There is a certain area I need to study because I have the potential to bring forth some new ideas.

> Divine Director, I'm with you,
> my vision one, no longer two,
> as karma's veil you do disperse,
> I see a whole new universe.
>
> **Divine Director, send the light,**
> **from blindness clear my inner sight,**
> **my vision free, my vision clear,**
> **your guidance is forever here.**

5. Divine Director, help me see that I cannot always be focused on one thing. I still need to have some time to relax, to do something different. In order to live a relatively active, normal life, I need to have time also to do something that is relaxing.

> Divine Director, I go up,
> electric light now fills my cup,
> consume in me all shadows old,
> bestow on me a vision bold.
>
> **Divine Director, send the light,**
> **from blindness clear my inner sight,**
> **my vision free, my vision clear,**
> **your guidance is forever here.**

6. Divine Director, help me see if I have volunteered, and made part of my Divine plan, to demonstrate how to walk the spiritual path while living an active life in society.

> Divine Director, heart of gold,
> my sacred labor I unfold,
> o blessed Guru, I now see,
> where my own plan is taking me.
>
> **Divine Director, send the light,**
> **from blindness clear my inner sight,**
> **my vision free, my vision clear,**
> **your guidance is forever here.**

7. Divine Director, help me gain a more selective vision of what is my focus in this lifetime and then select away the activities that are not compatible with that. Help me maintain a normal lifestyle or change my lifestyle in order to weed out these activities that are draining my energies and attention.

> Divine Director, by your grace,
> in grander scheme I find my place,
> my individual flame I see,
> uniqueness God has given me.

**Divine Director, send the light,
from blindness clear my inner sight,
my vision free, my vision clear,
your guidance is forever here.**

8. Divine Director, help me see that a truly rich person is one who has attention left over to focus on what is important for that person to bring forth.

Divine Director, vision one,
I see that I AM God's own Sun,
with your direction so Divine,
I am now letting my light shine.

**Divine Director, send the light,
from blindness clear my inner sight,
my vision free, my vision clear,
your guidance is forever here.**

9. Divine Director, help me be mindful of the fact that there are many activities in the world that are pulling on my attention. Help me keep my attention focused on what is the essence of my Divine plan.

Divine Director, what a gift,
to be a part of Spirit's lift,
to raise mankind out of the night,
to bask in Spirit's loving sight.

**Divine Director, send the light,
from blindness clear my inner sight,
my vision free, my vision clear,
your guidance is forever here.**

Sealing

In the name of the Divine Mother, I call to Mother Mary for the sealing of myself and all people in my circle of influence in the creative flow of the Divine Mother, the River of Life. I call for the multiplication of my calls by all representatives of the Divine Mother, so that we form the perfect figure-eight flow of "As Above, so below." Thus, I accept that this is fully manifest, because the mouth of the Lord, the Divine Mother that I AM, has spoken it. Amen.

13 | THE REWARD FOR SERVICE IS FREEDOM

I AM the Ascended Master Saint Germain. Now, you heard a magnificent discourse this morning from Jesus where he talked about the need to be able to look back at your life and have no regrets and reason that whatever you went through was because you needed the experience. Well, my beloved, as you may be beginning to realize, we sometimes like to present you with certain, what seems like contradictions, like enigmas. So I will present you with one.

The ability to admit you have been wrong

You have heard Jesus say that you should be able to look back at your life with no regrets. Then, I will submit to you: What is the most important characteristic or ability of a student on the higher levels of the spiritual path who is beginning to see, or is willing to see, the higher aspects of his or her Divine plan? Well, it is precisely, my beloved, the ability to admit that you have been wrong.

How do you reconcile that you should be able to look back at your life with no regrets with having to admit that you have been wrong? Well, the ego will take Jesus' teaching and say: "Well, this means I should look back at my life and I should never see that I have been wrong. I have never been wrong, I have never done anything wrong, I've just needed that experience so I never need to feel that I was wrong, and now Saint Germain is saying I should be able to admit when I was wrong."

Let us give you a little more teaching, a little different perspective, on this. You see, my beloved, it is all a matter of what you put into the word "you." "You" should be able to admit that "you" have been wrong. Is it the same you that I am talking about? What is the you that can be wrong? It is the separate self. Can the separate self ever admit that it has been wrong? No—it is not capable of it. What can admit that it has been wrong? The Conscious You—*when* it is conscious. The Conscious You can at the same time that it is admitting that it has been wrong, see that what was wrong was the external self, the separate self. In seeing this, it can separate itself from that self. Therefore, you realize that while you are admitting that not everything you did in life was perfect, you are at the same time separating yourself from the self that caused you to do this.

This is why you can look back at your life with no regrets. You can actually see that there were certain things you did in your life that were wrong. Jesus was not in any way implying that everything you did was okay, was acceptable, was right according to any normal common-sense standard. He is not implying that you should look back at your life and say: "Well, I just did it because I needed the experience so I don't need to learn anything from it." Obviously, you need to learn from it, you need to look at what was the psychology of the separate self that caused you to do this. Therefore, when you uncover that psychology, you can see the decision behind it, you can consciously change that decision and that is when you can let the separate self die. At that point, of course, you should have no regrets because you have come up higher and that is what life is all about.

Using and abusing the violet flame

I have, many, many years ago through a previous ascended master dispensation, publicly given awareness of and the tools to invoke the violet flame energy, which I chose to call it. We have not necessarily emphasized this as much in this dispensation, partly because so much was said on it previously, but we have, of course, explained what the violet flame is. The violet flame is in a way the cosmic eraser. It is an energy of such a vibration that it can be used to erase any lower energy, any fear-based energy in the four levels of the material universe.

When you do something, it produces a certain amount of energy, sometimes also called "karma," and before you are completely free of that, you need to consume the karma. A very efficient way to do this is to invoke the violet flame and use it to consume that energy. Now, I have also said previously that some students in previous dispensations have abused this dispensation of the violet flame. Whenever they did something that created misqualified energy, they used the violet flame to consume the energy but they were not willing to look at the psychology behind it. They just did the same thing again next week, and then again they used the violet flame to erase that but it did not really promote their spiritual progress. It is much like some Catholics that can sin, then they go to confession, feel they have been forgiven of their sin and then they lightheartedly go out and sin all over again. They know they can always go back to confession and the priests just have to absolve them of all of their sins.

Well, this is, of course, not what we want to see because this binds you to a treadmill of your unresolved psychology that you cannot get out of. The violet flame actually helps you not get out of it because, instead of being more and more burdened by the energy, you can avoid feeling that burden so you can continue doing what you are doing. This, of course, is not what we desire to see. That is why, in this dispensation, we have given you so many tools about the psychology and resolving these issues so you can be free of them.

The importance of being wrong

Nevertheless, what I wish to give you here is that there comes a point where you have begun to gain greater and greater clarity over your Divine plan, but there can still be something that is holding you back from seeing the next level. What is holding you back is precisely this inability or unwillingness to say: "That was wrong."

We have, of course, given many teachings about duality. When I say you have to be willing to admit you were wrong, I am simply using the concept, the words, that are commonly used among people today. We could specify this more in that what you have to be willing to see and admit is that you have had a view of life, a view of yourself, a view and understanding of spiritual teachings that was not the highest possible.

Do you understand, my beloved, that you can look at so many areas of the world, and let us, as an example, use the field of religion. Someone has grown up in the Christian faith, in the Catholic church, for example. They have been indoctrinated with the belief that the Catholic church is the only road to salvation, the only true church. The person has accepted this belief and has believed it. Now, at some point in life, the person begins to see that there are certain contradictions in Catholic doctrine, certain things that cannot be explained, certain things that do not make sense, certain things in the history of the church that just cannot be in alignment with Christ—but the person is reluctant to admit this at the conscious level. What is the psychological mechanism? You can say it is ego, you can say it is whatever, but if you really look at the psychological mechanism, it is that many people feel that if they admit that the beliefs that they had, that they adopted at a certain point in the past, if they admit that those beliefs were not the highest possible, that means they would have been wrong and they are not willing to admit that they have been wrong. In some cases, it can be simple pride. You are spiritual students and for most of you, pride is not the dominant element of your consciousness. What is the mechanism that applies to many spiritual students?

Doubting your intuition

Well, this messenger went through it when he was younger. He was in a certain meditation movement. He felt that he had been intuitively led to go into that movement. Therefore, he assumed that when his intuition told him to go into a certain teaching, that was a genuine teaching and movement. After some years, he began to have doubts about the validity of the movement. He was at first very reluctant to admit this because he was afraid to acknowledge that the movement was not genuine, not the highest possible. The reason he was afraid to acknowledge this was that, then he felt his intuition would have been wrong for telling him to go into the movement.

If his intuition was wrong and he could not trust his intuition, then what could he trust? He was subconsciously afraid of being thrown into a state of doubt, a no-mans-land of not feeling he could trust anything. There came a point where he was admitting that the movement was not genuine or the highest possible and he left the movement. For a couple of years, he went through a state of being angry, feeling betrayed by his intuition and even deciding he would never again engage in another spiritual movement. Well, as you might know from yourself, whenever you make these kinds of decisions: "I'm never again going to do this," sure enough, you are going to have to do it. Fortunately, this messenger came to a point where he was willing to again trust his intuition when it told him to go into the next spiritual movement, which was an ascended master teaching and a genuinely sponsored organization. It still took him many years to resolve, in his mind, why his intuition had told him to go into the meditation movement. It required him to come to the understanding that on the spiritual path, it is not a matter of being right as the ego sees it. It is a matter of having certain experiences that shift your consciousness. He realized, after quite some time, that his intuition had been genuine when telling him to go into the meditation movement because it was part of his Divine plan to have that experience, as he needed to learn something from it. However, his outer mind had interpreted his intuition to mean that when he was told to go into it, it must be a genuine movement.

You can recognize in yourself, perhaps, a similar pattern where you feel you had to do something, you feel prompted by your intuition to do something. You happily walk down the road that your intuition is pointing you to, and suddenly "wham-bam" you are standing in mud up to your ears and you are saying: "Why did you tell me to do this?"

You need to recognize, again, that you did need that experience and then, obviously, you can go through the same reasoning as I described and realize that it was because you needed to learn something. You needed to shift your consciousness and you could only do this through the actual experience.

How to overcome limitations

You can also take this a step further and you can recognize that the attitude and the beliefs you had about what you did, well, in a certain sense (in a worldly sense) you would say they were "wrong" because they were not in alignment with a higher reality. What I am saying here is this: When you look at the religious field, for example, you can say: "Why are there so many people who are still in an outer way loyal to the Catholic church? Why do they go to church even if they don't go every Sunday? Why are they members of the church when they don't ever go to church?"

Well, my beloved, it is in a large part because they are not willing to admit that their Catholic beliefs or their belief in the Catholic church were wrong. I understand that there is a stigma, there is a trauma, associated with being wrong because the fallen ones have created a consciousness that is very pervasive in the world, saying that if you are wrong it is "bad" and it leads to certain dire consequences and punishments and going to hell and this and that. You are ascended master students and we have given you the tools to pull yourself above that fallen consciousness. You realize that by being wrong, you are not going to be condemned to hell because, as we have said, there is nothing you cannot overcome. The thing is, how do you overcome something unless you look at it and honestly admit that you need to let it go instead of holding on to it.

Look at the world of religion again. Look how you have the old concept of Christian apologetics, which is a movement that is meant to justify and explain the Christian faith. What are these Christian beliefs based on? The errors inserted by the Catholic church seventeen centuries ago! Are they getting anywhere by seeking to explain away what was erroneous in the beginning? No, of course not! They are just putting themselves into denial, and in denial you are not going to be able to see the higher aspects of your Divine plan.

This willingness to admit: "My beliefs were limited and therefore I need to just let them go and open my mind to a higher realization, a higher experience," this is the key ingredient of a student on the path who wishes to see the higher levels of his or her Divine plan. So many times you see this, even among ascended master students, that they have a certain belief, a certain view, for example, the view of ascended masters. It is not in alignment with reality, it is holding the students back at a lower level of consciousness, they cannot progress beyond that level. Because they are not willing to admit that their beliefs are not the highest possible, are not in alignment with truth and that they were "wrong," how can they move on? How can they be free of it?

Now, in the ascended master organization that this messenger was a member of, there was a popular concept that whenever you had some issue come up in your psychology and you told this to somebody and said: "What do I do with this?," the people would say: "Oh, just put it into the violet flame." People would think that anything, any uncomfortability, anything that had come up in their psychology, they just needed to put it into the violet flame. This messenger once heard a young student in that movement say: "They always say to me: 'Just put it into the violet flame,' and I do but it keeps coming back!" Of course, this is true. If you do not resolve the underlying psychology, it is going to keep coming back. You can give violet flame over and over again and it may resolve the energies that are misqualified so you feel lighter, you do not feel so burdened by it. But the violet flame cannot resolve your psychology because that can only be done by you making a conscious decision.

Explaining why you were not wrong

You see here that what we are telling you is that as you go to higher levels of your spiritual path, you have the potential to see higher levels of your Divine plan. What have we told you? You come into embodiment at a certain level of consciousness. Your Divine plan was made from a higher level of consciousness. How are you going to see the higher levels of your Divine plan? Only by reaching that level of consciousness. How are you going to reach that level of consciousness? Only by looking at the beliefs you had at a lower level of consciousness and admitting, acknowledging consciously they were not the highest possible. Some of them were potentially completely out of alignment with reality and therefore erroneous or wrong. If you cannot admit that you have been wrong, you cannot progress beyond a certain point.

We have, of course, seen in the religious field, in the political field, in the scientific field and even among ascended master students that they can go into these almost endless blind alleys of trying to explain why their beliefs were not wrong or why they were not wrong for having those beliefs. It is quite frankly amazing to see the imagination that people will use in order to explain why their beliefs were not wrong after all or why they were not wrong for having them. All that is really necessary is to say: "I had those beliefs because that was what I could see at the time. Now, I have risen to a higher level of consciousness and I can see more but in order to really implement what I can see, I have to let go of my former beliefs. When I was a child I spoke as a child. Now, I am a man and I should speak as a man, instead of holding on to my childhood beliefs."

My beloved, we see this over and over again. Spiritual seekers have a longing to find something all of their life. They find a spiritual teaching, whatever it may be. Their outer minds reason: "This must be the ultimate spiritual teaching and the ultimate guru." They decide with their outer minds, perhaps halfway unconsciously: "I'm going to be in this movement the rest of my life and then I will ascend" (or be enlightened or whatever). When it comes to the point where they have now had all of the growth they can have from that movement, their minds are closed. They are not willing to listen to their intuition who is guiding them to go on to another teaching or another approach to the teaching. Their minds have become rigid, have become solidified around the belief that what they are doing, what they have, is enough.

This belief is wrong. It is always wrong because growth is an ongoing process. You have all done this and there is no shame in it. I am not blaming you, I am simply pointing out what is happening. You have all had these points where you thought, now you had reached some ultimate understanding, some ultimate belief and this was what you were supposed to do because you all have elements of the ego and what does the ego want? It wants to feel secure.

There is no shame in admitting this, it is just what we all went through when we were in embodiment because it is part of the human condition. The thing is, those who progress on the spiritual path are those who are willing to look at themselves and see this: "My ego, my separate selves, they have this tendency. It's not really me who actually believes that I didn't have to look for another teaching, it was a separate self that's part of my ego and I am *not* that separate self. I am more than this! Therefore the 'I' that I truly am is willing to look at that self and see that the beliefs of that self were *wrong!* They were outdated, they were limited and I am letting them go! I am opening my mind to seeing something that I couldn't see through the filter of those limited beliefs! I am liquefying my mind so it isn't solidified around a certain point, a certain belief"!

That, my beloved, is the difference between those who progress to the higher levels of their Divine plan and manifest the highest potential of their Divine plan and those who stop at some point before they reach their highest potential. We, of course, do not want to see you stop before the goal that you yourselves defined for yourselves for this lifetime. It was not forced upon you, it was what *you* wanted. It is not what *I* want for you. It is what *you* wanted for yourself. I am just reminding you. I am not forcing you. I am just reminding you of what you actually decided you wanted before you came into embodiment and I am reminding you of how to get there.

Forgetting your own mistakes

How does the violet flame fit into this? Well, say if you look back at your life and say: "What I did, what I believed was not the highest possible."

Perhaps you have even done certain things that clearly put you into a fear-based state of mind and produced misqualified energy. Then, you do two things. You use the violet flame to envelop that entire situation, to consume the energies. Then, you use the tools and teachings we have on internal spirits, separate selves, primal self to uncover the belief behind it and to change that belief—and thereby let that separate self die. Then, you accept, my beloved, that now you are done with it—it is over. It is to the point where it does not even exist anymore!

There is a sentence in the Bible that the Lord says: "I shall remember their sins no more." Well, my beloved, it may be that God is able to forget your sins but are you? Are you able to forget the so-called "mistakes" you have made? What I am saying here is this: You can use the violet flame to consume the energy, then the energy is gone. It is not there anymore, it is as if it never existed. You can let that separate self die and then the separate self is not there anymore. It is as if that separate self never existed. But! There can still be an element of your consciousness, and it is not actually the Conscious You, it is another separate self. There can still be that element of your consciousness that remembers what you did and is projecting that you need to continue to remember this. You need to somehow feel sorry for it, or you need to somehow compensate for it or you need to whatever—put your attention on it. What I am telling you is that once you have done the clean-up work, what you need to do is to step back and see that there is this other separate self (perhaps even fallen beings or other people) projecting this upon you. Then you need to say: "You are not me. I don't want you in my life anymore! I am letting you die!" Then, you need to accept that you do not actually need to remember this anymore. You do not need to put your attention on it whatsoever.

Letting go of people who will not let go

Many of you will actually be tested time and time again because the fallen beings will keep projecting this at you, reminding you of this. Maybe there are people in your family or in your relationships who will keep reminding you of "what you did to me those many years ago" and why you should still feel sorry for it because they feel sorry for themselves for it. They have not resolved the psychology that caused them to react. They have not resolved the energy, they have not let go of it. Then, again, you have to say: "Okay, I respect free will and I respect that you have your free will. If you want to hold on to what happened in the past, I respect your right to do this. But I have equal respect for my own free will, that I have a right to put this behind me. If you are not willing to do the same, that's fine but I am putting it out of my life. I am putting myself out of my misery."

My beloved, you then have the option, in some cases, that if a person that is in your family or in your relationships will not let go of the past, you may come to a point where you say: "I just have to let you go. I just have to let you out of my life, to select you out of my life because it isn't constructive for me to be associated with a person who keeps revolving around the past and is not willing to overcome it." This is a right you have, my beloved, regardless of how they blame you and how they tell you: "You can't just leave me, you can't just walk away from me." My beloved, you have the right to do this, if you feel this is right for you. I am not telling you what to do, I am telling you, you have the right to make that choice even if other people will not let go of the past.

Seeing more subtle beliefs

My beloved, truly, you cannot overcome a limited belief without seeing that it was limited. Now, how do you see that a belief is limited? Well, at least at a certain level, you see that it is limited compared to a belief that is higher, that is broader, that is more expansive. This brings up one of these catch-22s that people can get into.

They have a limited belief. Take for example, again, many Catholics. If you have ever tried to convince certain Catholics of the limitations of the Catholic doctrine and the Catholic church, you can experience that it is as if they are not even hearing what you are saying. That is because they are in a catch-22 where they cannot see that their beliefs are limited because they have no frame of reference to compare them to. The reason they do not have a frame of reference is because their minds are so locked on their beliefs that they cannot see that there is a broader understanding.

Naturally, you are spiritual students, you have already been willing to open your minds to a higher understanding on so many areas, on so many things. What you will find, some of you, is that even though you are open to a new understanding in many areas, there are still a few holy cows walking around in the meadow of your consciousness—or lying down chewing the cud, *chewing, chewing, chewing, chewing,* being perfectly content to *chew, chew, chew*. Then, once in a while, they regurgitate your beliefs into their mouth again and then they *chew, chew, chew* once more! This is a separate self that is that way. You can have a situation where you have overcome some separate selves already and you know the process but there is something you have not seen. That is where I submit to you that one way to expose these limited beliefs, these holy cows, could be when you are provoked by a teaching we give, when you are disturbed by something. When there is something that really irks you, really disturbs your comfortability. It is not necessarily that you see right away the limiting beliefs behind it. You may actually have to do some work on it. You need to see: "Why am I disturbed? Why does this provoke me?" Then, you need follow that, go beyond the feeling and try to see what is the belief you have that makes you comfortable—and the cow is just lying there: *chewing*. Then, consider what is the higher understanding we are seeking to convey to you. When you open your mind to this, you can grasp that higher understanding because we have said to you that when you are at the 56th level of consciousness, you can grasp the teaching at the 57th level, or the awareness that is associated with the 57th level. But you have to open your mind, you cannot have your mind fixated on a certain belief.

When you open your mind, you will see it. If you are willing to acknowledge that your previous belief was limited or "wrong," then you can move forward. I am simply saying that some of you are advanced students and you have followed the path, you have applied the teachings you have already dismissed a lot of these holy cows. Some of you are sitting there thinking: "Well, do I have anything left, what beliefs do I have that I'm fixated on?" And you do not really see anything. Some of you do not have much left but I submit that all of you could benefit from at least surveying yourself and saying: "Is there still anything that disturbs me?" For example, when you read the *My Lives* book, was there something that provoked you? Was there something that disturbed you? Then, follow it, go beyond the feeling, what is the belief behind it? You will see there is a cow lying there… *chewing, chewing, chewing.* When you see it, you can say: "Aha! That's what Saint Germain was talking about—you're outta here!"

No ultimate level on earth

My beloved, it is our joy to see you go through this process. Do you understand? We are not blaming you, we are not coming across with this: "You're not good enough." It is our joy to see when you break through some limited belief and suddenly the weight falls off your shoulders. Like this messenger has described that even after being on the path for forty years, all of the teachings, all of the work on psychology that he has done had never actually touched the core of his primal self. It was not until he received the teachings from Jesus on the primal self this December, just these few months ago, that he really broke through and was able to see something, was able to let it go and feel that a giant weight was lifted from him.

He is not even claiming that he is done with this, (because he has learned not to make those kind of claims over the years). What I am saying is this: If a person who has been that long on the path still has some cows chewing away at the cud, then perhaps it would be wise for all of you to say: "Do I have anything? Is there anything I'm just not seeing? How could I come to see it, because truly I do want to step up to the higher vision of my Divine plan. I do want to make maximum progress. I do want to reach that level of consciousness where I can be myself."

Another way to discover if you have holy cows is simply this: Do you feel you are being yourself? Do you feel free to express yourself without being afraid of the reaction? Another way is: What is your attitude to the material realm, to this earth? Are you comfortable being here, do you feel you can express yourself here, or do you feel some kind of resentment or limitation by being here? Well, again, there is some holy cow there that is holding you back because it is just not moving. Follow it, look at it and admit that it was a limited belief.

If you cannot admit that you have had a limited belief, my beloved, how can you rise to the next level of consciousness? What have we said? There are 144 levels of consciousness. There is an illusion associated with each level. When are you going to be free of all illusions? Well, when you rise to the 144th level and resolve that enigma so you are ready to ascend.

You could say: What is a very common characteristic in spiritual, New Age movements? There is this belief that you can reach some ultimate stage while you are still in embodiment on earth. You are enlightened, you are an unascended ascended master, you are ego-free, you have resolved your psychology, you are home free! So many people, including this messenger for many years, are thinking that it has to be possible to come to a point where you have worked through your psychology and now you are free of this.

They are pursuing this goal but who is it that can sometimes feel that it is home free? You see many people out there who make various declarations, such as that they have overcome the ego, they are enlightened, they are this, they are that. Who is it that is home free? Well, it is their egos because now they think that they no longer have to even look for the ego because they have already overcome it. That is when the ego can really lie down and say: "Ah, now I can relax and chew, chew, chew because he's never going to see me. He wouldn't even know me if I bit him in the leg."

It is wise to realize that this is an illusion projected by the fallen beings, magnified by many people who have good intentions but who just do not have enough understanding of the path. It is actually possible, as I said earlier, to make a certain decision that brings about a revolutionary shift where you are no longer longing for this state of being home free while you are in embodiment. You will be home free when you are ascended. Until then, do not bother pursuing this. Look for the next illusion that will bring you up to the next level of consciousness. *That*, my beloved, is a revolutionary shift in awareness that those who are truly successful on the spiritual path find a way to make. They are no longer chasing the pot of gold at the end of the rainbow. They are always looking for the next illusion, the next step up. When they see it, they are willing to admit: "Hey, that was limited, I was wrong." Not that "I" was wrong, you find another way to look at it so you do not even think in terms of right and wrong, but you say: "Okay—that's gotta go." It just becomes second nature and it is not something you have to struggle with.

The struggle to admit you are wrong

Many of you, including this messenger when he was younger, had to struggle severely, sometimes for years to admit that he had been wrong at a certain point. He can look back and admit this with a smile because he has gone beyond it, and so can you go beyond it but it may require some work. In the beginning, the ego will resist you for all it is worth. You will know – if you have ever been a farmer in a past life – that when a cow decides that it does not want to move, there are not any powers in heaven and on earth who can move a cow!

My beloved, be willing to wrestle with this because you will experience an enormous freedom if you can come to the point where you are beyond that resistance. You just admit that it was a limited belief and then you move on. Of course, what do you have to sacrifice there? You have to sacrifice, again, the belief in some ultimate teaching, some ultimate truth, some ultimate understanding that you could have. My beloved, recognize as we have said: You will not have an ultimate understanding of how the universe works as long as you are in embodiment on a dense-matter planet like earth. It *cannot* be done!

Shift into saying you have the highest understanding that you can have right now but there is a higher understanding at the next level of consciousness, and the next until the 144th level. Strive for that. Always have your mind be liquefied, be open to seeing that higher understanding. My beloved, when you are open and when you are willing, that is when we can really work with you. You can come to a point, as this messenger has sometimes sat there and wondered, how incredibly many insights you can receive from within in a very short period of time. Many of you have experienced the same thing.

There are periods in your life where it is as if every day or several times a day you have some revolutionary insight, you have an experience where you suddenly see a whole new perspective. This can be your daily experience and it can be a very joyful experience because at the lower levels where the ego still has some hold over you, the ego is projecting that if you give up an existing belief, you have lost something. It is a struggle, but when you make that shift, you realize: Well, giving up an existing belief, a limited belief, can only be a liberation and that is a joy, a relief, a new level of freedom. It has its own reward.

What's in it for me?

The ego will sometimes seek to make bargains. The ego of various students might even say to the ascended masters: "So, Saint Germain, you want me to give up this belief? What's in it for me? What do I get out of this?" There are ascended master students who have attempted to make bargains with us, even saying: "If I do this for you, what do I get out of it?"

My beloved, when you get beyond this, the reward is in the experience. It is built in when you experience greater freedom. *That* is its own reward. What other reward to you need? I am the master of freedom for earth. I need no other reward than experiencing the Flame of Freedom and expressing it whenever I have an opportunity.

Why have I volunteered to stay with earth and work on manifesting a golden age? What is in it for me? Do I hope to somehow be promoted to a higher level of ascended master? Do I think that some cosmic being is going to come down and there is going to be a grandiose ceremony and they are going to hang some kind of medal around my neck? No, the reward is feeling the flow of freedom through my Being.

Yes of course, there is an omega aspect, there is also a reward in seeing people being free. But the primary reward is just feeling that flow of freedom, and that is why, when you come to that point, the reward for your service is the service itself! It is just the experience of feeling the flow. *The flow*, my beloved. *The flow*—it is everything. The ego only knows still-stand, which is death. But the flow is life itself. Therefore, to paraphrase the old words: "I have put before you life and death. Choose Life. The Life that I AM."

14 | INVOKING THE ABILITY TO ADMIT BEING "WRONG"

In the name I AM THAT I AM, Jesus Christ, I call to all representatives of the Divine Mother, especially Saint Germain, to help me overcome all inability or unwillingness to admit when I have been "wrong," including…

[Make personal calls.]

Part 1

1. Saint Germain, help me see that the most important ability of a student on the spiritual path is the ability to admit that I have been wrong.

> O Saint Germain, you do inspire,
> my vision raised forever higher,
> with you I form a figure-eight,
> your Golden Age I co-create.

**O Saint Germain, what love you bring,
it truly makes all matter sing,
your violet flame does all restore,
with you we are becoming more.**

2. Saint Germain, help me see that the you that can be wrong is the separate self. The separate self can never admit that it has been wrong. Only the Conscious You can admit that it has been wrong—*when* it is conscious.

O Saint Germain, what Freedom Flame,
released when we recite your name,
acceleration is your gift,
our planet it will surely lift.

**O Saint Germain, what love you bring,
it truly makes all matter sing,
your violet flame does all restore,
with you we are becoming more.**

3. Saint Germain, help me see that the Conscious You can at the same time that it is admitting that it has been wrong, see that what was wrong was the external self, the separate self. In seeing this, it can separate itself from that self.

O Saint Germain, in love we claim,
our right to bring your violet flame,
from you Above, to us below,
it is an all-transforming flow.

**O Saint Germain, what love you bring,
it truly makes all matter sing,
your violet flame does all restore,
with you we are becoming more.**

4. Saint Germain, help me realize that while I am admitting that not everything I did in life was perfect, I am at the same time separating myself from the self that caused me to do this. This is why I can look back at my life with no regrets.

O Saint Germain, I love you so,
my aura filled with violet glow,
my chakras filled with violet fire,
I am your cosmic amplifier.

O Saint Germain, what love you bring,
it truly makes all matter sing,
your violet flame does all restore,
with you we are becoming more.

5. Saint Germain, help me see that there were certain things I did in my life that were wrong. Help me learn from it and look at what was the psychology of the separate self that caused me to do this.

O Saint Germain, I am now free,
your violet flame is therapy,
transform all hang-ups in my mind,
as inner peace I surely find.

O Saint Germain, what love you bring,
it truly makes all matter sing,
your violet flame does all restore,
with you we are becoming more.

6. Saint Germain, help me uncover that psychology, see the decision behind it and consciously change that decision, so I can let the separate self die. Then, I will have no regrets because I have come up higher and that is what life is all about.

O Saint Germain, my body pure,
your violet flame for all is cure,
consume the cause of all disease,
and therefore I am all at ease.

O Saint Germain, what love you bring,
it truly makes all matter sing,
your violet flame does all restore,
with you we are becoming more.

7. Saint Germain, help me see that there comes a point where I have greater clarity about my Divine plan, but there can still be something that is holding me back from seeing the next level. This is the inability or unwillingness to say: "That was wrong."

> O Saint Germain, I'm karma-free,
> the past no longer burdens me,
> a brand new opportunity,
> I am in Christic unity.

> **O Saint Germain, what love you bring,**
> **it truly makes all matter sing,**
> **your violet flame does all restore,**
> **with you we are becoming more.**

8. Saint Germain, help me recognize that I have had a view of life, myself and spiritual teachings that was not the highest possible.

> O Saint Germain, we are now one,
> I am for you a violet sun,
> as we transform this planet earth,
> your Golden Age is given birth.

> **O Saint Germain, what love you bring,**
> **it truly makes all matter sing,**
> **your violet flame does all restore,**
> **with you we are becoming more.**

9. Saint Germain, help me see the psychological mechanism that makes me feel that if I admit that the beliefs I had were not the highest possible, that means I would have been wrong.

> O Saint Germain, the earth is free,
> from burden of duality,
> in oneness we bring what is best,
> your Golden Age is manifest.

> O Saint Germain, what love you bring,
> it truly makes all matter sing,
> your violet flame does all restore,
> with you we are becoming more.

Part 2

1. Saint Germain, help me see if I am reluctant to admit something because I am afraid this would mean my intuition would have been wrong. And if I cannot trust my intuition, then what *can* I trust?

> O Saint Germain, you do inspire,
> my vision raised forever higher,
> with you I form a figure-eight,
> your Golden Age I co-create.
>
> **O Saint Germain, what love you bring,**
> **it truly makes all matter sing,**
> **your violet flame does all restore,**
> **with you we are becoming more.**

2. Saint Germain, help me see if I am subconsciously afraid of being thrown into a state of doubt, a no-mans-land of not feeling I can trust anything.

> O Saint Germain, what Freedom Flame,
> released when we recite your name,
> acceleration is your gift,
> our planet it will surely lift.
>
> **O Saint Germain, what love you bring,**
> **it truly makes all matter sing,**
> **your violet flame does all restore,**
> **with you we are becoming more.**

3. Saint Germain, help me see that on the spiritual path, it is not a matter of being right as the ego sees it. It is a matter of having certain experiences that shift my consciousness. Therefore, my intuition can be genuine even if my outer mind interprets it to have been wrong.

> O Saint Germain, in love we claim,
> our right to bring your violet flame,
> from you Above, to us below,
> it is an all-transforming flow.
>
> **O Saint Germain, what love you bring,**
> **it truly makes all matter sing,**
> **your violet flame does all restore,**
> **with you we are becoming more.**

4. Saint Germain, help me recognize when the attitude and the beliefs I have are not in alignment with a higher reality. Help me avoid falling into the trap of thinking this means I am wrong.

> O Saint Germain, I love you so,
> my aura filled with violet glow,
> my chakras filled with violet fire,
> I am your cosmic amplifier.
>
> **O Saint Germain, what love you bring,**
> **it truly makes all matter sing,**
> **your violet flame does all restore,**
> **with you we are becoming more.**

5. Saint Germain, help me overcome the stigma associated with being wrong that the fallen ones have created, namely that if I am wrong it is "bad" and it leads to dire consequences.

> O Saint Germain, I am now free,
> your violet flame is therapy,
> transform all hang-ups in my mind,
> as inner peace I surely find.

14 | Invoking the ability to admit being "wrong"

> **O Saint Germain, what love you bring,**
> **it truly makes all matter sing,**
> **your violet flame does all restore,**
> **with you we are becoming more.**

6. Saint Germain, help me realize that by being wrong, I am not going to be condemned to hell because there is nothing I cannot overcome. Yet I cannot overcome something unless I look at it, and honestly admit that I need to let it go instead of holding on to it.

> O Saint Germain, my body pure,
> your violet flame for all is cure,
> consume the cause of all disease,
> and therefore I am all at ease.

> **O Saint Germain, what love you bring,**
> **it truly makes all matter sing,**
> **your violet flame does all restore,**
> **with you we are becoming more.**

7. Saint Germain, help me see that if I cannot admit when I have been "wrong," I will put myself into denial. In denial I cannot see the higher aspects of my Divine plan.

> O Saint Germain, I'm karma-free,
> the past no longer burdens me,
> a brand new opportunity,
> I am in Christic unity.

> **O Saint Germain, what love you bring,**
> **it truly makes all matter sing,**
> **your violet flame does all restore,**
> **with you we are becoming more.**

8. Saint Germain, help me see that the key ingredient for a student on the path, when I wish to see the higher levels of my Divine plan, is the willingness to admit: "My beliefs were limited and therefore I need to just let them go and open my mind to a higher realization, a higher experience."

O Saint Germain, we are now one,
I am for you a violet sun,
as we transform this planet earth,
your Golden Age is given birth.

**O Saint Germain, what love you bring,
it truly makes all matter sing,
your violet flame does all restore,
with you we are becoming more.**

9. Saint Germain, help me realize that I will see the higher levels of my Divine plan only by reaching a higher level of consciousness. I will reach that level of consciousness only by looking at the beliefs I adopted at a lower level of consciousness, and consciously acknowledging that they were not the highest possible.

O Saint Germain, the earth is free,
from burden of duality,
in oneness we bring what is best,
your Golden Age is manifest.

**O Saint Germain, what love you bring,
it truly makes all matter sing,
your violet flame does all restore,
with you we are becoming more.**

Part 3

1. Saint Germain, help me avoid going into these endless blind alleys of trying to explain why my beliefs were not wrong or why I was not wrong for having those beliefs. Help me say: "I had those beliefs because that was what I could see at the time. Now, I have risen to a higher level of consciousness and I can see more, but in order to really implement what I can see, I have to let go of my former beliefs."

O Saint Germain, you do inspire,
my vision raised forever higher,

with you I form a figure-eight,
your Golden Age I co-create.

O Saint Germain, what love you bring,
it truly makes all matter sing,
your violet flame does all restore,
with you we are becoming more.

2. Saint Germain, help me see if I have had all of the growth I can have from a certain movement or belief system. Help me listen to my intuition who is guiding me to go on to another teaching or another approach to the teaching.

O Saint Germain, what Freedom Flame,
released when we recite your name,
acceleration is your gift,
our planet it will surely lift.

O Saint Germain, what love you bring,
it truly makes all matter sing,
your violet flame does all restore,
with you we are becoming more.

3. Saint Germain, help me overcome the illusion that I have reached some ultimate understanding, some ultimate belief. Help me see this is only the ego that wants to feel secure.

O Saint Germain, in love we claim,
our right to bring your violet flame,
from you Above, to us below,
it is an all-transforming flow.

O Saint Germain, what love you bring,
it truly makes all matter sing,
your violet flame does all restore,
with you we are becoming more.

4. Saint Germain, help me see that those who progress on the spiritual path are those who are willing to look at themselves and see: "My ego, my separate selves, have a certain tendency. It's not really me who actually believes that I don't have to look for another teaching, it's a separate self that's part of my ego and I am *not* that separate self. I am more than this!"

O Saint Germain, I love you so,
my aura filled with violet glow,
my chakras filled with violet fire,
I am your cosmic amplifier.

O Saint Germain, what love you bring,
it truly makes all matter sing,
your violet flame does all restore,
with you we are becoming more.

5. Saint Germain, the "I" that I truly am is willing to look at that self and see that the beliefs of that self were *wrong!* They were outdated, they were limited and I am letting them go! I am opening my mind to seeing something that I couldn't see through the filter of those limited beliefs! I am liquefying my mind so it isn't solidified around a certain point, a certain belief!

O Saint Germain, I am now free,
your violet flame is therapy,
transform all hang-ups in my mind,
as inner peace I surely find.

O Saint Germain, what love you bring,
it truly makes all matter sing,
your violet flame does all restore,
with you we are becoming more.

6. Saint Germain, help me see that even when I have used the violet flame to consume the energy and let the separate self die, there can still be a separate self that remembers what I did and is projecting that I need to continue to remember this. I need to feel sorry for it, compensate for it or put my attention on it.

O Saint Germain, my body pure,
your violet flame for all is cure,
consume the cause of all disease,
and therefore I am all at ease.

**O Saint Germain, what love you bring,
it truly makes all matter sing,
your violet flame does all restore,
with you we are becoming more.**

7. Saint Germain, help me step back and see that there is a separate self projecting this upon me, and then say: "You are not me. I don't want you in my life anymore! I am letting you die!"

O Saint Germain, I'm karma-free,
the past no longer burdens me,
a brand new opportunity,
I am in Christic unity.

**O Saint Germain, what love you bring,
it truly makes all matter sing,
your violet flame does all restore,
with you we are becoming more.**

8. Saint Germain, I accept that I do not actually need to remember this anymore. I do not need to put my attention on it whatsoever.

O Saint Germain, we are now one,
I am for you a violet sun,
as we transform this planet earth,
your Golden Age is given birth.

**O Saint Germain, what love you bring,
it truly makes all matter sing,
your violet flame does all restore,
with you we are becoming more.**

9. Saint Germain, help me respect my own free will and my right to put things behind me. Help me let go of people who will not let go of the past. Help me accept that I have a right to do what I feel is right for me.

> O Saint Germain, the earth is free,
> from burden of duality,
> in oneness we bring what is best,
> your Golden Age is manifest.
>
> **O Saint Germain, what love you bring,**
> **it truly makes all matter sing,**
> **your violet flame does all restore,**
> **with you we are becoming more.**

Part 4

1. Saint Germain, help me see if there are still a few holy cows walking around in the meadow of my consciousness. I may see them only when I am disturbed by something, such as a spiritual teaching.

> O Saint Germain, you do inspire,
> my vision raised forever higher,
> with you I form a figure-eight,
> your Golden Age I co-create.
>
> **O Saint Germain, what love you bring,**
> **it truly makes all matter sing,**
> **your violet flame does all restore,**
> **with you we are becoming more.**

2. Saint Germain, help me see why this is disturbing me, then follow it, go beyond the feeling and see what is the belief I have that makes me comfortable. I am opening my mind to the higher understanding you are seeking to convey to me.

> O Saint Germain, what Freedom Flame,
> released when we recite your name,

acceleration is your gift,
our planet it will surely lift.

O Saint Germain, what love you bring,
it truly makes all matter sing,
your violet flame does all restore,
with you we are becoming more.

3. Saint Germain, help me survey myself and see if there is still something that disturbs me. Help me follow it, go beyond the feeling and see the belief behind it. Help me let this belief go.

O Saint Germain, in love we claim,
our right to bring your violet flame,
from you Above, to us below,
it is an all-transforming flow.

O Saint Germain, what love you bring,
it truly makes all matter sing,
your violet flame does all restore,
with you we are becoming more.

4. Saint Germain, is there anything I'm just not seeing? Help me come to see it, because I do want to step up to the higher vision of my Divine plan. I want to make maximum progress. I want to reach the level of consciousness where I can be myself.

O Saint Germain, I love you so,
my aura filled with violet glow,
my chakras filled with violet fire,
I am your cosmic amplifier.

O Saint Germain, what love you bring,
it truly makes all matter sing,
your violet flame does all restore,
with you we are becoming more.

5. Saint Germain, help me see the holy cows that are preventing me from being myself and expressing myself without being afraid of the reaction. Help me see my attitude to the material realm and whether I am comfortable being here.

> O Saint Germain, I am now free,
> your violet flame is therapy,
> transform all hang-ups in my mind,
> as inner peace I surely find.
>
> **O Saint Germain, what love you bring,**
> **it truly makes all matter sing,**
> **your violet flame does all restore,**
> **with you we are becoming more.**

6. Saint Germain, help me overcome the belief that I can reach some ultimate stage while I am still in embodiment on earth. Help me let go of the illusion that it is possible to come to a point where I have worked through my psychology and now I am free of everything.

> O Saint Germain, my body pure,
> your violet flame for all is cure,
> consume the cause of all disease,
> and therefore I am all at ease.
>
> **O Saint Germain, what love you bring,**
> **it truly makes all matter sing,**
> **your violet flame does all restore,**
> **with you we are becoming more.**

7. Saint Germain, help me make the decision that brings about a revolutionary shift, where I am no longer longing for this state of being home free while I am in embodiment. I am looking for the next illusion that will bring me up to the next level of consciousness. Help me make it second nature for me to see the next illusion and admit: "Hey, that was limited, it's gotta go."

> O Saint Germain, I'm karma-free,
> the past no longer burdens me,

a brand new opportunity,
I am in Christic unity.

**O Saint Germain, what love you bring,
it truly makes all matter sing,
your violet flame does all restore,
with you we are becoming more.**

8. Saint Germain, help me come to the point where I am beyond the resistance to seeing a limited belief. I just admit that it was a limited belief and then I move on. Help me have my mind liquefied and open to seeing a higher understanding so that you can really work with me.

O Saint Germain, we are now one,
I am for you a violet sun,
as we transform this planet earth,
your Golden Age is given birth.

**O Saint Germain, what love you bring,
it truly makes all matter sing,
your violet flame does all restore,
with you we are becoming more.**

9. Saint Germain, help me make it a daily experience that I receive new insights from you. Help me see that giving up an existing belief, a limited belief, can only be a liberation, a joy, a relief, a new level of freedom. Help me experience that the freedom I attain is its own reward and that I need no other reward for walking the path.

O Saint Germain, the earth is free,
from burden of duality,
in oneness we bring what is best,
your Golden Age is manifest.

**O Saint Germain, what love you bring,
it truly makes all matter sing,
your violet flame does all restore,
with you we are becoming more.**

Sealing

In the name of the Divine Mother, I call to Mother Mary for the sealing of myself and all people in my circle of influence in the creative flow of the Divine Mother, the River of Life. I call for the multiplication of my calls by all representatives of the Divine Mother, so that we form the perfect figure-eight flow of "As Above, so below." Thus, I accept that this is fully manifest, because the mouth of the Lord, the Divine Mother that I AM, has spoken it. Amen.

15 | THE JUDGMENT OF CHRIST AND YOUR DIVINE PLAN

I AM the Ascended Master Jesus, and it is my intent with this discourse to give you some teachings that will not apply to all people, certainly not all people who in a wider sense might find this teaching. It applies to many of you, and I advise you not to sit there and judge with the outer mind whether it applies to you or not. You cannot know that with the outer mind and cannot necessarily know it at your present level of awareness. You will know it when you rise to the higher levels of your Divine plan and have a clearer vision of these higher levels.

People who ignore or deny dark forces

Now, my beloved, if you look at planet earth today, you can see, as we have talked about earlier, that there are many different groupings of people who are at many different levels of consciousness, have many different belief systems, many world views. However, what I wish to bring to your attention here is that there is a segment of the spiritual field (the New Age, mystical, esoteric, open-minded people) who have come to believe that either there is no darkness, no dark forces, or that you, as a spiritual person, should not put your attention upon them because by doing so you give them power.

Naturally, we have given you, through this dispensation, many teachings on the fallen beings. We gave the teachings on the concept of avatars and how you come to earth and you are exposed to the trauma by the fallen beings. Is it, then, truth or reality what these people say, that either dark forces do not exist or that you should not put your attention upon them? Well, this is a delicate matter in the sense that there are a few people on earth for whom it is not necessary to put their attention on dark forces.

Actually, anyone who is an avatar, you have to put your attention on learning about fallen beings and what they do because they were the ones who attacked you when you came to this mission, they were the ones who caused you to create your primal self. As long as you are not willing to look at the existence of dark forces and how they could have influenced you in the past, well, you cannot free yourself from the primal self. If you do not free yourself from the primal self, then you cannot fulfill the highest potential of your Divine plan.

The sad reality is that there are actually tens of thousands, even hundreds of thousands, of people in the New Age field who have a high potential in their Divine plans, but as long as they maintain this attitude that they should ignore dark forces, not put their attention upon it, they have cut themselves off from fulfilling the higher potential of their Divine plans. They have gone to a certain level and they might feel very comfortable there, partly because they feel: "There are no dark forces attacking me." Of course, the dark forces are not attacking them because they are not a threat to the dark forces.

What the dark forces fear most

What is a threat to the dark forces? What is it they desperately want to avoid? Well, they want to avoid that a human being in physical embodiment rises to the level where he or she can consciously acknowledge that you have a level of Christhood and because of that you have the opportunity and the authority to challenge the fallen beings and their presence on earth. This is what they are mortally afraid of because they know that once you step up to that level, it is impossible for them to stop you. They know that if they try to stop you, it will bring about their judgment.

What I am leading you towards is the realization that for many of you, and for some of those who will find this teaching in a broader area, it is the highest aspects of your Divine plan that you bring the judgment of Christ upon the fallen beings and their consciousness. When you look at my life, you see how I would confront the fallen beings, and you may look at yourselves today and then consider what this means for you today.

It does not necessarily mean the same as what you saw in my life, but it does mean that you need to come to a point where you acknowledge that this is part of your Divine plan. You notice from within—not because I am telling you, not because you are reading this dictation. I do not want you to read this and then decide with the outer mind that: "I'm going to go on a crusade and expose the fallen beings and challenge them." It has to come from within and it will only come, my beloved, when you have resolved the birth trauma that the fallen beings used to paralyze you and prevent you from being who you are on this planet.

You are defined by your birth trauma

You understand, my beloved, that there is a certain mechanism that can come into play even when you have the teachings that you have had, up until the teachings on the birth trauma. It is almost as if, as a spiritual student, you can go into a state of mind where you think it is a matter of getting more and more understanding about the spiritual path, even more and more understanding about the ego, about psychology, about healing your psychology. It is almost as if you create a self that thinks you are making progress, but if you look carefully at this self, it also thinks that the ultimate breakthrough is out there in the future. Some day, it will happen, if you continue to do what you are doing now. As my beloved brother, Saint Germain, said: There is a time for evolutionary progress and there are certain times where you need to make a revolutionary shift in consciousness.

The revolutionary shift you need to make, if you want to step up to a higher level, is to recognize that what defines you as a being in embodiment on earth is your birth trauma. It has defined you from your first embodiment. All of these other things that you might have done (various therapies, studying various teachings, practicing spiritual tools) they have all been helpful in bringing an evolutionary change and you have progressed by doing it. But they will actually not truly shift your consciousness because they are not touching the birth trauma. It is as if they are circling around it but not getting to it. That is why you need to make the shift and realize that there comes that point where you know from within (because you recognize the truth in what we are saying) that the next step for you is to look at this birth trauma directly. You cannot walk around it and you cannot skirt the issue. You cannot focus on other things, you cannot think it just happens one day, that if you keep doing invocations and studying the teachings – poof – it is going to happen. It is *not* going to happen. You may need to make a conscious decision to confront this, to go right into it and to discover how the fallen beings paralyze you.

The book *My Lives* describes one way. Naturally, the fallen beings have various ways of doing this. Some of you have been given your birth trauma by being lured by your good intentions, by being lied to and then by being betrayed. There are other scenarios that come into play. Until you discover that birth trauma, you cannot actually manifest and accept your Christhood, you cannot accept yourself as the Christ on earth. Why is that? Because, my beloved, what was it in essence that the fallen beings did when they exposed you to the birth trauma? Well, they created a division in your being, in your four lower bodies. The core of this division is not actually fear, even though you might think it is. The core of the division is doubt. The most insidious enemy on the spiritual path is actually doubt.

Overcoming your core doubt

You come here as an avatar with the best of intentions and then the fallen beings expose you to this trauma—and suddenly you begin to doubt: "Should I have come here? Do I have a right to come here? Am I welcome here? Can I ever be myself and express myself on this planet? Should I change myself into somebody else so that people can accept me?" All of these various doubts, an almost infinite variety of doubts.

You see this in yourselves in many cases where you can be very quick to doubt yourself. There is a good side of this in the sense that you are open-minded and you are open to seeing things in yourself and changing yourself. This is a positive. It is what has helped you grow on the path. You must recognize that there is also a potential danger with this because you see some people on earth who are completely closed-minded. They are absolutely convinced that they are right and they seemingly, at least on a surface level, have no doubt about being right. Of course, at a very deep level all people have various doubts but many people have managed to put on a facade, a persona, where they project that they are right and they know they are right and they seemingly have none of the doubts.

Some of you know people like this and some of you have sat there and wondered: "How can they be so sure about themselves? Why am I doubting myself so much?" Many of you will recognize that you have this tendency (especially when you are confronted with these very dominant, very strong personalities, as they call it) to doubt yourself. "Oh, maybe they are right?" Then, suddenly you will go into a loop in the mind and this loop is created by the linear mind, the analytical mind.

What can the analytical mind do? It can always come up with arguments for or against any viewpoint, any topic. It can argue from both sides of the issue. When you have this tendency to go into doubt, then your analytical mind can always present an argument for why you might actually be wrong or maybe you should not speak up? Maybe you should not challenge that person? Maybe that person is right after all? Maybe they just have a right to be the way they are and maybe you should just ignore it and submit to them, or go away and leave them where they are without challenging them?

You understand what I said earlier: The greatest fear of the fallen beings is to have the Living Christ in embodiment who challenges them. What have they done? They have attempted with every avatar that came to this earth to insert an element of doubt so that you do not dare to challenge them. The absolutely last thing they want is for you to reach a certain level of Christhood and then challenge them. They have done everything possible to prevent this, and their main tool is this element of doubt they have inserted into you.

It is only when you look at the birth trauma consciously that you will discover what it is you doubt about your right to be here, your right to be the Living Christ in embodiment, your right to challenge the fallen beings, your right to express who you are, your higher spiritual identity. Only when you look at the doubt, will you be able to see that the fallen beings used a specific viewpoint, a specific belief, to insert this doubt. That belief is an illusion. Why is it an illusion? Because it is dualistic and this means that when you look at this belief in isolation, it might seem valid. When you step back and realize that in duality every single viewpoint has an opposite polarity, then you can see the opposite polarity of the viewpoint that caused your doubt. Then, you can see that you can also come up with valid viewpoints to support that polarity and that is when you can see that none of them are the ultimate reality.

Selecting out the existential doubt

Do you understand, my beloved? The fallen beings can only operate with duality. Duality is always a polarity. How do the fallen beings take on any appearance of authority? How do they manage to make people believe that here is one viewpoint, a dualistic viewpoint, that is an absolute truth? Well, they can only do this by ignoring the opposite dualistic polarity, by downplaying it, by hiding it, by making people ignore it or doubt it. Therefore, they elevate the one polarity as the absolute truth. Sometimes they also present the opposite polarity as evil and, of course, you can see this all over the world where there is raised up: truth and error, truth and the lie, capitalism–communism, Christianity–all other religions and so forth and so on. So many of these dualistic polarities where one is wholly good and the other is wholly bad.

When you see this at the personal level, in your own birth trauma, how you took in a certain belief that caused you to doubt your right to be here—and then you see that it has an opposite polarity and you could argue forever for or against these two polarities, you can step back and say: "Enough with the argumentation. I am letting this primal self die. I am simply selecting out the doubt from my being." The most important thing you can select out at the higher levels of your Divine plan is what we might call an existential doubt in your right to be here.

My beloved, one of the more common patterns created by the fallen beings (and one that this messenger has not realized consciously until I am giving this teaching), is to make you think that because you have done or said something here on earth (in this situation that caused your birth trauma) that was not perfect, then you do not have the right to challenge the fallen beings. In other words, you think you should be perfect and if you are not perfect, then you should not challenge them. Many of you can recognize this.

This messenger had an interesting experience driving to this conference where he, in conversation, without any forethought said: "You know I've actually never discovered anything evil in my own being." Then, he paused because he was shocked by this statement as he had never thought about it before. The fact of the matter is that with all of his willingness to observe himself, to go into his psychology, he has never discovered an element of evil in his being. The same will hold true for most of you and most of the people who will read this teaching. The same holds true, my beloved, for every avatar. There is no evil in your being—there never was.

Even with all the traumas you have experienced on this planet, you have not allowed an element of evil into your being.

Therefore, my beloved, what does this mean? Well, it means you are not a fallen being. You are not like the fallen beings. Therefore, even though you may not be perfect according to some worldly standard, you have the right to challenge the fallen beings.

How to challenge fallen beings

You have the right, not necessarily to come out and accuse them of being wrong because the fallen beings love to create this dualistic battle where somebody says: "You're wrong!" and then the other goes into an immediate defensive reaction and comes back and says: "No, *you're* wrong!" Then, you have an ongoing struggle that goes on indefinitely.

It is actually not a matter of challenging the fallen beings by saying: "You're wrong." The real way to challenge the fallen beings is to say: "There is an alternative to your way of looking at life. There is an alternative to your way of looking at everything! There is a different way. There is a different level of consciousness than what you have." What is the alternative? Well, ultimately, and in the most universal sense, it is the Christ, the Christ consciousness, which is the alternative to the fallen consciousness.

Of course, this can be expressed in many specific ways. You can go into any area of life and as you come to these higher levels of your Divine plan, you will build the discernment where you can go in and many of you will see that you actually have the ability to do this. It starts with an ability to read vibration. Many of you have in your discussions here expressed how, at some point, you found some spiritual teaching or guru or some idea and you just felt: "Oh, this is not for me. I am not going to go into that." This is the beginning of discernment where you are able to read vibration.

Your outer mind cannot put words on why and what it is but as you move higher in Christhood you begin to be able to express this in words. You begin to be able to go into almost any aspect of life, or at least areas where you have some knowledge and expertise, and you can identify: "This is a dualistic idea. This is an unbalanced view." You do not need to go out publicly and accuse this of being evil or fallen beings or whatever. You can find a way to use words that people can relate to and accept. You can express that this is not the highest possible viewpoint and there is an alternative. This is one way to challenge the fallen consciousness.

Dealing with personal attacks

Now, for some of you, it may also be on a more personal level where you meet people who are either fallen beings or who are in the fallen consciousness and you challenge them directly. Some of you have chosen to have fallen beings in your families or in your relationships. It is not necessary, my beloved, to challenge the fallen beings by going into a dualistic conflict with them. In fact, it might be constructive, at least for a while, to adopt the mindset that you are not challenging the fallen *beings,* you are challenging the fallen *consciousness* because it is easier for you to keep it at an impersonal level. You see, my beloved, the fallen beings when they feel challenged, what will they do? They will always accuse you back. You might come and say: "I do not agree with the ideas you are promoting," but a fallen being will per instinct attack you personally.

How do you deal with this personal attack that you might be exposed to and, for example, this messenger has certainly been exposed to any number of times? Well, it is very difficult to deal with it as long as you have that doubt in your being. As the open-minded, self-aware, self-critical person you are, you always consider when someone says something about you: "Could they be right? Do I need to change? Am I too aggressive? Am I this, am I that?" Again, how do you get rid of the doubt? Well, only by looking at your birth trauma.

When you come to the point where you realize that you do have a right to be here and there is nothing evil in your being, you are not challenging other people in order to put them down or be critical but you have a right to express who you are. You can actually come to a point where you are not challenging the fallen consciousness with the outer intent of challenging the fallen consciousness. You are not deliberately going out and looking for: "What is wrong, what is bad, what are wrong ideas, what can I challenge?" You are just being yourself, you are beginning to express yourself, what you know, the insights you have, the experiences you have had. In so doing, of course, you will challenge the fallen consciousness and sometimes you will meet fallen beings who will feel personally attacked by you because they always take everything personally. The only way to really deal with this is that you do not take their reaction personally because, again, you are not doing this because you have a personal agenda—right? You can recognize, if you look back at your life, that when you say something, when you express a viewpoint, you want other people to agree with you because then you will feel validated. If they disagree with you, then it will stir up the wound you have in yourself, the insecurity, the doubt and then you will feel bad. You have a personal agenda of wanting other people to agree with you in order to avoid feeling bad inside yourself. This is what I mean by a personal agenda for an avatar.

My beloved, an avatar does not have the personal agendas that the fallen beings have of manipulating other people so that they can get something. This is, we might say, the wounded personal agenda of avatars where you seek to change other people to compensate for your own wound. Of course, when you get rid of the wound, you no longer need to do this. You are not even doing it anymore with the attitude that you have to change something on earth. As we have said, you come to that point of simply being yourself, radiating what comes to you from your higher being, co-creating, and this is going to challenge the fallen beings.

Making the Christhood switch

However, as we have said, there can come these points where you have resolved the birth trauma, you have consumed the energy, you have let go of this separate self, perhaps the primal self, but there is another separate self that somehow has come to think that you should not be challenging, or you should not be direct, or you should not be unkind, or any number of such things. In other words, you are actually ready to begin to express your Christhood and challenge the fallen ideas but there is that separate self in you that is blocking it because you think you should not do this for whatever reason.

Maybe you think that: "I am a spiritual person, I should be kind and gentle with everybody," as many well-meaning people in the New Age field think. You need to be willing to look at that separate self and say: "What is the way of expressing my Christhood that I saw when I was at the highest level of awareness? What was it that I decided I wanted to express?" Then, you look at this self and say: "I'm not going to let this self stand in my way. I am going to let it die and I'm going to make a revolutionary conscious switch in my mind that I am willing to be the Living Christ in action. I am willing to express whatever comes to me from my I AM Presence even when it challenges or offends other people." My beloved, we have said before that Christhood is not a popularity contest, that it is not something that will make you popular or will make other people comfortable. You will see that when I walked the earth on the dusty roads of Palestine, sometimes I would meet people who, just by encountering my Presence, would become so uncomfortable because the light that I radiated stirred up their own inner demons (so to speak) and suddenly those demons would scream and yell out at me. I am not saying this will necessarily happen to you, but I am saying that you need to recognize that the more light you have, the more there will be some people that will be uncomfortable when they encounter the light. You need to get to the point where you are not using other people's reactions to say: "Oh, did I do something wrong? Is there something wrong with me? Shouldn't I have done this?"

You come to the point, again, where you accept free will. You make this conscious shift that you accept free will. You accept that you have a right to be who you are. You accept that other people have a right to react to that according to their level of consciousness. Then again, you have a right to continue to be who you are, regardless of their reaction. Their reaction is what? It is a result, ultimately, of their own choices.

They may have a psychological pattern, they may have some internal spirits, they may have some demons possessing them that are causing the reaction so they are not making a conscious choice. Ultimately, when you look back at the history of that lifestream, that lifestream made certain choices that brought them to their present level of awareness. Their reaction to you is a result of their choices. That, my beloved, is *their* free will, not *your* free will. You have no authority over their free will. When you fully recognize that you have no authority over another person's free will, you also recognize you have no responsibility for their choices or the consequences.

The Bodhisattva ideal

This is where we might need to realize that as an avatar, many of you came here because you looked at the earth, you looked at the suffering on earth and you felt compassion for the people who were suffering. This is an ideal that is expressed in the East, especially related to Kuan Yin, as the Bodhisattva ideal. The way it is told in the East was that Kuan Yin had come to the point where she had qualified for her ascension, or nirvana as they call it, and she could move on from the earth. As she was ready to leave, she took one last look back and she heard the cries of the world, those who were suffering and she decided to remain with earth in order to help people overcome that suffering. Well, this is a Bodhisattva ideal of someone who had qualified for their ascension and still chose to remain with the earth. But it can be just as easily translated to many avatars who also decided to come to earth because you heard the cries of the world, you saw the suffering.

What have we given you? What has this messenger realized as a result of processing the teachings on the birth trauma? It is that as an avatar you were not in the ascended state of consciousness when you decided to come to earth. You had a higher level of consciousness, you came from a natural planet. Again, there was no evil in your being but still you had something unresolved, something you had not learned. What was it you had not learned? Well, it was the absoluteness of free will. This is one of the biggest challenges you find.

My beloved, you could argue that the only problem the fallen beings have is that they have not fully experienced and accepted the absoluteness of free will. They are still seeking to find ways to manipulate free will, the free will of others, or to stretch their own free will in what they think will give them greater freedom because they do not realize that they *have* absolute freedom.

You understand? Some fallen beings will not acknowledge that they have absolute free will. They have in their minds created this epic drama that God is limiting their free will. Therefore, the only way to express their free will is to rebel against God by doing the opposite of what God wants them to do. They just do not acknowledge that the God who wants them to do something is of their own creation and exists only in their own minds. Whereas the real Creator has said: "You have complete free will." It is one of the greatest challenges of a self-aware being, fallen or not, to recognize the absoluteness of free will.

As an avatar, you did not fully grasp the absoluteness of free will. When you looked down on earth and saw that people were suffering, you could only reason that something had gone wrong because they had made the wrong choices. It was your task, your self-appointed task, to go down and help them make better choices—not by manipulating them but in various other ways. Is it your task as an avatar to come here and do something about other people's choices.

The fundamental difference of free will

Absolutely not! According to the Law of Free Will, this is *not* your task. Does this mean you cannot help people? No, it does not. There is a fundamental difference between having the mindset that you need to do something to change other people and having the mindset that you are here to show them that there is an alternative to their current state of consciousness. It is a *fundamental* difference.

It may not seem as such a big difference but when you process this idea in your minds, and ask for inner direction, you can come to the point where you make one of these revolutionary shifts that Saint Germain talked about. Suddenly, you realize how fundamental that difference is. *That,* my beloved, is going to be your greatest challenge as an avatar on earth. You are going to have to be willing to do what Saint Germain talked about: Admit that you were wrong. It is not that you were wrong—wrong in a bad, evil sense for coming to earth. But you have to admit that the attitude that you had, that brought you to earth, needs to go. It was unbalanced. It was imperfect. It was not the ultimate. It was not the Christ consciousness. You have to be willing to admit this because until you admit this as an avatar, you cannot get out of here.

As long as you think that your reason for coming to earth, or that your success on earth, was to change somebody else, to change their free-will choices, you cannot let go of this planet. There will be some other task you have to do, some problem you have to solve, some epic struggle you have to fulfill. It can go on, my beloved, indefinitely. That is one of the things we wanted to show you in the book *My Lives* where it took two million years for me to get over the illusion that brought me here. It can take even longer.

Is it in your Divine plan to ascend?

You need to recognize that if it is in your Divine plan that you can ascend after this lifetime, what will it take for you to ascend? Sometimes, and especially in previous ascended master organizations, students get this almost mechanical view of the ascension. You think that if you do this, and if you do that and if you understand this and if you understand that – poof – you will ascend! Again, there will never be a "poof!" What will it take to ascend? It will take (as this messenger saw in an intuitive flash many years ago) that you come to the point where you are standing there in front of that gate. If you walk through it, you have ascended. Before you can walk through it, you must look back on earth. I know there are stories about those who looked back and were turned into a pillar of salt but this is not going to happen when you are at the level of your ascension. You *must* look back. You must hear the cries of the world. *Then* you must survey your being and say: "Is there anything on earth that I cannot leave behind?"

Only when you realize that there is nothing in your being that is pulling on you to stay on earth, only *then* can you turn around and make that choice: "I am leaving this planet for good. I am giving up the possibility of influencing this planet that I can only have by being in physical embodiment. I am giving it up! I am selecting it out!" Then, you can ascend but it is a choice and it must be a fully conscious choice. There cannot be anything in your being you have not looked at because then the prince of this world has something in you and he will pull you back.

Now, here is another thing. We recognize that whenever we give a teaching, it may cause some people to interpret it in a slightly imbalanced way. We have given many teachings on the ascension, and many ascended master students over the decades have gotten the idea that the only thing that really matters, the only thing you should really do as an ascended master student, is strive for your ascension. You need to ascend as quickly as possible, certainly after this lifetime, if at all possible or in the next lifetime. This is the case for *some* of you but it is not the case for *all* of you.

What are we on the verge of bringing in on this planet? Saint Germain's Golden Age! There are beings in embodiment, including avatars, who want to be part of manifesting Saint Germain's Golden Age. This, of course, is not going to happen fully at the end of your lifetime even if you are young at the present moment. There may be some of you where it is not in your Divine plan that you ascend after this lifetime because you want to take succeeding embodiments in order to help manifest Saint Germain's Golden Age or even experience Saint Germain's Golden Age. This is what you can only discern when you come to the higher levels of your Divine plan and, again, you can only really discern this when you resolve the birth trauma.

Recognize this, my beloved: Many avatars, because of the intensity and the pain involved with the birth trauma, have a desire to get out of here because they think they will get away from their birth trauma. Of course, when you ascend you will get away from your birth trauma but you do not ascend until you have looked at it, confronted your birth trauma. There is this escape mechanism where people feel: "Oh, it's too much to deal with the birth trauma so I'm just going to focus on making my ascension and I'm sure I can do this without confronting my birth trauma." It cannot be done!

Again, what will enable you to be a part of bringing forth Saint Germain's Golden Age? What will enable you to experience it and really enjoy it? It is that you resolve your birth trauma. It does not mean that when you resolve your birth trauma, you will automatically ascend, that you will have to ascend. Now, you can choose to remain on earth and say: "Well, you know, now I have been struggling with this birth trauma for two million years, I sure would like to experience this planet without it." There is absolutely nothing wrong with you making that choice, my beloved—even if you have the option to ascend.

Yes, of course, as was said in previous dispensations, it has a positive effect on the earth when someone ascends. It pulls up on the collective consciousness. Certainly, when someone has resolved their birth trauma and starts expressing their Christhood, it also has a positive effect if you stay in embodiment. Again, this is not something that is forced upon you. There have been people who were ascended master students who almost felt forced to make their ascension or strive for their ascension because they had to do this to help the earth. You have an absolute right to make the determination: "I want to stay in embodiment and help bring about Saint Germain's Golden Age." If, my beloved, all of you ascended tomorrow, who would bring about the golden age? [Someone in the audience responds "We!"] No, because you would be ascended and when you are ascended, you cannot bring it into physical manifestation.

To ascend or not to ascend

My beloved, there have been previous ages on earth (we have talked about root races and so forth), there have been cycles where a civilization had gradually risen to a very high level and there was a certain group of lifestreams who had been instrumental in bringing this civilization to that high level. In doing so, the reason they were instrumental in raising their civilization was that they had raised their own consciousness and started to manifest Christhood. In doing so, of course, they had qualified for their ascension. They had the free-will choice: Would they ascend or not? There have been cases where so many of these mature lifestreams chose to ascend at the same time that after they went out of embodiment, the civilization very quickly went into a downward spiral and collapsed. There were not enough people in embodiment, so to speak, to hold the spiritual balance and to keep the civilization in an upward spiral. In some cases, this meant that the fallen beings could move in, take up leadership and bring the civilization down.

You have to be careful and recognize there is always a balance to be found. Now again, we are not looking back and blaming these people for choosing to ascend. It was their right to make that choice and it was the challenge of those who had seen these examples and were at lower levels. Would they step up and fill the vacuum or would they allow the fallen beings to come in and fill the vacuum? That was their choice and their challenge. It was perfectly all right as to how it played itself out.

What I am simply saying to you is that as an ascended master student, you do not have to fixate your mind on thinking: "I have to ascend after this lifetime." There is nothing you *have* to do. You can certainly serve life, serve the earth, serve Saint Germain by remaining in embodiment when you have resolved that birth trauma and are therefore much more able to be an open door.

Your Divine plan was not forced upon you

Free will is absolute and therefore in the realm of free will, there can be no absolutes that you *should* or you *should not*. You see, it is important for you to come to this point because, my beloved, in order to fulfill the highest potential of your Divine plan, you must overcome this sense that there is something forced upon you. You can even have a separate self that has heard about the concept of a Divine plan and has studied our teachings but it still feels that this was forced upon you. Maybe even that you yourself forced your Divine plan upon yourself! That is what this self feels.

You need to identify if you have that tendency and then you need to look at it and say: "I no longer need this self. I am letting you die." You cannot fulfill the highest potential of your Divine plan until you have full and absolute acceptance of it. In other words, you cannot feel that you made choices before you came into embodiment, and now that you are here and you see how difficult it is to be in physical embodiment and how things are on earth, you are not sure you can live up to those choices or fulfill those choices. You are not even sure you are *willing* to fulfill those choices so you feel a certain conflict in you. It is almost like you are, as I said 2,000 years ago, "a house divided against itself" concerning your Divine plan.

If there is a division in you, between what is in your Divine plan that you yourself chose to put in there and then there is a separate self that has a different will, then you need to look at that. You cannot fulfill the highest potential of your Divine plan as long as you are dragging this self around with you.

Again, you need to have this revolutionary shift of looking at this and saying: "Okay, I'm willing to take a look at this, I'm willing to go into it, I'm willing to experience what the belief is behind it." Then, you see the unreality of the reason and you say: "No, that isn't actually my choice. It might be the choice of the separate self. I see that it was because of whatever created the separate self, a trauma, a false belief, whatever it was, but I now see it and I choose to let it die. I choose to then embrace what I actually put in my Divine plan because I am willing to rise to the level of consciousness from which I put those elements in my Divine plan." Only when you let go of that separate self, can you actually rise to that. Only then can you embrace your Divine plan—fully embrace it.

My beloved, when you look at my life as it was 2,000 years ago, if you are really honest, you will be able to see that I was the Living Christ, but I was in some way the *reluctant* Living Christ. You see this, for example, in the situation when before what led to my arrest and crucifixion, I was sitting in the Garden of Gethsemane. Some say I was sweating drops of blood, some say I was not sweating drops of blood but that is not really the point. The point is that I was saying: "God, if it be thy will, let this pass from me." Then, I nevertheless said: "Not my will but thine be done."

But, what does that show you? It shows you that even I, at the level of Christhood that I had, there was still a division in my being where I felt there was the will I had here and there was a higher will. Was it God that was forcing this upon me? No, I had chosen this when I had made my Divine plan. I had chosen but there was still a part of my outer being, my outer personality, a separate self, that had not fully embraced and accepted that. What I am saying is: This was, of course, perfectly in order. This was 2,000 years ago, a much more dense consciousness. I was one of the forerunners for demonstrating the Christ consciousness. It was perfectly fine but in today's age, you have the potential to step up higher, overcome this division in yourself and fully embrace your Divine plan.

That is, of course, what I desire to see from you, my beloved. Does that mean that you will manifest a higher level of Christhood than I manifested 2,000 years ago? "*Yes!* It might mean that for you!" Do you not think that is what I want for you? Do you think, my beloved, as the ascended master Jesus Christ, I have some ego ambition that: "I was the one who demonstrated Christhood on earth and I never want anyone to surpass me?"

I want you to do greater works than I did. I said it 2,000 years ago. It is not my problem that you have not believed me! I am at peace with that, I leave that to your free will, I just point out to you that this is how I look at it. It will be my supreme joy to see many people – 10,000 people – manifest a higher level of Christhood than I could manifest 2,000 years ago, even by, as I have said before, expressing that Christhood in a somewhat "normal" lifestyle.

My beloved, it has been my supreme joy to give you this discourse and to actually see the shifts in the consciousness of those of you who have absorbed it. It will be my joy to see how it will spread like rings in the water and help more and more people come to that point of fully accepting the highest potential of your Divine plan—fully accepting your own choices.

16 | INVOKING THE VISION OF MY PERSONAL CHRISTHOOD

In the name I AM THAT I AM, Jesus Christ, I call to all representatives of the Divine Mother, especially Jesus, to help me overcome the illusions that prevent me from accepting and expressing my Christhood, including…

[Make personal calls.]

Part 1

1. Jesus, help me see that the dark forces desperately want to avoid that I rise to the level where I can consciously acknowledge that I have a level of Christhood, and because of that I have the opportunity and the authority to challenge the fallen beings and their presence on earth.

O Jesus, blessed brother mine,
I walk the path that you outline,

a great example to us all,
I follow now your inner call.

**O Jesus, let the Fire of Joy,
consume the devil's subtle ploy,
transfigured is our planet earth,
the golden age is given birth.**

2. Jesus, help me see that the dark forces are mortally afraid of this because they know that once I step up to that level, it is impossible for them to stop me. They know that if they try to stop me, it will bring about their judgment.

O Jesus, open inner sight,
the ego wants to prove it's right,
but this I will no longer do,
I want to be all one with you.

**O Jesus, let the Fire of Joy,
consume the devil's subtle ploy,
transfigured is our planet earth,
the golden age is given birth.**

3. Jesus, help me see if it is the highest aspect of my Divine plan that I bring the judgment of Christ upon the fallen beings and their consciousness. Help me see what confronting the fallen beings, as you did, means for me today.

O Jesus, I now clearly see,
the Key of Knowledge given me,
my Christ self I hereby embrace,
as you fill up my inner space.

**O Jesus, let the Fire of Joy,
consume the devil's subtle ploy,
transfigured is our planet earth,
the golden age is given birth.**

4. Jesus, help me acknowledge if this is part of my Divine plan. Help me see that this is not a decision with the outer mind. It must come from within, and it will only come when I resolve the birth trauma that the fallen beings used to paralyze me and prevent me from being who I am on this planet.

> O Jesus, show me serpent's lie,
> expose the beam in my own eye,
> as Christ discernment you me give,
> in oneness I forever live.
>
> **O Jesus, let the Fire of Joy,**
> **consume the devil's subtle ploy,**
> **transfigured is our planet earth,**
> **the golden age is given birth.**

5. Jesus, help me see that there is a certain mechanism that can make me think it is a matter of getting more and more understanding about the spiritual path. Help me see if I have created a self that thinks I am making progress, but also that the ultimate breakthrough is out there in the future.

> O Jesus, I am truly meek,
> and thus I turn the other cheek,
> when the accuser attacks me,
> I go within and merge with thee.
>
> **O Jesus, let the Fire of Joy,**
> **consume the devil's subtle ploy,**
> **transfigured is our planet earth,**
> **the golden age is given birth.**

6. Jesus, help me make the revolutionary shift and recognize that what defines me as a being in embodiment on earth is my birth trauma. It has defined me from my first embodiment.

> O Jesus, ego I let die,
> surrender ev'ry earthly tie,
> the dead can bury what is dead,
> I choose to walk with you instead.

> **O Jesus, let the Fire of Joy,**
> **consume the devil's subtle ploy,**
> **transfigured is our planet earth,**
> **the golden age is given birth.**

7. Jesus, help me make the shift and realize that there comes a point where I know from within that the next step is to look at this birth trauma directly. I am making a conscious decision to confront this, to go right into it and to discover how the fallen beings paralyze me.

> O Jesus, help me rise above,
> the devil's test through higher love,
> show me separate self unreal,
> my formless self you do reveal.

> **O Jesus, let the Fire of Joy,**
> **consume the devil's subtle ploy,**
> **transfigured is our planet earth,**
> **the golden age is given birth.**

8. Jesus, help me see the individual scenario that caused my birth trauma, so I can expose the division in my being that was created by the fallen beings. Help me see the core of this division, namely the doubt inserted by the fallen beings.

> O Jesus, what is that to me,
> I just let go and follow thee,
> with this I do pass ev'ry test,
> to find with you eternal rest.

> **O Jesus, let the Fire of Joy,**
> **consume the devil's subtle ploy,**
> **transfigured is our planet earth,**
> **the golden age is given birth.**

9. Jesus, help me see how my best intentions were used by the fallen beings to expose me to the trauma that made me doubt: "Should I have come here? Do I have a right to come here? Am I welcome here? Can I ever be myself and express myself on this planet? Should I change myself into somebody else so that people can accept me?"

> O Jesus, fiery master mine,
> my heart now melting into thine,
> I love with heart and mind and soul,
> the God who is my highest goal.
>
> **O Jesus, let the Fire of Joy,**
> **consume the devil's subtle ploy,**
> **transfigured is our planet earth,**
> **the golden age is given birth.**

Part 2

1. Jesus, help me see the cases where I am very quick to doubt myself. Help me recognize if I tend to doubt myself when I am around strong personalities who are convinced they are right.

> O Jesus, blessed brother mine,
> I walk the path that you outline,
> a great example to us all,
> I follow now your inner call.
>
> **O Jesus, let the Fire of Joy,**
> **consume the devil's subtle ploy,**
> **transfigured is our planet earth,**
> **the golden age is given birth.**

2. Jesus, help me see when I go into a loop that is created by the linear mind, because it can always come up with arguments for or against any viewpoint. It can argue from both sides of the issue.

O Jesus, open inner sight,
the ego wants to prove it's right,
but this I will no longer do,
I want to be all one with you.

**O Jesus, let the Fire of Joy,
consume the devil's subtle ploy,
transfigured is our planet earth,
the golden age is given birth.**

3. Jesus, help me see that when I have this tendency to go into doubt, then my analytical mind can always present an argument for why I might be wrong or why I should not speak up or challenge that person.

O Jesus, I now clearly see,
the Key of Knowledge given me,
my Christ self I hereby embrace,
as you fill up my inner space.

**O Jesus, let the Fire of Joy,
consume the devil's subtle ploy,
transfigured is our planet earth,
the golden age is given birth.**

4. Jesus, help me see that because the greatest fear of the fallen beings is to have the Living Christ in embodiment who challenges them, they have attempted with every avatar that came to this earth to insert an element of doubt so that we do not dare to challenge them.

O Jesus, show me serpent's lie,
expose the beam in my own eye,
as Christ discernment you me give,
in oneness I forever live.

**O Jesus, let the Fire of Joy,
consume the devil's subtle ploy,
transfigured is our planet earth,
the golden age is given birth.**

5. Jesus, help me see that the absolutely last thing the fallen beings want is for me to reach a certain level of Christhood and then challenge them. They have done everything possible to prevent this, and their main tool is this element of doubt they have inserted into me.

> O Jesus, I am truly meek,
> and thus I turn the other cheek,
> when the accuser attacks me,
> I go within and merge with thee.
>
> **O Jesus, let the Fire of Joy,**
> **consume the devil's subtle ploy,**
> **transfigured is our planet earth,**
> **the golden age is given birth.**

6. Jesus, help me see that it is only when I look at the birth trauma consciously that I will discover what is my doubt about my right to be here, my right to be the Living Christ in embodiment, my right to challenge the fallen beings, my right to express my higher spiritual identity.

> O Jesus, ego I let die,
> surrender ev'ry earthly tie,
> the dead can bury what is dead,
> I choose to walk with you instead.
>
> **O Jesus, let the Fire of Joy,**
> **consume the devil's subtle ploy,**
> **transfigured is our planet earth,**
> **the golden age is given birth.**

7. Jesus, help me look at the doubt and see that the fallen beings used a specific viewpoint, a specific belief, to insert this doubt. That belief is an illusion because it is dualistic.

> O Jesus, help me rise above,
> the devil's test through higher love,
> show me separate self unreal,
> my formless self you do reveal.

**O Jesus, let the Fire of Joy,
consume the devil's subtle ploy,
transfigured is our planet earth,
the golden age is given birth.**

8. Jesus, help me see that a dualistic viewpoint means that when I look at this belief in isolation, it might seem valid. Help me step back and realize that in duality, every single viewpoint has an opposite polarity. I can see both what caused my doubt and the opposite polarity. This means none of them are the ultimate reality.

O Jesus, what is that to me,
I just let go and follow thee,
with this I do pass ev'ry test,
to find with you eternal rest.

**O Jesus, let the Fire of Joy,
consume the devil's subtle ploy,
transfigured is our planet earth,
the golden age is given birth.**

9. Jesus, help me see how, in my birth trauma, I took in a certain belief that caused me to doubt my right to be here. Help me see that it has an opposite polarity and I could argue forever for or against these two polarities.

O Jesus, fiery master mine,
my heart now melting into thine,
I love with heart and mind and soul,
the God who is my highest goal.

**O Jesus, let the Fire of Joy,
consume the devil's subtle ploy,
transfigured is our planet earth,
the golden age is given birth.**

Part 3

1. Jesus, help me step back and say: "Enough with the argumentation. I am letting this primal self die. I am simply selecting out the doubt from my being." Help me select out my existential doubt in my right to be here.

> O Jesus, blessed brother mine,
> I walk the path that you outline,
> a great example to us all,
> I follow now your inner call.
>
> **O Jesus, let the Fire of Joy,**
> **consume the devil's subtle ploy,**
> **transfigured is our planet earth,**
> **the golden age is given birth.**

2. Jesus, help me see if the fallen beings have made me think that because I have done or said something imperfect here on earth, then I do not have the right to challenge them. Help me see if I think I should be perfect, so if I am not perfect, then I should not challenge them.

> O Jesus, open inner sight,
> the ego wants to prove it's right,
> but this I will no longer do,
> I want to be all one with you.
>
> **O Jesus, let the Fire of Joy,**
> **consume the devil's subtle ploy,**
> **transfigured is our planet earth,**
> **the golden age is given birth.**

3. Jesus, help me see that there is no element of evil in my being—there never was. Even with all the traumas I have experienced on this planet, I have not allowed an element of evil into my being.

> O Jesus, I now clearly see,
> the Key of Knowledge given me,

my Christ self I hereby embrace,
as you fill up my inner space.

**O Jesus, let the Fire of Joy,
consume the devil's subtle ploy,
transfigured is our planet earth,
the golden age is given birth.**

4. Jesus, help me see that I am not like the fallen beings, so even though I may not be perfect according to some worldly standard, I have the right to challenge the fallen beings.

O Jesus, show me serpent's lie,
expose the beam in my own eye,
as Christ discernment you me give,
in oneness I forever live.

**O Jesus, let the Fire of Joy,
consume the devil's subtle ploy,
transfigured is our planet earth,
the golden age is given birth.**

5. Jesus, help me see that this does not mean I accuse the fallen beings of being wrong according to their dualistic standard. It means that I say: "There is an alternative to your way of looking at life. There is an alternative to your way of looking at everything! There is a different way. There is a different level of consciousness than what you have."

O Jesus, I am truly meek,
and thus I turn the other cheek,
when the accuser attacks me,
I go within and merge with thee.

**O Jesus, let the Fire of Joy,
consume the devil's subtle ploy,
transfigured is our planet earth,
the golden age is given birth.**

16 | Invoking the vision of my personal Christhood

6. Jesus, help me build the discernment based on the ability to read vibration and identify: "This is a dualistic idea. This is an unbalanced view." Help me express that this is not the highest possible viewpoint and there is an alternative.

> O Jesus, ego I let die,
> surrender ev'ry earthly tie,
> the dead can bury what is dead,
> I choose to walk with you instead.
>
> **O Jesus, let the Fire of Joy,**
> **consume the devil's subtle ploy,**
> **transfigured is our planet earth,**
> **the golden age is given birth.**

7. Jesus, help me see if I have chosen to have fallen beings in my family or in relationships. Help me adopt the mindset that I am not challenging the fallen *beings,* I am challenging the fallen *consciousness* so I can keep it on an impersonal level.

> O Jesus, help me rise above,
> the devil's test through higher love,
> show me separate self unreal,
> my formless self you do reveal.
>
> **O Jesus, let the Fire of Joy,**
> **consume the devil's subtle ploy,**
> **transfigured is our planet earth,**
> **the golden age is given birth.**

8. Jesus, help me see that when the fallen beings feel challenged, they will per instinct accuse me and attack me personally. Help me see that it is difficult to deal with this personal attack as long as I have doubt in my being.

> O Jesus, what is that to me,
> I just let go and follow thee,
> with this I do pass ev'ry test,
> to find with you eternal rest.

> O Jesus, let the Fire of Joy,
> consume the devil's subtle ploy,
> transfigured is our planet earth,
> the golden age is given birth.

9. Jesus, help me realize that I *do* have a right to be here and there is nothing evil in my being, so I am not challenging other people in order to put them down or be critical. I have a right to express who I am.

> O Jesus, fiery master mine,
> my heart now melting into thine,
> I love with heart and mind and soul,
> the God who is my highest goal.

> O Jesus, let the Fire of Joy,
> consume the devil's subtle ploy,
> transfigured is our planet earth,
> the golden age is given birth.

Part 4

1. Jesus, help me reach the point where I am not challenging the fallen consciousness with the outer intent of challenging the fallen consciousness. I am not deliberately looking for what is wrong, I am just being myself and expressing myself.

> O Jesus, blessed brother mine,
> I walk the path that you outline,
> a great example to us all,
> I follow now your inner call.

> O Jesus, let the Fire of Joy,
> consume the devil's subtle ploy,
> transfigured is our planet earth,
> the golden age is given birth.

16 | Invoking the vision of my personal Christhood

2. Jesus, help me see that the fallen beings will feel personally attacked by me because they always take everything personally. The only way to deal with this is that I do not take their reaction personally, because I am not doing this because I have a personal agenda.

> O Jesus, open inner sight,
> the ego wants to prove it's right,
> but this I will no longer do,
> I want to be all one with you.
>
> **O Jesus, let the Fire of Joy,**
> **consume the devil's subtle ploy,**
> **transfigured is our planet earth,**
> **the golden age is given birth.**

3. Jesus, help me overcome the mechanism of expressing a viewpoint and wanting other people to agree with me because then I will feel validated. If they disagree with me, then it will stir up the wound I have in myself and then I will feel bad.

> O Jesus, I now clearly see,
> the Key of Knowledge given me,
> my Christ self I hereby embrace,
> as you fill up my inner space.
>
> **O Jesus, let the Fire of Joy,**
> **consume the devil's subtle ploy,**
> **transfigured is our planet earth,**
> **the golden age is given birth.**

4. Jesus, help me see if I have a personal agenda of wanting other people to agree with me in order to avoid feeling bad inside myself, in order to compensate for my own wound.

> O Jesus, show me serpent's lie,
> expose the beam in my own eye,
> as Christ discernment you me give,
> in oneness I forever live.

**O Jesus, let the Fire of Joy,
consume the devil's subtle ploy,
transfigured is our planet earth,
the golden age is given birth.**

5. Jesus, help me heal the wound and overcome the attitude that I have to change something on earth. Help me be myself, radiating what comes to me from my higher being, and challenge the fallen beings that way.

O Jesus, I am truly meek,
and thus I turn the other cheek,
when the accuser attacks me,
I go within and merge with thee.

**O Jesus, let the Fire of Joy,
consume the devil's subtle ploy,
transfigured is our planet earth,
the golden age is given birth.**

6. Jesus, help me see if I have a separate self that thinks I should not be challenging, I should not be direct, I should not be unkind. Help me see if I am ready to express my Christhood and challenge the fallen ideas, but there is a separate self that is blocking it because I think I should not do this.

O Jesus, ego I let die,
surrender ev'ry earthly tie,
the dead can bury what is dead,
I choose to walk with you instead.

**O Jesus, let the Fire of Joy,
consume the devil's subtle ploy,
transfigured is our planet earth,
the golden age is given birth.**

7. Jesus, I am willing to look at that separate self and say: "What is the way of expressing my Christhood that I saw when I was at the highest level of awareness? What was it that I decided I wanted to express?"

O Jesus, help me rise above,
the devil's test through higher love,
show me separate self unreal,
my formless self you do reveal.

**O Jesus, let the Fire of Joy,
consume the devil's subtle ploy,
transfigured is our planet earth,
the golden age is given birth.**

8. Jesus, help me look at this self and say: "I'm not going to let this self stand in my way. I am going to let it die and I'm going to make a revolutionary conscious switch in my mind that I am willing to be the Living Christ in action. I am willing to express whatever comes to me from my I AM Presence even when it challenges or offends other people."

O Jesus, what is that to me,
I just let go and follow thee,
with this I do pass ev'ry test,
to find with you eternal rest.

**O Jesus, let the Fire of Joy,
consume the devil's subtle ploy,
transfigured is our planet earth,
the golden age is given birth.**

9. Jesus, help me accept that Christhood is not a popularity contest, that it is not something that will make me popular or will make other people comfortable.

O Jesus, fiery master mine,
my heart now melting into thine,
I love with heart and mind and soul,
the God who is my highest goal.

**O Jesus, let the Fire of Joy,
consume the devil's subtle ploy,
transfigured is our planet earth,
the golden age is given birth.**

Part 5

1. Jesus, help me recognize that the more light I have, the more there will be some people who will be uncomfortable when they encounter the light. Help me avoid using other people's reactions to say: "Oh, did I do something wrong? Is there something wrong with me? Should I not have done this?"

> O Jesus, blessed brother mine,
> I walk the path that you outline,
> a great example to us all,
> I follow now your inner call.
>
> **O Jesus, let the Fire of Joy,**
> **consume the devil's subtle ploy,**
> **transfigured is our planet earth,**
> **the golden age is given birth.**

2. Jesus, help me come to the point where I accept free will. I make the conscious shift that I accept free will. I accept that I have a right to be who I am. I accept that other people have a right to react to that according to their level of consciousness. I have a right to continue to be who I am, regardless of their reaction, because their reaction is a result of their own choices.

> O Jesus, open inner sight,
> the ego wants to prove it's right,
> but this I will no longer do,
> I want to be all one with you.
>
> **O Jesus, let the Fire of Joy,**
> **consume the devil's subtle ploy,**
> **transfigured is our planet earth,**
> **the golden age is given birth.**

16 | Invoking the vision of my personal Christhood

3. Jesus, help me see that other people made certain choices that brought them to their present level of awareness. Their reaction to me is a result of their choices. I have no authority over their free will, and therefore I have no responsibility for their choices or the consequences.

> O Jesus, I now clearly see,
> the Key of Knowledge given me,
> my Christ self I hereby embrace,
> as you fill up my inner space.
>
> **O Jesus, let the Fire of Joy,
> consume the devil's subtle ploy,
> transfigured is our planet earth,
> the golden age is given birth.**

4. Jesus, help me see if I came here as an avatar because I felt compassion for the people who were suffering. Help me see that as an avatar I was not in the ascended state of consciousness when I decided to come to earth. I had something unresolved because I had not learned the absoluteness of free will.

> O Jesus, show me serpent's lie,
> expose the beam in my own eye,
> as Christ discernment you me give,
> in oneness I forever live.
>
> **O Jesus, let the Fire of Joy,
> consume the devil's subtle ploy,
> transfigured is our planet earth,
> the golden age is given birth.**

5. Jesus, help me see that when I looked down on earth and saw that people were suffering, I could only reason that something had gone wrong because they had made the wrong choices. It was my self-appointed task to go down and help them make better choices, to do something about other people's choices.

> O Jesus, I am truly meek,
> and thus I turn the other cheek,

when the accuser attacks me,
I go within and merge with thee.

**O Jesus, let the Fire of Joy,
consume the devil's subtle ploy,
transfigured is our planet earth,
the golden age is given birth.**

6. Jesus, help me fully accept that according to the Law of Free Will, this is *not* my task. Help me see the fundamental difference between having the mindset that I need to do something to change other people, and having the mindset that I am here to show them that there is an alternative to their current state of consciousness.

O Jesus, ego I let die,
surrender ev'ry earthly tie,
the dead can bury what is dead,
I choose to walk with you instead.

**O Jesus, let the Fire of Joy,
consume the devil's subtle ploy,
transfigured is our planet earth,
the golden age is given birth.**

7. Jesus, I am asking for your inner direction so I can come to the point where I make the revolutionary shift of realizing how fundamental that difference is.

O Jesus, help me rise above,
the devil's test through higher love,
show me separate self unreal,
my formless self you do reveal.

**O Jesus, let the Fire of Joy,
consume the devil's subtle ploy,
transfigured is our planet earth,
the golden age is given birth.**

8. Jesus, I am willing to admit that I was wrong. It is not that I was wrong for coming to earth. I admit that the attitude that brought me to earth needs to go. It was unbalanced. It was imperfect. It was not the ultimate. It was not the Christ consciousness. I am willing to admit this because until I admit this as an avatar, I cannot get out of here.

> O Jesus, what is that to me,
> I just let go and follow thee,
> with this I do pass ev'ry test,
> to find with you eternal rest.
>
> **O Jesus, let the Fire of Joy,**
> **consume the devil's subtle ploy,**
> **transfigured is our planet earth,**
> **the golden age is given birth.**

9. Jesus, help me see that as long as I think that my reason for coming to earth was to change somebody else, I cannot let go of this planet. There will be some other task I have to do, some problem I have to solve, some epic struggle I have to fulfill and it can go on indefinitely.

> O Jesus, fiery master mine,
> my heart now melting into thine,
> I love with heart and mind and soul,
> the God who is my highest goal.
>
> **O Jesus, let the Fire of Joy,**
> **consume the devil's subtle ploy,**
> **transfigured is our planet earth,**
> **the golden age is given birth.**

Part 6

1. Jesus, help me see if it is in my Divine plan that I ascend after this lifetime. Help me see that for me to ascend, I will have to come to the point where I can look at earth, survey my being and say: "Is there anything on earth that I cannot leave behind?"

O Jesus, blessed brother mine,
I walk the path that you outline,
a great example to us all,
I follow now your inner call.

**O Jesus, let the Fire of Joy,
consume the devil's subtle ploy,
transfigured is our planet earth,
the golden age is given birth.**

2. Jesus, help me see that only when I realize that there is nothing in my being that is pulling on me to stay on earth, can I turn around and make that choice: "I am leaving this planet for good. I am giving up the possibility of influencing this planet that I can only have by being in physical embodiment. I am giving it up! I am selecting it out!"

O Jesus, open inner sight,
the ego wants to prove it's right,
but this I will no longer do,
I want to be all one with you.

**O Jesus, let the Fire of Joy,
consume the devil's subtle ploy,
transfigured is our planet earth,
the golden age is given birth.**

3. Jesus, help me see that ascending is a choice and it must be a fully conscious choice. There cannot be anything in my being I have not looked at, because then the prince of this world has something in me and he will pull me back.

O Jesus, I now clearly see,
the Key of Knowledge given me,
my Christ self I hereby embrace,
as you fill up my inner space.

**O Jesus, let the Fire of Joy,
consume the devil's subtle ploy,
transfigured is our planet earth,
the golden age is given birth.**

4. Jesus, help me see if it is *not* in my Divine plan that I ascend after this lifetime, because I want to take succeeding embodiments in order to help manifest Saint Germain's Golden Age or even experience Saint Germain's Golden Age.

O Jesus, show me serpent's lie,
expose the beam in my own eye,
as Christ discernment you me give,
in oneness I forever live.

**O Jesus, let the Fire of Joy,
consume the devil's subtle ploy,
transfigured is our planet earth,
the golden age is given birth.**

5. Jesus, help me see if I, because of the intensity and the pain involved with the birth trauma, have a desire to get out of here because I think I will get away from my birth trauma. Help me accept that I do not ascend until I have looked at and confronted my birth trauma.

O Jesus, I am truly meek,
and thus I turn the other cheek,
when the accuser attacks me,
I go within and merge with thee.

**O Jesus, let the Fire of Joy,
consume the devil's subtle ploy,
transfigured is our planet earth,
the golden age is given birth.**

6. Jesus, help me see that what will enable me to be a part of bringing forth Saint Germain's Golden Age is that I resolve my birth trauma. Once I resolve the trauma, I can actually enjoy being in embodiment on earth.

O Jesus, ego I let die,
surrender ev'ry earthly tie,
the dead can bury what is dead,
I choose to walk with you instead.

**O Jesus, let the Fire of Joy,
consume the devil's subtle ploy,
transfigured is our planet earth,
the golden age is given birth.**

7. Jesus, help me see that even if I have qualified for my ascension, I have an absolute right to make the determination: "I want to stay in embodiment and help bring about Saint Germain's Golden Age."

O Jesus, help me rise above,
the devil's test through higher love,
show me separate self unreal,
my formless self you do reveal.

**O Jesus, let the Fire of Joy,
consume the devil's subtle ploy,
transfigured is our planet earth,
the golden age is given birth.**

8. Jesus, help me avoid fixating my mind on thinking: "I have to ascend after this lifetime." There is nothing I *have* to do. I can serve life, serve the earth, serve Saint Germain by remaining in embodiment, when I have resolved the birth trauma and I am able to be an open door.

O Jesus, what is that to me,
I just let go and follow thee,
with this I do pass ev'ry test,
to find with you eternal rest.

**O Jesus, let the Fire of Joy,
consume the devil's subtle ploy,
transfigured is our planet earth,
the golden age is given birth.**

16 | Invoking the vision of my personal Christhood

9. Jesus, help me accept that free will is absolute and therefore in the realm of free will, there can be no absolutes that I *should* or I *should not*. Help me overcome the sense that there is something forced upon me, so I can fulfill the highest potential of my Divine plan.

> O Jesus, fiery master mine,
> my heart now melting into thine,
> I love with heart and mind and soul,
> the God who is my highest goal.
>
> **O Jesus, let the Fire of Joy,**
> **consume the devil's subtle ploy,**
> **transfigured is our planet earth,**
> **the golden age is given birth.**

Part 7

1. Jesus, help me see if I have a separate self that has heard about the concept of a Divine plan, but still feels that this was forced upon me, maybe even that I myself forced my Divine plan upon myself.

> O Jesus, blessed brother mine,
> I walk the path that you outline,
> a great example to us all,
> I follow now your inner call.
>
> **O Jesus, let the Fire of Joy,**
> **consume the devil's subtle ploy,**
> **transfigured is our planet earth,**
> **the golden age is given birth.**

2. Jesus, help me identify if I have that tendency and then look at it and say: "I no longer need this self. I am letting you die."

> O Jesus, open inner sight,
> the ego wants to prove it's right,

but this I will no longer do,
I want to be all one with you.

O Jesus, let the Fire of Joy,
consume the devil's subtle ploy,
transfigured is our planet earth,
the golden age is given birth.

3. Jesus, help me overcome the sense that I made choices before I came into embodiment, and now that I am here and see how difficult it is, I am not sure I can live up to those choices.

O Jesus, I now clearly see,
the Key of Knowledge given me,
my Christ self I hereby embrace,
as you fill up my inner space.

O Jesus, let the Fire of Joy,
consume the devil's subtle ploy,
transfigured is our planet earth,
the golden age is given birth.

4. Jesus, help me see if I am not sure I am *willing* to fulfill those choices because there is a certain conflict in me. Help me see if I am a house divided against myself concerning my Divine plan.

O Jesus, show me serpent's lie,
expose the beam in my own eye,
as Christ discernment you me give,
in oneness I forever live.

O Jesus, let the Fire of Joy,
consume the devil's subtle ploy,
transfigured is our planet earth,
the golden age is given birth.

5. Jesus, help me see if there is a division in me between what is in my Divine plan that I myself chose to put in there, and then a separate self that has a different will.

O Jesus, I am truly meek,
and thus I turn the other cheek,
when the accuser attacks me,
I go within and merge with thee.

**O Jesus, let the Fire of Joy,
consume the devil's subtle ploy,
transfigured is our planet earth,
the golden age is given birth.**

6. Jesus, help me have a revolutionary shift of looking at this and saying: "Okay, I'm willing to take a look at this, I'm willing to go into it, I'm willing to experience what is the belief behind it."

O Jesus, ego I let die,
surrender ev'ry earthly tie,
the dead can bury what is dead,
I choose to walk with you instead.

**O Jesus, let the Fire of Joy,
consume the devil's subtle ploy,
transfigured is our planet earth,
the golden age is given birth.**

7. Jesus, help me see the unreality of the reason and say: "No, that isn't actually my choice. It might be the choice of the separate self. I see that it was because of whatever created the separate self, but I now choose to let it die. I choose to then embrace what I actually put in my Divine plan, because I am willing to rise to the level of consciousness from which I put those elements in my Divine plan."

O Jesus, help me rise above,
the devil's test through higher love,
show me separate self unreal,
my formless self you do reveal.

**O Jesus, let the Fire of Joy,
consume the devil's subtle ploy,
transfigured is our planet earth,
the golden age is given birth.**

8. Jesus, help me accept that I have the potential to step up higher, overcome this division in myself and fully embrace my Divine plan.

O Jesus, what is that to me,
I just let go and follow thee,
with this I do pass ev'ry test,
to find with you eternal rest.

**O Jesus, let the Fire of Joy,
consume the devil's subtle ploy,
transfigured is our planet earth,
the golden age is given birth.**

9. Jesus, help me accept that you want me to manifest a higher level of Christhood than you manifested 2,000 years ago. You want me to do greater works than you did. It will be your supreme joy to see many people manifest a higher level of Christhood than you could manifest 2,000 years ago, by expressing our Christhood in a somewhat "normal" lifestyle.

O Jesus, fiery master mine,
my heart now melting into thine,
I love with heart and mind and soul,
the God who is my highest goal.

**O Jesus, let the Fire of Joy,
consume the devil's subtle ploy,
transfigured is our planet earth,
the golden age is given birth.**

Sealing

In the name of the Divine Mother, I call to Mother Mary for the sealing of myself and all people in my circle of influence in the creative flow of the Divine Mother, the River of Life. I call for the multiplication of my calls by all representatives of the Divine Mother, so that we form the perfect figure-eight flow of "As Above, so below." Thus, I accept that this is fully manifest, because the mouth of the Lord, the Divine Mother that I AM, has spoken it. Amen.

17 | THE OMEGA PERSPECTIVE ON JUDGMENT

I AM the Ascended Master Mother Mary. My beloved, when you experience a discourse like the one you have just experienced from Jesus, I am reminded of when I was in embodiment with Jesus and would sometimes sit there almost in a state of awe when I heard him speak. It was said in the Bible that no man spoke as this man and certainly Jesus has a way with words that is very unique and very beautiful. Even as an ascended master, I can certainly experience, of course, a dictation. I experience it in a different way because I experience both the ascended being who is speaking as he is in the ascended realm but I also experience what is coming through the messenger.

When you consider the difficulty, the distance in vibration, the distance in the level of consciousness, when you consider how dense the earth is, then you see the difficulty of bringing the Being of an ascended master through words spoken in this realm. You must admire the ability of Jesus to bring forth so much of his Being in this dense realm. Yet you must almost be in awe of the whole process of how this is even possible to communicate from the ascended realm through an unascended messenger.

Sometimes we know that our students can come to take this for granted and feel that: "Oh well, it seems so easy—the messenger just gets up there and closes his eyes and then it starts flowing." When you consider the density of this realm, it truly is a unique process that you should not become comfortable with, to the point where you take it for granted.

The omega side of judgment

What I wish to do today is to bring you, sort of the omega perspective on Jesus' discourse. Every time we talk about bringing the judgment of Christ and challenging the fallen beings, there is always a certain percentage of you who have a reaction to this. It is not that I am in any way condemning you for having this reaction. I am going to point out to you that there are two aspects of why you have a reaction, why you might feel hesitant, why you might feel this is not for you: "Does this really apply to me? What should I do? I don't see myself as an outgoing person" and many other thoughts you might have.

Well, my beloved, as Jesus said, the primary weapon of the fallen beings is doubt and many of you, of course, have this doubt. In fact, all of you who have not resolved your birth trauma will have doubt, the doubt of the fallen beings. There is part of the reaction you can have that is simply based on this. You have not resolved your primal self, therefore you feel this hesitation. I can assure you that when you resolve the primal self, you will no longer feel that hesitation, at least when you make the shift that Jesus talked about.

Nevertheless, what I want to get to is that, as Jesus said, it is not for all of you, in your Divine plan to ascend after this lifetime. Likewise, it is not for all of you that it is in your Divine plan to go out and challenge the fallen beings in some overt way. What Jesus was talking about was the alpha aspect of challenging the fallen beings where you speak out about their ideas and perhaps you are even willing to confront them on the personal level and let them attack you so they can receive that judgment of Christ. For others of you, this is not in your Divine plan, this is not how you specified expressing Christhood in your Divine plan. Of course, Christhood as everything else has an alpha and an omega side.

What is the omega way of challenging the fallen beings and bringing the judgment of Christ on the fallen beings? Well my beloved, it is to love them. This may be on a personal level where you have chosen to be in a relationship, whether it be family or another relationship, with fallen beings. You have chosen to closely associate yourself with certain fallen beings. If you tune in and see what is in your Divine plan, you may realize that it would actually be a misunderstanding for you to decide with your outer mind, based on the teachings that have been given, that: "Now I need to challenge these people." If you have a dominant personality in your sphere of acquaintances, you decide: "I need to challenge that person." Or if you get a sense that a certain person might be a fallen being, you think you need to challenge them.

I am asking you to tune in and not to start challenging anybody until you know what is in your Divine plan, until you feel that this comes from within. It is not that you need to have a visual impression of your Divine plan and then you go out and challenge the fallen beings. You go on your intuition. If you feel intuitively prompted to challenge someone, you do, but you do not decide with your outer mind that you should challenge them.

Especially those of you who feel hesitant, I am asking you to first of all work on your birth trauma. Even when you overcome the birth trauma, I am asking you to tune in and see: "Is it actually my choice to go out and challenge people? Or was it my choice to love people instead?" Then, you need to recognize that in order to fulfill your highest desire and potential for your Divine plan, we are not talking about loving the fallen beings in a human way. We are talking about loving them in what we have called an unconditional way and I would like to talk about the difference.

Human love and unconditional love

You see, my beloved, an unconditional way, an unconditional love, can only be brought forth when you have resolved your birth trauma—when you are an avatar. If you are not an avatar but one of the original inhabitants of the earth, you need to rise to a high level of Christhood before you can express unconditional love because conditional love is, of course, based on unresolved psychology. It is often what we have called possessive love where you think you love somebody but you are doing it because you think that person can give you something that either completes yourself or obscures your wound so you do not feel it. That is why, when people are in love, they are in a state of euphoria, they do not feel their wounds, they are on cloud nine and everything is wonderful.

It is simply because they are not seeing the wound right now, they are not dealing with it. Then, when the honeymoon is over, now they start feeling their wounds again. Then, they project: "Oh, this person wasn't the true love that I'm longing for, so I need to look for somebody else." This can, of course, go on over and over and over again.

As long as you have these wounds, and especially the birth trauma, you will not be able to be the open door for unconditional love. You can take the situation described in the *My Lives* book with the judgment of Lucifer where the protagonist expresses unconditional love for Lucifer—and that is Lucifer's final opportunity: Will he respond to someone he has known in physical embodiment expressing that unconditional love? If the fallen being does not respond to unconditional love, then that is the judgment of that fallen being, the judgment of Christ.

There may be some of you who feel that this is what you are meant to do. You have a certain person in your sphere of influence and you feel you should not challenge them. It is not your role to change them, it is simply your role to show them a different way, a different state of consciousness and therefore to ultimately come to a point where you can express unconditional love. Perhaps these are not necessarily fallen beings, perhaps they are human beings, they may be original inhabitants of the earth, they may even be other avatars, who can be transformed when they experience a different form of love than they have experienced here on earth.

This is certainly one way to demonstrate that there is a different state of consciousness. In other words, it is perfectly correct in the alpha aspect of Christhood to express certain viewpoints and ideas and to even challenge other ideas and explain why they are dualistic and why they are not the highest possible. The omega aspect is to demonstrate a different state of consciousness, through unconditional love, through loving other people. Of course, this applies to your family members as well, whether they are fallen beings or not. I am not, of course, telling you to go around looking at every person you meet and trying to judge with the outer mind: "Is this a fallen being or not?" Then, you can create all these criteria in your mind that when people behave such and such, they must be fallen beings.

My beloved, we have seen in previous ascended master dispensations where an entire organization with thousands of members could develop a very judgmental culture. In some cases, people where convinced that these other people are fallen beings and we have seen how this can develop into almost like a competition sport where people compete about being able to expose who is a fallen being and who is not. They go around accusing other people, and they basically think that anybody who disagrees with them must be a fallen being. This is, of course, not a balanced state to be in and this is not what we are encouraging.

Neither are we encouraging you to go into what is found in the world that is called sympathy for the devil, where you think that you have to love everybody. Jesus spoke about the people in the New Age community who will not acknowledge anything evil but there are other people who may acknowledge that there is evil in the world but they think the way to overcome it is through love. It is true, the way to overcome evil is through love but it has to be *unconditional* love. Otherwise, if it is *possessive* love, then they will simply use that love to pull you into a reactionary pattern.

Relationships with fallen beings

There are indeed some of you who will need to see that in order to step up to the highest potential of your Divine plan, you need to recognize that you have been in relationships with a certain fallen being for many lifetimes. You will need to come to that point where you identify this and then you need to look at what are the wounds, what are the mechanisms, that have tied you to this fallen being. You need to look at what are the beliefs behind it, and ultimately you will come to the realization that at some level of your being, you thought that you could change that fallen being by being in a relationship, by loving them—you could change them.

That is when you need to step up and internalize what Jesus said about the absoluteness of free will. You are not here to change anyone else, fallen being or not. You could say, you are *especially* not here to change the fallen beings. The original inhabitants of the earth, if you attempt to change them, in many cases they will ignore you. Fallen beings will not ignore you if you attempt to change them, they will use you, they will use your desire to change them, to tie you to them and to, at the very least, extract your energy, steal your energy. In other cases, they will actually manipulate you or even seek to destroy you through your desire to reform a fallen being.

You really have, as an avatar, to come to a point where you recognize if you have been in this pattern, if you have a desire to change the fallen beings. Then, you have to completely let that go, you have to let that self die. You cannot manifest Christhood if you are in this state, which is basically a reactionary pattern to the fallen beings. The desire to reform the fallen beings will always spring from your birth trauma where you were exposed to them for the first time. You were shocked, and then you somehow created this, in many cases, very long step-by-step reasoning process that led you to conclude that what the fallen being have done to you, demonstrated what they have done to the planet. The best way that you could help change the planet was to select a specific fallen being, go into a close relationship with that fallen being and try to reform them.

This, then, becomes part of your primal self. There can be many other things as part of the primal self where you think you have to bring about certain changes on earth. One of them is the desire to change a fallen being. You cannot truly resolve your primal self until you first look at this desire to change a fallen being and let go of it. You give it up because you recognize the absoluteness of free will, you recognize that is not why you are here.

The desire to change a fallen being is not the core of your primal self. The core of your primal self is your reaction to the trauma or the violence you were exposed to or the deception (whatever it may be). In response to that trauma, you created the self that wants to reform a fallen being. You could say it is an aspect of your primal self but it was not how your primal self started. That is why, in order to get down to the core of your primal self, you have to first let go of this desire to reform a fallen being.

Can fallen beings be reformed?

This, of course, brings up the topic: "Can fallen beings be reformed?" I will ask you to consider a more specific question: "Could *I* ever reform a fallen being?" The answer to that is: "No, absolutely not." There is nothing that *you* could do or say that would reform a fallen being. For that matter, there is nothing you could do or say that would change any other human being. Why is this? Because of free will. Now, does this mean you are powerless, that it is pointless of you to be here? No!

What does it take for another human being to change, what would it take for a fallen being to be changed, then go on an upward path? They have to make a choice. You cannot force other people's choices. You can force their behavior and this is what the fallen beings have been attempting to do. They have also been attempting to manipulate and deceive you into making various choices

Ultimately, you have no power to force another person's choice. You can, as the fallen beings do, take advantage of that person's psychology and thereby push their choices. You understand what I am saying: Even if you push other peoples choices, this is not going to reform them, it is not going to reform a fallen being, it is not going to change the other people in a positive direction where they grow.

You can change them in a negative direction by forcing their choices but you cannot *force* a positive choice. It must come from within that lifestream, and in many cases it only comes when they have had enough of certain experiences. Of course, what you *can* do is you can inspire them to make a higher choice by showing them that there is an alternative to their state of consciousness, there is a higher way. By inspiring them, by demonstrating to them, you may cause them to make another choice. It is not you that is reaching into their minds and creating a change, it is them voluntarily making a different choice.

Of course, if they had not seen you demonstrate this higher state of consciousness (as Jesus has said: If he had not demonstrated that you can walk the earth in the Christ Consciousness), they would not have had the option. *That* is what you can do. You can give them the option but you cannot force their choice Of course, you can do what the fallen beings are doing and try to force peoples choices in a downward direction but, my beloved, that surely is not why you are here as an avatar. Look at the mess that is existing on earth and what is the cause of it? It is that the fallen beings have forced people to make choices that put them in a downward spiral. As I am saying, you cannot force somebody to make choices that will put them in an upward spiral. You need, as an avatar, to completely let go of this desire to reform or change any other person. Only *then*, can you be the open door for unconditional love.

You cannot have unconditional love

Why am I saying that you cannot *have* human love but you can *be the open door* for unconditional love? Well, because human love is possessive and that means you can possess it, you can own it. There are people in the world, even many who think they are spiritual and New Age people, who think they are very loving people. They are loving in a human way where they are subconsciously using that love to get something from people.

In some cases, they are not having an evil intent, they are not actually manipulating other people in a direct manner. They have this personal inner desire to be seen as very loving. When they express love towards other people, it is so that they can get these other people to validate their inner desire to be seen as loving. "Oh, you're such a loving person," and then they feel validated, the ego feels validated.

You cannot own unconditional love, you cannot own non-possessive love but you can open yourself to it as you can open yourself to Christhood. What is unconditional love? Well, it is the omega aspect of the Christ consciousness. You cannot own the Christ consciousness, you cannot force the Christ consciousness. You cannot, with the outer mind (the dualistic mind, the analytical mind) *force*. You can pretend to be the Christ, but it does not make you the Christ. You can try to create phenomena that seem to show you have great power of mind over matter, as even the book describes Lucifer was able to do. This is not Christhood. You can have human love and you can make people think that you are so loving, but this is not Christ love. Christ love, as we have said: The Holy Spirit bloweth where it listeth, but it flows wherever there is an opening. There has to be an opening and if you have a desire to change other people, there will not be an opening in your being through which unconditional love can flow.

It is very, very possible that if you express unconditional love towards a fallen being, they will reject it. They will feel disturbed by it, they might even accuse you or they might withdraw from you and want to have nothing to do with you. This you need to accept. We have talked about the revolutionary shifts. We have said that there can come a point where you have resolved your psychology, you have resolved your primal self and your birth trauma, you have consumed the energy, you have let the self die but there is another separate self that still can have a certain attachment.

For example, you feel that if you are the open door for unconditional love, then you should not be rejected, people should not reject you. There are actually people who have come to the point, to the level of Christhood, where they could be the open door for expressing unconditional love towards another person. Then, that love was rejected and the person, because they had that separate self, could sometimes go into a downward spiral of being so disturbed that this love was rejected that it actually took them down in consciousness. They might even have decided never again to express unconditional love.

You need to recognize that even when you are able to be the open door for unconditional love, there can still be that separate self that has some kind of image of what should happen when you express unconditional love. You can, for that matter, also have a self that has some kind of image of what should happen when you speak your truth and challenge the fallen beings or when you express your higher being.

Avoiding feeling rejected

You see my beloved, again, Christhood (being the Living Christ, expressing Christhood) does not mean you are completely perfect, that you have resolved every aspect of your psychology, that you are at the 144th level. You can, even when you go beyond the 48th level, have glimpses where you express Christhood or even a certain higher form of love. When you go beyond the 96th level, you can have glimpses (and more and more frequent glimpses, even longer periods) where you are in the Christ consciousness. You are expressing unconditional love but you still, of course, have to get up to the 144th level. This means that there are still illusions you have not overcome, and some of these illusions can be related to you thinking that other people should respond in a pure manner when you are approaching them in a pure manner.

You see my beloved, avatars have come from natural planets. On a natural planet you are used to that when you do something for others with pure intentions, they will not turn around and accuse you of being a bad person. When you do something for a fallen being, or even human beings on earth, they may indeed reject you in a very aggressive, nasty, very unkind, accusatory manner. Even when you come to that point where you can express Christhood, whether the alpha or omega aspect, you still need to be aware that there can be a self, or an illusion, you have not let go of that causes you to feel rejected or go into other negative reactions when other people do not respond the way you expect them to respond.

In these cases, you then need to be willing to look at yourself and take this as an opportunity to overcome another illusion, to let another separate self go, so you can rise to the next level up where you can express more unconditional love and be more non-attached to how people receive it. Ultimately, in order to express the fullness of unconditional love, you need to be completely non-attached to how other people respond to it because you are not doing it with any intention. The rose that grows in the garden has no intention of pulling people who walk by into sticking their nose into the flower. It does not feel rejected when they rush by, tapping on their smart phones because they have to absolutely answer that latest SMS!

It can be painful to express Christhood

This is the higher levels of Christhood. I understand that it is not the lower levels of Christhood. You do not need to blame yourself for having this reaction. We do not in any way want to discourage you from expressing Christhood. Again, you do not have to be perfect to express Christhood. At the lower levels you will have situations, you will have moments, where you are the open door and there is something flowing through you, whether a higher idea, whether unconditional love. Then, suddenly, the spell is broken, so to speak. Now, you are out of it, back to your normal level of consciousness and that means that you are now using your normal level of consciousness to react to the consequences of you expressing Christhood. In other words, you react to other people's reactions, not at the level of Christhood that you just expressed but with your normal level of consciousness.

My beloved, this is inevitable, this is part of the path to Christhood. You may think that this did not happen to Jesus but of course it happened to Jesus. He also had a period where he was very hesitant about expressing his Christhood, where he was very sensitive about people's reactions to it. You see, my beloved, we have all gone through this phase and we have no desire whatsoever to discourage you. What we want you to realize is that it is inevitable. You have to go through this interim phase where you switch in and out of Christhood and where you, therefore, inevitably will react with your normal level of consciousness to the consequences of expressing your Christhood.

This means that it can be painful and it can be difficult. You can even feel you have done something wrong. You were too strong, you were too forceful or you were too loving and too kind or whatever. You need to learn to see through this and see that this reaction in you is an opportunity for you to step up to the next level of consciousness, to overcome the illusion associated with your present level and to step up to a higher level where you can express more Christhood. As you become consciously aware of this process, you can quickly make that shift where now you no longer blame yourself, you are not coming down on yourself, you are not feeling you are imperfect. You just realize the absolute truth that we have actually been trying to tell you in the path to self-mastery books.

Reacting at your level of consciousness

Nada made great efforts to help you see in the sixth book [*The Mystical Initiations of Peace*] that there comes the point on the path where you recognize that you are not at the highest level of consciousness. You will recognize that you are at the 87th level, not the 144th level. You are not required to be able to deal with life on earth the way you can at the 144th level. It is perfectly all right, perfectly acceptable to us as ascended masters, that you react to life at the 87th level—or whatever level you are at.

We are never demanding or expecting that should react with a higher level. We are never blaming you for not reacting with a higher level. I realize there have been previous ascended master teachings and organizations where they have created a culture where people were blamed for not been perfect. Again, we had to start somewhere.

What you have the potential to step up to is to actually, in a sense, make peace with yourself as you are right now. This does not mean that you stop your growth and that you go into this state and thinking: "Ah Nah, I'm ego-free now, I'm perfect, I don't need to grow, I don't need to look at myself." You can make peace with being at the level of consciousness you are at instead of blaming yourself or instead of feeling that you are behind and you should really be at the higher level.

We do not want you to live the rest of your time in embodiment always feeling behind, always feeling that you are not good enough. You *are* good enough at the level of consciousness you are at and there is no reason to blame yourself for reacting at that level of consciousness, even reacting to when you have expressed Christhood and what other people do with it.

Your reaction, when you are willing to look at it, is the opportunity to see the illusion of your present level and rise to the next level. It has always been that way and it always *will* be that way. This was the same 2,000 years ago when Jesus came closer to the 144th level. It is the same for every one of us who has been in embodiment, and it will not change as long as the earth is not a natural planet. Of course, there can be a shift where what is now the lowest level of consciousness is no longer allowed on earth.

There is nothing wrong with matter

The basic mechanics of the path is that you are at a certain level. Your reaction is the way it is. By looking at it, you can see the illusion at that level so you can rise to the next level. This is the basic mechanics of the spiritual path. It may not seem as glamorous as some people want to make out the path to be, but I trust that many of you are at the point where you are saying: "I've had enough of the illusions, I've had enough of the delusions of grandeur, I just wanna know how the path works so I can make the fastest progress and I can get above these unbalanced, negative, self-blaming reactions and be at peace with being here."

My beloved, how do you ultimately be at peace with being here? Well, you need to resolve the birth trauma because that is what took you out of the peace you had when you came as an avatar. As part of this process, even when you have resolved the birth trauma, there will still be a separate self that you need to look at. It can be individual for each one, but it is the separate self you created in reaction to the material realm, the matter realm, the mother realm, as it is on earth. You realize that as an avatar, you came from a natural planet where matter was not as dense. This means many things but one of the things it means is that there were not the kind of consequences you see on earth. Mind was much more powerful in terms of changing matter. Matter was more responsive to mind on a natural planet.

You are used to that you could do something that you might call a mistake. It created a physical consequence but when you were willing to step back and change your consciousness, you could undo that physical consequence. When you came down here on earth and recognized that you could make a choice here on earth and it would create a physical consequence that you could not overcome for the rest of that lifetime (and it might even follow you in other lifetimes), you were shocked at this. You were shocked at how dense matter was.

Now, take care of noticing that this had nothing to do with the fallen beings as such and the birth trauma they exposed you to. It was simply your reaction to the fact that matter is so dense on earth that you can create consequences that you cannot easily undo and it might linger for a long time. This created a separate self in reaction to this where you often went into a negative reaction to the mother realm. You often felt that you could not be comfortable, you could not be at peace, in the mother realm and that there was something wrong with the mother realm, that the mother realm should not be this way.

You need to come to that revolutionary shift where you are willing to look at that and actually come to accept that planet earth is a teaching device for a certain range of consciousness. Therefore, in order to give people the lessons they need to have, matter needs to be as dense as it is.

Matter needs to be as unresponsive to mind as it is, or the vast majority of people on earth would not learn their lessons.

Now you, as an avatar, are not having to learn the same lessons that most other people on earth have to learn. Therefore, you can overcome this, but you can only overcome it if you are willing to look at it. If you are willing to come to the point of accepting that there is nothing wrong with matter.

Your reaction to matter

It was your reaction to matter that caused you to think there was something wrong with matter. It is *your* responsibility to resolve that separate self. Only when you do, will you be free to actually embrace being in physical embodiment.

In order to rise above a certain level of Christhood, you have to be at peace with being in physical embodiment. This was much more difficult to do at Jesus' time and that is why even he could not do it fully. In today's age, you have that potential. Those of you who want to stay in embodiment in order to bring in Saint Germain's Golden Age, it is very important for you to come to this point where you overcome the desire to get out of here. You overcome the sense that there is something wrong with matter for being the way it is. You accept being here, you accept matter for what it is.

Of course, how can you accept matter the way it is unless you can accept yourself fully and how can you accept yourself fully unless you overcome the birth trauma? You see how this all ties together. You see why we did not give these teachings about your Divine plan before we had given the teachings on the birth trauma. When you are an avatar, everything, my beloved, revolves around the birth trauma. It is, as they say, the three-hundred-pound gorilla in the room that nobody wants to talk about. Only, of course, your primal self is neither a gorilla nor does it weigh three hundred pounds. It is just this almost unreal self that is not nearly as difficult to resolve as you might think. It is just a matter of using the tools, using the exercise I gave to go down, go through the gardens, go into the theatre and just see it [This exercise is in the book *Healing Your Spiritual Traumas*].

Once you shift out of the primal self, you will be amazed at how seemingly effortless it was. Of course, we understand that you cannot force this with the outer mind. You cannot use the primal self to switch out of the primal self.

Keep using the tools

The way you look at everything on earth, the way you look at a teaching, is through the filter of the primal self. That is why we have given you teachings that are meant to trick your outer mind. That is why we have given you exercises that can gradually take you to that point where, now you can make that shift, now it happens spontaneously. You have to be willing to apply the tools, to go through the process. You have to be willing to open your mind to see something you have not seen before, even to see the primal self. You have to be aware that as the Conscious You, you can separate yourself from the primal self and that is the only way you can look at it from the outside. It is the only way you can see it. You have the tools.

Again, my beloved, do not get into this reaction of saying: "Oh, Mother Mary said we have all the tools, but I still can't see this primal self. What am I doing wrong?" This is the primal self talking. Again, keep using the tools. My beloved, if you have had your primal self for two million years, you do not have to blame yourself if you cannot resolve it in one week after getting the teaching. It may take time but it does not matter so much how long it takes, as long as it happens. As long as it happens in this lifetime, then you will have broken through and you will have fulfilled the highest potential for your Divine plan as an avatar.

With this, my beloved, I want to express my gratitude and the gratitude of all of us for having come to this conference. This does not mean I seal the conference, I leave that to the Buddha, but I want to express the gratitude of the mother for your willingness, not only to come to the conference but also your willingness to apply the teachings we have given in these books about the primal self and so on.

Surely, if there had not been a critical mass of students (both those who are here and those who are not here) who had applied these teachings, we would not have been able to bring forth what we have given here. I trust you recognize that this is a step up. It certainly is a step up from all other teachings you find out there about the concept of a Divine plan. It will empower many people to actually break through to that higher level and therefore begin to fulfill their highest potential. We are grateful that we have been able to bring forth these tools. We, of course, have always been able to bring them forth but you are beginning to realize – are you not – that we cannot just give everything we have. It must be an interactive process where only when people accept a teaching and apply it, can we give the higher teaching.

To those who have, more shall be given. That is the principle behind multiplying the talents. We are grateful that you have multiplied the talents so we can multiply your efforts and bring forth more. It is a beautiful dance, is it not?

18 | INVOKING PEACE WITH BEING HERE

In the name I AM THAT I AM, Jesus Christ, I call to all representatives of the Divine Mother, especially Mother Mary, to help me overcome everything in my psychology that prevents me from feeling at peace with being here, including…

[Make personal calls.]

Part 1

1. Mother Mary, help me see if hearing about bringing the judgment of Christ and challenging the fallen beings, triggers a resistance in me.

> O Blessed Mary's Song of Life,
> consuming every form of strife.
> As I attune to sound so fair,
> each cell is healthy, I declare.

**O Mother Mary, generate,
the song that does accelerate,
my mind into a peaceful state,
God's perfect love I radiate.**

2. Mother Mary, help me see if this reaction is based on the doubt that is the primary weapon of the fallen beings. Help me see if I feel hesitation because I have not resolved my primal self.

As life's own song I ever hear,
it does consume all sense of fear.
In tune with Mother's symphony,
from all diseases I AM free.

**O Mother Mary, generate,
the song that does accelerate,
my mind into a peaceful state,
God's perfect love I radiate.**

3. Mother Mary, help me see if it is not in my Divine plan to ascend after this lifetime or to go out and challenge the fallen beings in some overt way.

In Mother's love I do transcend,
and all my struggles hereby end.
For when with Mother's eye I see,
no imperfection touches me.

**O Mother Mary, generate,
the song that does accelerate,
my mind into a peaceful state,
God's perfect love I radiate.**

4. Mother Mary, help me see if it is in my Divine plan to challenge the fallen beings and bring the judgment of Christ in the omega way. Help me see if I have chosen to be in a relationship with fallen beings.

I see that healing must begin
by finding Living Christ within.

For as I see with single eye,
each cell the light does amplify.

**O Mother Mary, generate,
the song that does accelerate,
my mind into a peaceful state,
God's perfect love I radiate.**

5. Mother Mary, help me tune in and not start challenging anybody until I know what is in my Divine plan, until I feel that this comes from within. If I feel intuitively prompted to challenge someone, I will, but I will not decide with my outer mind.

In Mother's music I am free,
from memories of a lesser me.
My vision in a perfect state,
that all my cells regenerate.

**O Mother Mary, generate,
the song that does accelerate,
my mind into a peaceful state,
God's perfect love I radiate.**

6. Mother Mary, I am willing to work on my birth trauma. Help me see if it is my choice to go out and challenge people, or whether I chose to love people instead.

O Mother's Love, sweet melody,
from imperfections I AM free.
O Mother Mary, sound of sounds,
within my heart your love abounds.

**O Mother Mary, generate,
the song that does accelerate,
my mind into a peaceful state,
God's perfect love I radiate.**

7. Mother Mary, help me recognize that in order to fulfill the highest desire and potential for my Divine plan, I cannot love the fallen beings in a human way but in an unconditional way.

Through Mother's beauty so sublime,
transcending bounds of space and time.
All cells beyond the mortal tomb,
as they are whole in Mother's womb.

**O Mother Mary, generate,
the song that does accelerate,
my mind into a peaceful state,
God's perfect love I radiate.**

8. Mother Mary, help me see that unconditional love can only be brought forth when I have resolved my birth trauma, because conditional love is based on unresolved psychology.

In resonance with life's own song,
in life's harmonics I belong.
The blueprint of my perfect state
does every cell reconsecrate.

**O Mother Mary, generate,
the song that does accelerate,
my mind into a peaceful state,
God's perfect love I radiate.**

9. Mother Mary, help me recognize possessive love where I think I love somebody but I am doing it because I think that person can give me something that either completes me or obscures my wound so I do not feel it.

The tuning fork in every cell
is now attuned to Mother's bell.
From curse of death I AM now free,
I claim my immortality.

**O Mother Mary, generate,
the song that does accelerate,
my mind into a peaceful state,
God's perfect love I radiate.**

Part 2

1. Mother Mary, help me see if I have certain persons in my sphere of influence and it is not my role to change them, it is my role to show them a different way by expressing unconditional love.

O Blessed Mary's Song of Life,
consuming every form of strife.
As I attune to sound so fair,
each cell is healthy, I declare.

**O Mother Mary, generate,
the song that does accelerate,
my mind into a peaceful state,
God's perfect love I radiate.**

2. Mother Mary, help me see that the omega aspect of Christhood is to demonstrate a different state of consciousness through unconditional love, through loving other people.

As life's own song I ever hear,
it does consume all sense of fear.
In tune with Mother's symphony,
from all diseases I AM free.

**O Mother Mary, generate,
the song that does accelerate,
my mind into a peaceful state,
God's perfect love I radiate.**

3. Mother Mary, help me avoid looking at every person I meet and trying to create criteria in my mind to judge whether they are fallen beings.

In Mother's love I do transcend,
and all my struggles hereby end.
For when with Mother's eye I see,
no imperfection touches me.

O Mother Mary, generate,
the song that does accelerate,
my mind into a peaceful state,
God's perfect love I radiate.

4. Mother Mary, help me recognize if I have been in relationships with a certain fallen being for lifetimes. Help me identify this and then expose the wounds and mechanisms that have tied me to this fallen being.

I see that healing must begin
by finding Living Christ within.
For as I see with single eye,
each cell the light does amplify.

O Mother Mary, generate,
the song that does accelerate,
my mind into a peaceful state,
God's perfect love I radiate.

5. Mother Mary, help me see the beliefs behind it, and see if, at some level of my being, I thought I could change that fallen being by being in a relationship, by loving them.

In Mother's music I am free,
from memories of a lesser me.
My vision in a perfect state,
that all my cells regenerate.

O Mother Mary, generate,
the song that does accelerate,
my mind into a peaceful state,
God's perfect love I radiate.

6. Mother Mary, help me step up and internalize the absoluteness of free will. I am not here to change anyone else, fallen being or not. I am *especially* not here to change the fallen beings.

> O Mother's Love, sweet melody,
> from imperfections I AM free.
> O Mother Mary, sound of sounds,
> within my heart your love abounds.
>
> **O Mother Mary, generate,**
> **the song that does accelerate,**
> **my mind into a peaceful state,**
> **God's perfect love I radiate.**

7. Mother Mary, help me see that if I attempt to change the fallen beings, they will use my desire to change them to tie me to them and to steal my energy, manipulate me or seek to destroy me.

> Through Mother's beauty so sublime,
> transcending bounds of space and time.
> All cells beyond the mortal tomb,
> as they are whole in Mother's womb.
>
> **O Mother Mary, generate,**
> **the song that does accelerate,**
> **my mind into a peaceful state,**
> **God's perfect love I radiate.**

8. Mother Mary, help me recognize if I have been in this pattern, if I have a desire to change the fallen beings. Help me to completely let that go, let that self die.

> In resonance with life's own song,
> in life's harmonics I belong.
> The blueprint of my perfect state
> does every cell reconsecrate.

> O Mother Mary, generate,
> the song that does accelerate,
> my mind into a peaceful state,
> God's perfect love I radiate.

9. Mother Mary, help me see that I cannot manifest Christhood if I am in a reactionary pattern to the fallen beings. The desire to reform the fallen beings will spring from my birth trauma where I was exposed to them for the first time.

> The tuning fork in every cell
> is now attuned to Mother's bell.
> From curse of death I AM now free,
> I claim my immortality.

> O Mother Mary, generate,
> the song that does accelerate,
> my mind into a peaceful state,
> God's perfect love I radiate.

Part 3

1. Mother Mary, help me see if after my birth trauma I created this reasoning process that led me to conclude, that the best way I could help change the planet was to select a specific fallen being, go into a close relationship with that fallen being and try to reform them.

> O Blessed Mary's Song of Life,
> consuming every form of strife.
> As I attune to sound so fair,
> each cell is healthy, I declare.

> O Mother Mary, generate,
> the song that does accelerate,
> my mind into a peaceful state,
> God's perfect love I radiate.

2. Mother Mary, help me see if part of my primal self is the desire to change a fallen being. Help me see that I cannot truly resolve my primal self until I look at this desire and let go of it. Help me give it up because I recognize that this is not why I am here.

> As life's own song I ever hear,
> it does consume all sense of fear.
> In tune with Mother's symphony,
> from all diseases I AM free.
>
> **O Mother Mary, generate,**
> **the song that does accelerate,**
> **my mind into a peaceful state,**
> **God's perfect love I radiate.**

3. Mother Mary, help me see that the core of my primal self is my reaction to the trauma, violence or deception. Help me see if, in response to that trauma, I created the self that wants to reform a fallen being. Help me let go of this desire to reform a fallen being.

> In Mother's love I do transcend,
> and all my struggles hereby end.
> For when with Mother's eye I see,
> no imperfection touches me.
>
> **O Mother Mary, generate,**
> **the song that does accelerate,**
> **my mind into a peaceful state,**
> **God's perfect love I radiate.**

4. Mother Mary, help me see and accept that I cannot reform a fallen being. There is nothing that *I* could do or say that would reform a fallen being—or any other human being.

> I see that healing must begin
> by finding Living Christ within.
> For as I see with single eye,
> each cell the light does amplify.

> O Mother Mary, generate,
> the song that does accelerate,
> my mind into a peaceful state,
> God's perfect love I radiate.

5. Mother Mary, help me see that this does not mean I am powerless or that it is pointless for me to be here. Although I have no power or desire to force the choices of other people, I do have the power to inspire them to make a higher choice by showing them that there is an alternative to their state of consciousness.

> In Mother's music I am free,
> from memories of a lesser me.
> My vision in a perfect state,
> that all my cells regenerate.

> O Mother Mary, generate,
> the song that does accelerate,
> my mind into a peaceful state,
> God's perfect love I radiate.

6. Mother Mary, help me see that I can give others the option but I cannot force their choice Help me to completely let go of this desire to reform or change any other person, so I can be the open door for unconditional love.

> O Mother's Love, sweet melody,
> from imperfections I AM free.
> O Mother Mary, sound of sounds,
> within my heart your love abounds.

> O Mother Mary, generate,
> the song that does accelerate,
> my mind into a peaceful state,
> God's perfect love I radiate.

7. Mother Mary, help me experience that I cannot own unconditional love, but I can open myself to it as I can open myself to Christhood. Unconditional love is the omega aspect of the Christ consciousness.

Through Mother's beauty so sublime,
transcending bounds of space and time.
All cells beyond the mortal tomb,
as they are whole in Mother's womb.

O Mother Mary, generate,
the song that does accelerate,
my mind into a peaceful state,
God's perfect love I radiate.

8. Mother Mary, help me see that if I have a desire to change other people, there will not be an opening in my being through which unconditional love can flow.

In resonance with life's own song,
in life's harmonics I belong.
The blueprint of my perfect state
does every cell reconsecrate.

O Mother Mary, generate,
the song that does accelerate,
my mind into a peaceful state,
God's perfect love I radiate.

9. Mother Mary, help me see that if I express unconditional love towards a fallen being, they are likely to reject it. Help me see if I have a separate self that has an attachment and feels that if I am the open door for unconditional love, then I should not be rejected.

The tuning fork in every cell
is now attuned to Mother's bell.
From curse of death I AM now free,
I claim my immortality.

O Mother Mary, generate,
the song that does accelerate,
my mind into a peaceful state,
God's perfect love I radiate.

Part 4

1. Mother Mary, help me see if I have expressed unconditional love that was rejected, and the separate self decided never again to express unconditional love.

> O Blessed Mary's Song of Life,
> consuming every form of strife.
> As I attune to sound so fair,
> each cell is healthy, I declare.
>
> **O Mother Mary, generate,**
> **the song that does accelerate,**
> **my mind into a peaceful state,**
> **God's perfect love I radiate.**

2. Mother Mary, help me recognize that even when I am able to be the open door for unconditional love, there can still be a separate self that has some kind of image of what should happen when I express unconditional love.

> As life's own song I ever hear,
> it does consume all sense of fear.
> In tune with Mother's symphony,
> from all diseases I AM free.
>
> **O Mother Mary, generate,**
> **the song that does accelerate,**
> **my mind into a peaceful state,**
> **God's perfect love I radiate.**

3. Mother Mary, help me see if I have a self, or an illusion, that causes me to feel rejected or go into other negative reactions when other people do not respond the way I expect them to respond.

> In Mother's love I do transcend,
> and all my struggles hereby end.

For when with Mother's eye I see,
no imperfection touches me.

**O Mother Mary, generate,
the song that does accelerate,
my mind into a peaceful state,
God's perfect love I radiate.**

4. Mother Mary, I am willing to look at myself and take this as an opportunity to overcome another illusion, to let another separate self go. Help me rise to the next level up where I can express more unconditional love and be non-attached to how people receive it.

I see that healing must begin
by finding Living Christ within.
For as I see with single eye,
each cell the light does amplify.

**O Mother Mary, generate,
the song that does accelerate,
my mind into a peaceful state,
God's perfect love I radiate.**

5. Mother Mary, help me be completely non-attached to how other people respond to me because I am not expressing love with any intention.

In Mother's music I am free,
from memories of a lesser me.
My vision in a perfect state,
that all my cells regenerate.

**O Mother Mary, generate,
the song that does accelerate,
my mind into a peaceful state,
God's perfect love I radiate.**

6. Mother Mary, help me accept that I will go through an interim phase where I switch in and out of Christhood, and where I inevitably will react with my normal level of consciousness to the consequences of expressing my Christhood.

> O Mother's Love, sweet melody,
> from imperfections I AM free.
> O Mother Mary, sound of sounds,
> within my heart your love abounds.

> **O Mother Mary, generate,**
> **the song that does accelerate,**
> **my mind into a peaceful state,**
> **God's perfect love I radiate.**

7. Mother Mary, help me learn to see through this and see that this reaction is an opportunity to step up to the next level of consciousness. Help me overcome the illusion associated with my present level and step up to a higher level where I can express more Christhood.

> Through Mother's beauty so sublime,
> transcending bounds of space and time.
> All cells beyond the mortal tomb,
> as they are whole in Mother's womb.

> **O Mother Mary, generate,**
> **the song that does accelerate,**
> **my mind into a peaceful state,**
> **God's perfect love I radiate.**

8. Mother Mary, help me become consciously aware of this process, so I can quickly make the shift of no longer blaming myself, but realizing the absolute truth that I do not need to be perfect in order to express Christhood.

> In resonance with life's own song,
> in life's harmonics I belong.
> The blueprint of my perfect state
> does every cell reconsecrate.

> O Mother Mary, generate,
> the song that does accelerate,
> my mind into a peaceful state,
> God's perfect love I radiate.

9. Mother Mary, help me make peace with myself as I am right now. Help me make peace with being at the level of consciousness I am at, instead of blaming myself or feeling that I am behind and I should really be at a higher level.

> The tuning fork in every cell
> is now attuned to Mother's bell.
> From curse of death I AM now free,
> I claim my immortality.

> O Mother Mary, generate,
> the song that does accelerate,
> my mind into a peaceful state,
> God's perfect love I radiate.

Part 5

1. Mother Mary, help me accept that I *am* good enough at the level of consciousness I am at. There is no reason to blame myself for reacting at that level of consciousness, even reacting to when I have expressed Christhood and what other people do with it.

> O Blessed Mary's Song of Life,
> consuming every form of strife.
> As I attune to sound so fair,
> each cell is healthy, I declare.

> O Mother Mary, generate,
> the song that does accelerate,
> my mind into a peaceful state,
> God's perfect love I radiate.

2. Mother Mary, help me see that my reaction is the opportunity to see the illusion of my present level and rise to the next level. It has always been that way and it always *will* be that way.

> As life's own song I ever hear,
> it does consume all sense of fear.
> In tune with Mother's symphony,
> from all diseases I AM free.
>
> **O Mother Mary, generate,**
> **the song that does accelerate,**
> **my mind into a peaceful state,**
> **God's perfect love I radiate.**

3. Mother Mary, help me accept that the basic mechanics of the path is that I am at a certain level. My reaction is the way it is. By looking at it, I can see the illusion at that level so I can rise to the next level.

> In Mother's love I do transcend,
> and all my struggles hereby end.
> For when with Mother's eye I see,
> no imperfection touches me.
>
> **O Mother Mary, generate,**
> **the song that does accelerate,**
> **my mind into a peaceful state,**
> **God's perfect love I radiate.**

4. Mother Mary, I have had enough of the illusions, I have had enough of the delusions of grandeur. I just want to know how the path works so I can make the fastest progress and I can get above these unbalanced, negative, self-blaming reactions and be at peace with being here.

> I see that healing must begin
> by finding Living Christ within.
> For as I see with single eye,
> each cell the light does amplify.

O Mother Mary, generate,
the song that does accelerate,
my mind into a peaceful state,
God's perfect love I radiate.

5. Mother Mary, help me see the separate self I created in reaction to the material realm, especially the fact that I can make a choice and it will create a physical consequence that I cannot overcome for the rest of my lifetime.

In Mother's music I am free,
from memories of a lesser me.
My vision in a perfect state,
that all my cells regenerate.

O Mother Mary, generate,
the song that does accelerate,
my mind into a peaceful state,
God's perfect love I radiate.

6. Mother Mary, help me see if I created a separate self in reaction to this where I went into a negative reaction to the mother realm. I felt that I could not be comfortable, I could not be at peace, in the mother realm. I reasoned there was something wrong with the mother realm, that the mother realm should not be this way.

O Mother's Love, sweet melody,
from imperfections I AM free.
O Mother Mary, sound of sounds,
within my heart your love abounds.

O Mother Mary, generate,
the song that does accelerate,
my mind into a peaceful state,
God's perfect love I radiate.

7. Mother Mary, I am willing to look at this and go through a revolutionary shift of accepting that planet earth is a teaching device. In order to give people the lessons they need, matter needs to be as dense as it is. Matter needs to be as unresponsive to mind as it is, or the vast majority of people on earth would not learn their lessons.

> Through Mother's beauty so sublime,
> transcending bounds of space and time.
> All cells beyond the mortal tomb,
> as they are whole in Mother's womb.

> **O Mother Mary, generate,**
> **the song that does accelerate,**
> **my mind into a peaceful state,**
> **God's perfect love I radiate.**

8. Mother Mary, help me accept that there is nothing wrong with matter. It was my reaction to matter that caused me to think there was something wrong with matter. It is *my* responsibility to resolve that separate self. Only when I do, will I be free to actually embrace being in physical embodiment.

> In resonance with life's own song,
> in life's harmonics I belong.
> The blueprint of my perfect state
> does every cell reconsecrate.

> **O Mother Mary, generate,**
> **the song that does accelerate,**
> **my mind into a peaceful state,**
> **God's perfect love I radiate.**

9. Mother Mary, help me rise to the level of Christhood where I am at peace with being in physical embodiment. Help me overcome the desire to get out of here. Help me overcome the sense that there is something wrong with matter for being the way it is. Help me accept being here and accept matter for what it is.

> The tuning fork in every cell
> is now attuned to Mother's bell.

From curse of death I AM now free,
I claim my immortality.

**O Mother Mary, generate,
the song that does accelerate,
my mind into a peaceful state,
God's perfect love I radiate.**

Sealing

In the name of the Divine Mother, I call to Mother Mary for the sealing of myself and all people in my circle of influence in the creative flow of the Divine Mother, the River of Life. I call for the multiplication of my calls by all representatives of the Divine Mother, so that we form the perfect figure-eight flow of "As Above, so below." Thus, I accept that this is fully manifest, because the mouth of the Lord, the Divine Mother that I AM, has spoken it. Amen.

19 | WITHDRAWING SPACE FROM CERTAIN IMBALANCED CONDITIONS

I AM the Ascended Master Gautama Buddha. What can a Buddha add to the discussion of your Divine plan? There may be a few ascended master students who have the potential in their Divine plans to manifest at least some degree of Buddhahood in this lifetime. However, many who are ready to manifest Buddhahood from past lives will not need an outer teaching, will not seek out an outer teaching or an outer teacher. Nevertheless, I will give some thoughts about what is the difference between Buddhahood and Christhood.

Out-breath and in-breath

Although we have talked about this to some degree not so long ago, what I wish to discourse on is that Christhood is a more *outgoing* activity.

Buddhahood is a more *ingoing* activity. You might say that Christhood is the *out-breath* and Buddhahood is the *in-breath*. When you came to this planet as avatars, you were in the Christhood phase. In a sense, you breathed yourself out to take embodiment on earth.

Many of you are in the ingoing phase. In a sense, all of you are in the ingoing phase of breathing yourself back in from all kinds of entanglements with this world. Some of you (as was said) may indeed choose to stay in embodiment in order to be part of Saint Germain's Golden Age. Still, in order to get to the point where you can fulfill that potential, you are going through that phase of the in-breath, pulling yourself away from entanglements with karmic circumstances, selecting out the things that distract you from your Divine plan, resolving your birth trauma, first of all, so that you can be in a neutral state of mind.

We might say that, in a sense, Buddhahood and Christhood could be seen as simply different levels of the same evolutionary process. As we have said many times, you do not have to be perfect to express Christhood. What does it mean to be perfect? In a sense, it means that you do not have to have completely resolved your psychology, including your birth trauma, in order to begin to express Christhood. What we have expressed is that you should not be afraid to express Christhood, that you need to begin to do so without thinking you have reached some ultimate stage. Buddhahood is, of course, also, regardless of what has been projected by the religion of Buddhism, not an ultimate stage. We have said, nothing that happens on earth is ultimate. Even in the ascended realm there is ongoingness so how could anything ever be ultimate? How could enlightenment be ultimate? How could nirvana be some static state?

There comes the point where you have resolved a very high degree of your psychology, including your birth trauma and your separate selves. Then, you could call this the higher stages of Christhood because there is now very little resistance in your four lower bodies to the light flowing through you. That is also the point where you can begin to shift, some of you (not all of you because many of you still want to be active in society) more into the Buddhic consciousness, the Buddhic awareness.

How the Buddha is active

It is not that the Buddha cannot be active in society. The Buddha, perhaps, finds a different way to be active in society. This is a very subtle thing, a very individual thing. You can see the difference in the life of Jesus where he was outgoing, going out, meeting the people, often confronting them, whereas I, as the Buddha, created an ashram and let the people come to me. This is somewhat the differences between two approaches.

In a sense, the outgoing Christ is like the outgoing aspect of God the Father, the expansive phase. The Buddha is like the Mother, the ingoing, the contracting phase. The out-breath and the in-breath.

Some of you will come to a point where you begin to realize that it is no longer really so important what you do on the outer. This does not mean you have to withdraw from active life in society, create an ashram or live in a secluded setting. You may still live a "normal life," having a family, having a job, having a career of some kind, but you are doing it in a different way.

You are realizing that these outer activities do not define you. They are not pulling all of your attention into these outer activities. Often, during the Christhood stage, you are very, very focused on what you are doing and your entire attention is pulled into it. You are in a sense absorbed by the activity. When you reach Buddhahood, it is almost as if you can be partaking of some activity but there is a part of your mind that is not absorbed in it.

What level of consciousness am I at?

How do you, then, get to that stage? For this I want to build on what Mother Mary talked about where you need to come to the point of making peace with being in embodiment, making peace with the Mother Realm, making peace with free will, making peace with being at your present level of consciousness. There can come a point where you are actually no longer thinking about: "What level of consciousness am I at?"

You know it is an ongoing process. You know you are doing whatever you can to rise higher in consciousness. You are not concerned about where you are at on the scale. You are striving without striving. You are not struggling. You are not even having a goal. You are not into a comparative state of mind.

You are, as we have expressed it in words, flowing with the River of Life. You are flowing with life. You do not even have a clear goal you are working towards. You do not even have a clear vision of some Divine plan where you are supposed to do various steps to reach a particular goal. You are almost flowing with life and whatever circumstances come up, you are not even deciding with the outer mind what to do. You just feel intuitively, and then you do it.

Being at peace in any situation

In order to really get to that stage, you have to make one of these revolutionary shifts of being at peace with whatever situation you are in. There comes a stage of Buddhahood where you can manifest the outer circumstances that you want. In order to get to that stage, you have to go through an interim stage where you have to recognize that you will not actually move beyond a certain circumstance until you can be in the circumstance and be non-attached and therefore be at peace. You have made peace with the circumstance.

When you resolve the birth trauma and accept free will, then you can make peace with whatever circumstance. You do not have any personal wound that you are trying to defend or compensate for. Therefore, you can set other people free to be in whatever consciousness they are in and outplay whatever they are outplaying. This does not mean that if people are acting in an unbalanced manner and do not want to change, that you have to stay in the circumstance. You are, however, not running away from it to protect your personal wounds.

You can be at the point where you can say to yourself: "Could I stay in this circumstance and be at peace?" Yes, you could. You realize that you could. You have reached a certain level of non-attachment and wholeness where you could be at peace in that circumstance even if other people are not at peace. When you have come to that realization, you can take the next step of asking yourself: "Well, does the fact that I *can* be at peace in this circumstance mean that I *want* to stay in this circumstance?" Then, you might choose to move out of it. This can be disturbing to people around you because you might not be able to give a reason that these people can understand for why you are moving out of that circumstance. You just are.

The explanation problem

My beloved, what is it that keeps many people from reaching what we have called Buddhic non-attachment? It is that there is some kind of drama, some kind of story, in their minds that they feel they have to live up to or they have to fulfill. We have talked about the epic dramas. Many of you still have this separate self that has built an image of how you are supposed to be as a spiritual person. As part of this, you have a separate self that feels that whatever you do, whatever you choose to do, you should be able to come up with an explanation for why you are doing this. Mind you, an explanation that makes sense to this separate self, possibly to other people, perhaps even to the fallen beings.

In other words, you have an explanation problem. You have a self that feels that you should be able to explain yourself, your motivation, your reason for doing what you are doing. This ties in with the idea of an epic drama or a story line where, as a spiritual person, you are doing certain things, you are not doing others and you are doing what you are doing for a specific reason and not for another reason. You certainly cannot do anything without being able to explain the reason you are doing it.

Many people cannot move into Buddhic non-attachment because in their own minds they have this story that must unfold, they have this epic drama, they have this view of a spiritual person. They feel they always have to live up to it and if they do not, they have to be able to explain it. Even when they do make decisions that are within their image, they still have to be able to explain why they do it.

What have we talked about? Being the open door for your I AM Presence but the I AM Presence is in the spiritual realm. The I AM Presence may have a motivation for expressing something through you. Can that motivation be expressed in words, especially the words that can be understood at a certain lower level of consciousness? We have talked about expressing your Divine individuality. That individuality is beyond this world. Can you necessarily give a rational, common-sense, fact-based, cause-and-effect explanation of why you are expressing something?

Your overall view of life

My beloved, especially in the Western world there are spiritual students who have made significant progress. They are actually ready to express some level of Buddhahood but they still have not overcome that separate self. If you listen carefully to what we have been saying, what we are actually saying is that you might consider that there are two processes going on in parallel on your spiritual path. There is a process that we have explained, namely that in your four lower bodies you have certain wounds or traumas. This has created internal spirits and separate selves even the primal self – which is still just a separate self among many – and these are in your four lower bodies. In order to resolve them and be free of them, you have to do a certain almost mechanical aspect of invoking the energy to transform the energy that makes up these selves. You also have to do the conscious work of going into them, seeing the belief or illusion they are based on, then consciously choosing a higher reality.

What we are saying now is that even when you have done this, there can still be a separate self that was created while you (for example) were influenced by your birth trauma and your primal self. That separate self now has a view of how you should be as a person, as a spiritual person, who has this birth trauma. Even if you have resolved the birth trauma itself, you also need to resolve the separate self that holds this image of how you should be.

You could also express this another way, namely that there is the process of resolving all of these things. We could say that the traumas, the wounds, the separate selves, the internal spirits are like magnets that are pulling on the awareness of the Conscious You. It is pulling the awareness into being identified with this. These are very specific things. Then, beyond that can be your overall view of life. It is quite possible (over the long time you have been in embodiment) that you have a certain level where you have all these wounds, traumas and separate selves. You have another level where you have built an overall view of life on earth and how you see yourself in relation to life on earth.

It is a separate self but it is almost helpful to think of it in a broader way, that it is your overall view of life. Many of you, especially when you have grown up in the western world, you have this very linear mindset of feeling that there is always cause and effect. What that means for you is that when you do something, it is an effect. Therefore, you must have a reason that you can explain to other people, especially the people who are affected by what you are doing. You also must have a reason that you can explain to yourself, including your outer mind even your separate selves. If you cannot, then sure enough there will be some separate self, maybe several, that will question what you are doing, perhaps even accuse you of doing something wrong.

There may also be other people, and, of course, the fallen beings are also spreading out this general awareness in the collective consciousness that you should always have a reason, and that reason should be acceptable according to a certain standard. If you are Catholic, there are certain things you are supposed to do. If you do not do them or if you do something differently, you must be able to explain it. Then, maybe you can still be allowed to do it. Certainly, if you do something that is not acceptable and you cannot explain it, then you will be condemned. It is the same in most other environments on earth, even spiritual and New Age organizations, even (as we have said) past ascended master organizations where there was a very, very strong tendency to judge each other.

What I am saying is that there comes a point where you are beginning to go into Buddhahood, where you can benefit from looking at this process, looking at your overall view of life. Then, you can say: "Well, there is this concept that when I do something, I should have a reason that I can explain but why should I do this? Why do I have to explain myself? I am an independent being with free will, so is everybody else. I have a near total respect for the free will of other people. Should I not have the same total respect for my own free will and therefore be able to say I have no obligation to explain why I do something? I don't even need to explain this to myself. If I am acting on an impulse from my I AM Presence, why should I be able to justify and explain this in a way that my linear mind can fit into the belief system it has been indoctrinated with in this lifetime and many previous lifetimes? Can I not look at this mind, look at it as a separate self but even look at it as an overall view of life that I have stepped into and then say: 'I don't want to adhere to this world view, this belief system anymore. I don't want to play out this epic drama. I don't want to continue this personal story of how I should be in the material universe. I am willing to break the barriers and step beyond this.'"

Holding space on earth

These are the highest stages of Christhood. These are the stages of Buddhahood, the beginning stages. Those of you who have it in your Divine plan to go through this, can use this teaching to quickly go through that process. When you come to the point where you are willing to do something that you cannot explain, and that you cannot justify in a way other people can understand and accept, or that your outer mind can understand and accept, then you will experience a new degree of freedom. This may not necessarily mean that you do some radical outer actions, but inside of you, you will feel a new freedom. This can lead you to a stage where you can consider what it actually means to be the Buddha in embodiment or to have a degree of Buddhic consciousness while you are in embodiment. This I will discourse on. Even though I know that few people are ready to understand it, I feel it is important to get this teaching into the physical octave.

It has been said that the Buddha holds space for earth. My position in the ascended hierarchy is the position of Lord of the World where I sit as the Buddha and I am holding space. This is difficult to express in words but what you can say is this: There is a certain built-in mechanism in the Ma-ter light and in space itself that certain manifestations would very quickly create a self-reinforcing downward spiral that, for a planet, for example, could cause the planet to self-destruct.

Basically, what we could say here is that if there was nothing mitigating this, then planets on which fallen beings embody would very quickly self-destruct. They would go into a downward spiral and they would simply be blown apart by the energies. What is actually happening in this process is not entirely similar but it can be illustrated by the process of a black hole. You know that in a black hole, when you go beyond a certain horizon, the laws of nature break down, time breaks down and even space breaks down. In other words, if a planet deteriorated to this level, space would contract and the planet would implode. What does the Buddha do? He sits there in the ascended realm and he is holding the spiritual balance that prevents the space of earth – the space in which earth can exist – from collapsing, from contracting into a singularity.

We could explain this in a different way by saying that even though everything is made out of the Ma-ter light (every structure you see on earth is made out of the Ma-ter light) no structure could be formed unless there was an empty space in which it could form. Before a planet can be created by the Elohim, *first* space must be defined, *then* the Ma-ter light can fill in structures and create structures in that space. The Buddha holds the space. The Elohim create the earth, then beings take embodiment and they now do whatever they do with the earth.

There comes a point where it is decided that earth will be a planet that will allow fallen beings to embody and now there needs to be a being with a Buddhic consciousness who can hold space for earth so that it does not collapse in upon itself. This was not, of course, me because I was not ascended at that time but this is the office I am now holding. There was another Buddha that held space back then and there have been a number of Buddhas since then.

There comes a point where you reach a certain level of Buddhahood where you can begin not only to understand this concept intellectually but you can begin to experience the reality of it inside yourself. Then, you can realize that when you reach a level of Buddhic consciousness while still being in physical embodiment, you can form a figure-eight flow with me, with the Buddha that I am. You see, as the Buddha, I have vowed to hold space for earth so that the beings who embody on earth can do whatever they want to do with their free will without causing the planet to collapse.

You are, of course, one of those who are in embodiment on earth so you can realize something profound. Why is there war on earth? Well, in an overall sense, I am holding the space that allows the fallen beings to create war. Is it only the fallen beings who decide whether there is war on earth? No, it is not. There is war on earth because the people in embodiment are allowing space for war to exist in their minds, in their four lower bodies and in the collective consciousness.

In other words, I am allowing space in an overall sense but what will actually manifest in the physical requires that there are people in embodiment who give space in their minds so that this can happen. The fact that I hold space does not mean that there *has to* be war on earth. Therefore, war is only there when those in embodiment allow it. What you can actually begin to do (when you reach these levels of Buddhic consciousness), is you can recognize that because you are in physical embodiment, because you have reached this level of non-attachment where you do not have a personal story or an epic drama that you are seeking to unfold, you are in the non-attached state of consciousness. Because you are non-attached, you actually have the option to decide that you will withdraw space from a certain dualistic manifestation. I do not suggest you start out with war because it is a big topic, but I suggest that you find something that appeals to you personally. Then, you contemplate that first, you withdraw space in your own four lower bodies from this but then you can start expanding this and gradually come to the point where you withdraw space from the collective consciousness.

What one Buddha can do

I will tell you that one person in the Buddhic consciousness can withdraw space from a certain manifestation—not war because that would require more people in the Buddhic consciousness. In other areas that do not have quite the same powerful momentum, you can actually withdraw space. It would be possible, as an example, for one person with a sufficient level of Buddhahood to withdraw space for pedophilia and that would mean that no pedophile would be able to embody on earth after that cutoff point.

There are, however, some areas where one Buddha cannot make the change but by withdrawing space, you make it easier for a critical mass of people to make the decision: "We no longer want this in our society or on our planet." As we move more and more into the golden age, there will be a growing global awareness—that you have already seen start growing, but it will grow even more. There will come a point where there will be this awareness that it is up to us to decide what we allow to manifest on the planet. That is where one Buddha in embodiment can withdraw space from a certain manifestation that then makes it much easier for a critical mass of people to come to that outer decision: "We want this planet to be free of slavery, human trafficking, drug abuse, manipulating the economy, all of these manifestations." Eventually, there can be such a strong momentum that enough people decide that we want this planet to be free of war. Then, it can happen. It *will* happen.

You see, my beloved, these are some teachings for some of you. Many of you can just ignore them. I suggest that you do not ignore this very concept that you can have resolved your primal self and other separate selves but there is still something missing that is the shift in your overall attitude, the way you look at yourself.

People who do not make progress

If you look at spiritual movements, you will see in many cases that there are people who have been in a certain movement, followed a certain teaching and even applied it and practiced certain techniques for decades and decades. They have a great understanding of the spiritual path, an intellectual, linear understanding. They may even have built a certain outer persona where they know how to "walk like a man, talk like a man," act like a spiritual person. Therefore, they can appear to be very spiritual, harmonious, balanced and in control. If you look at it with inner sight, you see that this is all outer. They have not actually changed their overall view of life and of themselves. Really, we could say that if we think about the 144 levels of consciousness, there are people who might have been following an ascended master teaching for thirty years but they have only risen from, say, the 60th level of consciousness to the 68th level of consciousness whereas they actually had the potential to rise much higher in that amount of time. Why have they not risen higher? It is because their overall view of themselves has not shifted. They have not been willing to go through that revolutionary shift.

As I said, there are some people who just have not made progress even though they have done all the outer things. There are also people who have done the outer things and have in a way acquired the attainment to be at a certain level of consciousness, but you have not shifted your overall view of life to the point where you accept that you have made progress. This messenger, a number of years ago, came to a point where he realized that there was a part of his ego that wanted to feel that he was an advanced spiritual student and wanted to be prideful about this. He realized that in order to avoid feeling prideful, he had not actually dared to acknowledge that he had made progress. He had to go through a process of saying: "Do I believe that spiritual teachings work? Well, if I believe they work and if I have applied them for so many years, I must have made progress because, if the teachings work, I should have made progress. And if I haven't made progress, why am I bothering to apply the teachings? And if I don't believe the teachings work, why am I bothering to apply them? If I believe they work and I have applied them, I must have made progress. What's wrong with acknowledging this?"

Accepting that you can be an instrument

He went through a shift where he recognized that he had made certain progress and that is why he could accept it when Jesus approached him and said: "Are you willing to do something for me?" He could accept that: "Yes, perhaps I am actually able to be an instrument." It is the same for you. Many of you have actually done the work, made the progress but there is still some shift you have not gone through so you cannot actually accept it.

You have the students who, although they have also studied the teachings and supposedly done the work, have not really shifted their consciousness on the inner. What they have done on the outer is that they have built this persona of thinking they are a spiritual person so they think they have more spiritual attainment than they have. Then, you have the students who have actually gone through the progress on the inner but they have an outer persona that does not allow them to see this so they do not acknowledge their progress.

Most of you are, of course, in the category where you have made progress, you have done the work but you just have not dared to acknowledge it. You have not dared to step back and see that there is some kind of separate self that is preventing you from realizing where you are at on the path and what your potential is at your present level.

This is something that applies to almost all of you. You could benefit from considering this and be willing to make that shift of acknowledging: "I am an advanced student on the path. I have some maturity. I have some spiritual attainment and therefore I am able to be the open door. I am able to serve. I am able to build my attunement with the ascended masters. I am able to know the next step of my Divine plan. I am actually able to do something on earth, not that I am the doer but I am able to be a co-creator with my I AM Presence and bring forth something that is valid, worthwhile, worthy, constructive, good."

How many of you have dared to acknowledge this in yourselves? My beloved, the Holy Spirit, your I AM Presence, the ascended masters, respect your free will. If you insist on holding on to a limited view of yourself, we, of course, are not going to impose ourselves on you and force you to be the open door. We cannot force the door open, only *you* can open it. Many of you can make that shift very quickly and just dare to accept that you are at a level of the spiritual path – it does not matter what level it is – where you could be the open door in some measure. Then, dare to accept that, dare to express it. Be at peace with it. Be at peace with whatever reaction you might get from your surroundings.

My beloved this was the discourse I wanted to bring. I also want to thank you for being here. I want to extend my gratitude to those who will study these teachings, apply them, apply the tools and therefore will begin to grasp higher aspects of their Divine plan and dare to execute them. With the gratitude of the Buddha, I seal you and I seal this conference. May my peace be with you always—when you want it!

20 | INVOKING MY BUDDHIC POTENTIAL

In the name I AM THAT I AM, Jesus Christ, I call to all representatives of the Divine Mother, especially Gautama Buddha, to help me see if reaching a level of Buddhahood is the highest potential in my Divine plan. Help me see what stands in the way of me accepting this potential, including…

[Make personal calls.]

Part 1

1. Gautama, help me see if I have the potential in my Divine plan to manifest some degree of Buddhahood in this lifetime.

> Gautama, show my mental state
> that does give rise to love and hate,
> your exposé I do endure,
> so my perception will be pure.

> Gautama, Flame of Cosmic Peace,
> unruly thoughts do hereby cease,
> we radiate from you and me
> the peace to still Samsara's Sea.

2. Gautama, help me see if I am in the ingoing phase of breathing myself back in from all entanglements with this world, pulling myself away from entanglements with karmic circumstances, selecting out the things that distract me from my Divine plan, resolving my birth trauma so I can be in a neutral state of mind.

> Gautama, in your Flame of Peace,
> the struggling self I now release,
> the Buddha Nature I now see,
> it is the core of you and me.

> Gautama, Flame of Cosmic Peace,
> unruly thoughts do hereby cease,
> we radiate from you and me
> the peace to still Samsara's Sea.

3. Gautama, help me know that Buddhahood is not an ultimate stage. Help me resolve my psychology, including my birth trauma, so there is little resistance in my four lower bodies to the light flowing through me. Help me shift into the Buddhic awareness.

> Gautama, I am one with thee,
> Mara's demons do now flee,
> your Presence like a soothing balm,
> my mind and senses ever calm.

> Gautama, Flame of Cosmic Peace,
> unruly thoughts do hereby cease,
> we radiate from you and me
> the peace to still Samsara's Sea.

4. Gautama, help me see that the Buddha can be active in society. Help me find my individual expression of Buddhahood.

Gautama, I now take the vow,
to live in the eternal now,
with you I do transcend all time,
to live in present so sublime.

**Gautama, Flame of Cosmic Peace,
unruly thoughts do hereby cease,
we radiate from you and me
the peace to still Samsara's Sea.**

5. Gautama, help me realize that it is not so important what I do on the outer. I may still live a "normal life," having a family, job and career, but I am doing it in a different way.

Gautama, I have no desire,
to nothing earthly I aspire,
in non-attachment I now rest,
passing Mara's subtle test.

**Gautama, Flame of Cosmic Peace,
unruly thoughts do hereby cease,
we radiate from you and me
the peace to still Samsara's Sea.**

6. Gautama, help me see that the outer activities do not define me. The outer activities are not pulling all of my attention into focusing on them. I am partaking of an activity but there is a part of my mind that is not absorbed in it.

Gautama, I melt into you,
my mind is one, no longer two,
immersed in your resplendent glow,
Nirvana is all that I know.

**Gautama, Flame of Cosmic Peace,
unruly thoughts do hereby cease,
we radiate from you and me
the peace to still Samsara's Sea.**

7. Gautama, help me come to the point where I am no longer thinking about what level of consciousness I am at. I am doing whatever I can to rise higher in consciousness, but I am not concerned about where I am at on the scale. I am striving without striving, without struggling.

> Gautama, in your timeless space,
> I am immersed in Cosmic Grace,
> I know the God beyond all form,
> to world I will no more conform.

> **Gautama, Flame of Cosmic Peace,**
> **unruly thoughts do hereby cease,**
> **we radiate from you and me**
> **the peace to still Samsara's Sea.**

8. Gautama, help me come to the point where I am not even having a goal. I am not into a comparative state of mind. I am flowing with the River of Life. I am flowing with life.

> Gautama, I am now awake,
> I clearly see what is at stake,
> and thus I claim my sacred right
> to be on earth the Buddhic Light.

> **Gautama, Flame of Cosmic Peace,**
> **unruly thoughts do hereby cease,**
> **we radiate from you and me**
> **the peace to still Samsara's Sea.**

9. Gautama, help me come to the point where I have no clear vision of some Divine plan where I am supposed to do various steps to reach a particular goal. I am flowing with life and whatever circumstances come up, I am not deciding with the outer mind what to do. I just feel intuitively, and then I do it.

> Gautama, with your thunderbolt,
> we give the earth a mighty jolt,
> I know that some will understand,
> and join the Buddha's timeless band.

**Gautama, Flame of Cosmic Peace,
unruly thoughts do hereby cease,
we radiate from you and me
the peace to still Samsara's Sea.**

Part 2

1. Gautama, help me make the revolutionary shift of being at peace with whatever situation I am in.

> Gautama, show my mental state
> that does give rise to love and hate,
> your exposé I do endure,
> so my perception will be pure.

> **Gautama, Flame of Cosmic Peace,
> unruly thoughts do hereby cease,
> we radiate from you and me
> the peace to still Samsara's Sea.**

2. Gautama, help me recognize that I cannot move beyond a certain circumstance until I can be in the circumstance and be non-attached and therefore be at peace. I have made peace with the circumstance.

> Gautama, in your Flame of Peace,
> the struggling self I now release,
> the Buddha Nature I now see,
> it is the core of you and me.

> **Gautama, Flame of Cosmic Peace,
> unruly thoughts do hereby cease,
> we radiate from you and me
> the peace to still Samsara's Sea.**

3. Gautama, help me come to the point where I do not have any personal wound that I am trying to defend or compensate for. I set other people free to be in whatever consciousness they are in and outplay whatever they are outplaying.

> Gautama, I am one with thee,
> Mara's demons do now flee,
> your Presence like a soothing balm,
> my mind and senses ever calm.

> **Gautama, Flame of Cosmic Peace,**
> **unruly thoughts do hereby cease,**
> **we radiate from you and me**
> **the peace to still Samsara's Sea.**

4. Gautama, help me see that this does not mean that I have to stay in the circumstance. Yet, I am not running away from it to protect my personal wounds.

> Gautama, I now take the vow,
> to live in the eternal now,
> with you I do transcend all time,
> to live in present so sublime.

> **Gautama, Flame of Cosmic Peace,**
> **unruly thoughts do hereby cease,**
> **we radiate from you and me**
> **the peace to still Samsara's Sea.**

5. Gautama, help me reach the level of non-attachment and wholeness where I can be at peace in a certain circumstance even if other people are not at peace. Help me see when it is time to move out of that circumstance.

> Gautama, I have no desire,
> to nothing earthly I aspire,
> in non-attachment I now rest,
> passing Mara's subtle test.

**Gautama, Flame of Cosmic Peace,
unruly thoughts do hereby cease,
we radiate from you and me
the peace to still Samsara's Sea.**

6. Gautama, help me see if there is some kind of drama, some kind of story, in my mind that I feel I have to live up to or fulfill. Help me see if I have this separate self that has built an image of how I am supposed to be as a spiritual person.

Gautama, I melt into you,
my mind is one, no longer two,
immersed in your resplendent glow,
Nirvana is all that I know.

**Gautama, Flame of Cosmic Peace,
unruly thoughts do hereby cease,
we radiate from you and me
the peace to still Samsara's Sea.**

7. Gautama, help me see if I have a separate self that feels that whatever I choose to do, I should be able to come up with an explanation for why I am doing this, an explanation that makes sense to this separate self, possibly to other people, perhaps even to the fallen beings.

Gautama, in your timeless space,
I am immersed in Cosmic Grace,
I know the God beyond all form,
to world I will no more conform.

**Gautama, Flame of Cosmic Peace,
unruly thoughts do hereby cease,
we radiate from you and me
the peace to still Samsara's Sea.**

8. Gautama, help me see if I have an explanation problem, if I have a self that feels that I should be able to explain myself, my motivation, my reason for doing what I am doing.

Gautama, I am now awake,
I clearly see what is at stake,
and thus I claim my sacred right
to be on earth the Buddhic Light.

**Gautama, Flame of Cosmic Peace,
unruly thoughts do hereby cease,
we radiate from you and me
the peace to still Samsara's Sea.**

9. Gautama, help me see if I have a self that is tied in with an epic drama or a story line where, as a spiritual person, I am doing certain things, I am not doing others and I am doing it for a specific reason, never doing anything without being able to explain the reason for doing it.

Gautama, with your thunderbolt,
we give the earth a mighty jolt,
I know that some will understand,
and join the Buddha's timeless band.

**Gautama, Flame of Cosmic Peace,
unruly thoughts do hereby cease,
we radiate from you and me
the peace to still Samsara's Sea.**

Part 3

1. Gautama, help me see if I have a story that must unfold, an epic drama. Help me see if I feel I always have to live up to it and if I do not, I have to be able to explain why not.

Gautama, show my mental state
that does give rise to love and hate,
your exposé I do endure,
so my perception will be pure.

> Gautama, Flame of Cosmic Peace,
> unruly thoughts do hereby cease,
> we radiate from you and me
> the peace to still Samsara's Sea.

2. Gautama, help me see that the motivation of my I AM Presence cannot be expressed in words, especially the words that can be understood by the outer mind. I cannot give a rational, common-sense, fact-based, cause-and-effect explanation of why I am expressing an aspect of my Divine individuality.

> Gautama, in your Flame of Peace,
> the struggling self I now release,
> the Buddha Nature I now see,
> it is the core of you and me.

> **Gautama, Flame of Cosmic Peace,
> unruly thoughts do hereby cease,
> we radiate from you and me
> the peace to still Samsara's Sea.**

3. Gautama, help me see if I am ready to express some level of Buddhahood but I still have a separate self that has a view of how I should be as a spiritual person based on my birth trauma. Even if I have resolved the birth trauma itself, I also need to resolve the separate self that holds this image of how I should be.

> Gautama, I am one with thee,
> Mara's demons do now flee,
> your Presence like a soothing balm,
> my mind and senses ever calm.

> **Gautama, Flame of Cosmic Peace,
> unruly thoughts do hereby cease,
> we radiate from you and me
> the peace to still Samsara's Sea.**

4. Gautama, help me see that the traumas, the wounds, the separate selves, the internal spirits are like magnets that are pulling the awareness of the Conscious You into being identified with these very specific things.

> Gautama, I now take the vow,
> to live in the eternal now,
> with you I do transcend all time,
> to live in present so sublime.
>
> **Gautama, Flame of Cosmic Peace,**
> **unruly thoughts do hereby cease,**
> **we radiate from you and me**
> **the peace to still Samsara's Sea.**

5. Gautama, help me see that beyond this is my overall view of life on earth and how I see myself in relation to life on earth.

> Gautama, I have no desire,
> to nothing earthly I aspire,
> in non-attachment I now rest,
> passing Mara's subtle test.
>
> **Gautama, Flame of Cosmic Peace,**
> **unruly thoughts do hereby cease,**
> **we radiate from you and me**
> **the peace to still Samsara's Sea.**

6. Gautama, help me see if I have this very linear mindset of feeling that there is always cause and effect. When I do something, it is an effect, therefore, I must have a reason that I can explain to other people and to myself.

> Gautama, I melt into you,
> my mind is one, no longer two,
> immersed in your resplendent glow,
> Nirvana is all that I know.

> Gautama, Flame of Cosmic Peace,
> unruly thoughts do hereby cease,
> we radiate from you and me
> the peace to still Samsara's Sea.

7. Gautama, help me see if I have separate selves that will question what I am doing, perhaps even accuse me of doing something wrong.

> Gautama, in your timeless space,
> I am immersed in Cosmic Grace,
> I know the God beyond all form,
> to world I will no more conform.

> Gautama, Flame of Cosmic Peace,
> unruly thoughts do hereby cease,
> we radiate from you and me
> the peace to still Samsara's Sea.

8. Gautama, help me look at my overall view of life and see if there is this concept that when I do something, I should have a reason that I can explain.

> Gautama, I am now awake,
> I clearly see what is at stake,
> and thus I claim my sacred right
> to be on earth the Buddhic Light.

> Gautama, Flame of Cosmic Peace,
> unruly thoughts do hereby cease,
> we radiate from you and me
> the peace to still Samsara's Sea.

9. Gautama, help me accept that I do not have to explain myself. I am an independent being with free will, so is everybody else. I have a near total respect for the free will of other people. Should I not have the same total respect for my own free will and therefore be able to say I have no obligation to explain why I do something? I don't even need to explain this to myself.

> Gautama, with your thunderbolt,
> we give the earth a mighty jolt,
> I know that some will understand,
> and join the Buddha's timeless band.
>
> **Gautama, Flame of Cosmic Peace,**
> **unruly thoughts do hereby cease,**
> **we radiate from you and me**
> **the peace to still Samsara's Sea.**

Part 4

1. Gautama, help me see that if I am acting on an impulse from my I AM Presence, why should I be able to justify and explain this in a way that my linear mind can fit into the belief system, that it has been indoctrinated with in this lifetime and many previous lifetimes?

> Gautama, show my mental state
> that does give rise to love and hate,
> your exposé I do endure,
> so my perception will be pure.
>
> **Gautama, Flame of Cosmic Peace,**
> **unruly thoughts do hereby cease,**
> **we radiate from you and me**
> **the peace to still Samsara's Sea.**

2. Gautama, help me look at this mind, look at it as a separate self but even look at it as an overall view of life that I have stepped into. Help me say: "I don't want to adhere to this world view, this belief system anymore. I don't want to play out this epic drama. I don't want to continue this personal story of how I should be in the material universe. I am willing to break the barriers and step beyond this."

> Gautama, in your Flame of Peace,
> the struggling self I now release,

the Buddha Nature I now see,
it is the core of you and me.

**Gautama, Flame of Cosmic Peace,
unruly thoughts do hereby cease,
we radiate from you and me
the peace to still Samsara's Sea.**

3. Gautama, help me reach the state of inner freedom where I can consider what it actually means to be the Buddha in embodiment or to have a degree of Buddhic consciousness while I am in embodiment.

Gautama, I am one with thee,
Mara's demons do now flee,
your Presence like a soothing balm,
my mind and senses ever calm.

**Gautama, Flame of Cosmic Peace,
unruly thoughts do hereby cease,
we radiate from you and me
the peace to still Samsara's Sea.**

4. Gautama, help me see when I reach the level of Buddhahood where I can experience the reality of what it means that the Buddha holds space for a specific manifestation on earth.

Gautama, I now take the vow,
to live in the eternal now,
with you I do transcend all time,
to live in present so sublime.

**Gautama, Flame of Cosmic Peace,
unruly thoughts do hereby cease,
we radiate from you and me
the peace to still Samsara's Sea.**

5. Gautama, help me realize that when I reach a level of Buddhic consciousness while still being in physical embodiment, I can form a figure-eight flow with you.

Gautama, I have no desire,
to nothing earthly I aspire,
in non-attachment I now rest,
passing Mara's subtle test.

**Gautama, Flame of Cosmic Peace,
unruly thoughts do hereby cease,
we radiate from you and me
the peace to still Samsara's Sea.**

6. Gautama, help me recognize that because I am in physical embodiment, because I have reached this level of non-attachment where I do not have a personal story or an epic drama that I am seeking to unfold, I have the option to decide that I will withdraw space from a certain dualistic manifestation.

Gautama, I melt into you,
my mind is one, no longer two,
immersed in your resplendent glow,
Nirvana is all that I know.

**Gautama, Flame of Cosmic Peace,
unruly thoughts do hereby cease,
we radiate from you and me
the peace to still Samsara's Sea.**

7. Gautama, help me find something that appeals to me personally. Help me contemplate that first, I withdraw space in my own four lower bodies from this, but then I expand this and gradually come to the point where I withdraw space from the collective consciousness.

Gautama, in your timeless space,
I am immersed in Cosmic Grace,
I know the God beyond all form,
to world I will no more conform.

Gautama, Flame of Cosmic Peace,
unruly thoughts do hereby cease,
we radiate from you and me
the peace to still Samsara's Sea.

8. Gautama, help me see if I have not shifted my overall view of life to the point where I accept that I have made progress. Help me step back and see if there is a separate self that is preventing me from realizing where I am at on the path and what my potential is at my present level.

Gautama, I am now awake,
I clearly see what is at stake,
and thus I claim my sacred right
to be on earth the Buddhic Light.

Gautama, Flame of Cosmic Peace,
unruly thoughts do hereby cease,
we radiate from you and me
the peace to still Samsara's Sea.

9. Gautama, I am willing to make the shift of acknowledging: "I am an advanced student on the path. I have some maturity. I have some spiritual attainment and therefore I am able to be the open door. I am able to serve. I am able to build my attunement with the ascended masters. I am able to know the next step of my Divine plan. I am actually able to do something on earth, not that I am the doer, but I am able to be a co-creator with my I AM Presence and bring forth something that is valid, worthwhile, worthy, constructive, good."

Gautama, with your thunderbolt,
we give the earth a mighty jolt,
I know that some will understand,
and join the Buddha's timeless band.

Gautama, Flame of Cosmic Peace,
unruly thoughts do hereby cease,
we radiate from you and me
the peace to still Samsara's Sea.

Sealing

In the name of the Divine Mother, I call to Mother Mary for the sealing of myself and all people in my circle of influence in the creative flow of the Divine Mother, the River of Life. I call for the multiplication of my calls by all representatives of the Divine Mother, so that we form the perfect figure-eight flow of "As Above, so below." Thus, I accept that this is fully manifest, because the mouth of the Lord, the Divine Mother that I AM, has spoken it. Amen.

www.ingramcontent.com/pod-product-compliance
Lightning Source LLC
Chambersburg PA
CBHW030520230426
43665CB00010B/694